NATURE AND GRACE

NATURE AND GRACE

Toward an Integral Perspective

James A. Carpenter

CROSSROAD • NEW YORK

1988

The Crossroad Publishing Company
370 Lexington Avenue, New York, N.Y. 10017

Printed in the United States of America

Library of Congress Cataloging-in-Publication Data

Carpenter, James A., 1928–
    Nature and grace : toward an integral perspective / James A.
Carpenter.

    p.   cm.
    Bibliography: p.
    Includes index.
    ISBN 0-8245-0858-0 :
    1. Grace (Theology)—History of doctrines.   2. Nature—Religious
aspects—Christianity—History of doctrines.   3. Creation—History
of doctrines.   4. Salvation—History of doctrines.   I. Title.
    BT761.2.C34   1988   87-34575
    234—dc19   CIP

For My Children
Andy, Mark, Amy, Andrew, and Elizabeth
With Hope
For The Future

Contents

Preface

DISCUSSION OF THE RELATION of nature and grace is out of favor in much contemporary theology. It is my belief that our present knowledge of the world and of our own human reality prompts a reconsideration of the issue and a new reckoning with its importance for the whole range of Christian thought and life. No Christian doctrine can be dealt with adequately without recourse to the nature and grace schema. Creation, redemption, and consummation entail nature and grace at every level of significant discussion, not to mention the church and the sacraments, the one place perhaps where both are prominent entries. But what it means to be human and what it might mean to affirm that the human and the divine were at one in Jesus as the Christ are frequently dealt with as though nature were a minor matter, something outside the realm of serious theological concern.

There are a number of reasons why many theologians today either reject or ignore the nature and grace doctrine, some of which we will be considering in the following studies. It is enough to say here that a primary reason is to be found in the almost exclusive emphasis on history in much, if not most, theology of the past half-century and more. Grace in theology of this kind is considered in relation to history all too often without taking into account, or simply assuming, the manifest fact that history has its basis in the much larger continuum of nature. With the rise of history as virtually the all-consuming interest in theology, a great spate of human hubris ensued. Anthropocentricity, already entrenched in the tradition, reached new proportions.

The studies here, while simply studies and therefore discrete in themselves, have a unifying theme: the need to move out of entrapment in anthropocentricity into a liberating theocentricity. The nature and grace scheme, recast to meet present requirements, could, I believe, help us with this pressing need. So far as I can see, it is not merely one of many perspectives but among the chief perspectives that can enable theology to escape the impasse in which it finds itself at present. This work is designed to be diagnostic and at the same time to point toward a more integral perspective regarding the theology of nature and grace.

The method used is to expose the views of the theologians under consideration, then offer critical assessments of them and suggestions for further reflection. In some cases, as with Metz, Moltmann, and Westermann, it seemed necessary to deal with a number of issues midstream. This relieves perhaps the sameness of approach, affording a more direct access to the interaction of the theologies of these figures and my own deliberations. It seemed to me, however, that a less straightforward method than the one generally employed might cloud the issues and needlessly complicate an already greatly complicated area of thought.

While the term *nature* has many interpretations, it is used here in its inclusive sense but will perforce focus on nature as immediately experienced, both within and without ourselves and the realm in between. That our understanding of nature is historically conditioned goes without saying. We now know that nature itself has a "history" in the sense that it has developed and changed through billions of years. We now know too that the extent of nature is well-nigh infinite, and that what we know of it is minute. Despite this, we do know something of the reaches of its structure. If our science is at all accurate, nature is something like "the mighty alphabet for infant minds" of which Coleridge spoke in the last century. Limited as our knowledge of it is, we have reason to believe that we have not entirely misread it and are getting a little further along with the alphabet. The more we read of it, however, the more we know what might be read. We know that we are enveloped in mystery that verges on the absolute. To know this is already to know a great deal, but to have discerned something of the "measure, order and form" within the mystery, such as afforded by modern science, is to have a basis for grasping what nature might be, sufficiently so at least for us to have some idea of what we are talking about when we speak of it. No plea that we do not know what nature is, or that we cannot think "nature" as a whole, can exempt us from the responsibility and necessity of trying to reckon with it theologically.

The term *grace* as used here is understood in the classical sense as God's free gift of God's own power and presence to the world of creatures, not only to human creatures, but to everything created. The limitation of the operation and the effect of grace to human consciousness, common enough in tradition, is one of the roots of the exaltation of history at the expense and neglect of nature. A broader, more inclusive understanding of grace is needed, one commensurate with the broader conception of nature entertained in our time.

I am grateful to the following publishers for permission to use quotations from their copyright works: Augsburg Publishing House, for Claus Westermann, *Genesis I-II* (Copyright 1974, Neukirchen Verlag; E.T., 1983, Augsburg and SPCK); Crossroad Publishing Company, for Karl Rahner, *Theological Investigations*; Fortress Press, for Jürgen Moltmann, *The Future of Creation*; John Knox Press, for Claus Westermann, *Elements of Old Testament Theology*; Macmillan Publishing Company, for Alfred North Whitehead, *Adventure of Ideas, Modes of Thought, Process and Reality,* and *Science and the Modern World*; Cambridge University Press for nonexclusive world rights on the works of Whitehead used, and University of Chicago Press, for Paul Tillich, *Systematic Theology.*

It remains to be said that I am grateful to the General Theological Seminary for time to work on this book, for financial, secretarial, and research assistance. I want to thank my faculty colleagues for criticisms and suggestions, without any endorsement implied on their part, and two former students, Gretchen Zimmerman and Fredrica De Chuna, for editorial help and advice. I am especially grateful to Frank Oveis, editor of Crossroad, for his generous help and to Stacey Sauls, my student assistant, who helped me check the references and prepare the index, and who saved me from many errors, both of commission and omission.

JAMES A. CARPENTER

CHAPTER 1

Augustine and the West

FEW MORE FATEFUL MOMENTS in the development of Western thought can be found than that in which Augustine of Hippo declared that grace pertained not to "the constitution," but to "the cure," the restitution of nature.[1] A few years earlier, in 412, with wonted rhetorical balance, he put the matter a little differently: "not that by nature grace is denied, but rather by grace nature is repaired."[2] Many years afterwards, in his *Retractions*, he sought to clarify his thought and perhaps in some sense to qualify the way it had been interpreted: "I defend grace, not indeed as opposed to nature, but as that which controls and liberates nature."[3]

This qualification, if such it was, went largely unheeded by those who came after Augustine. The leading tendency of his anti-Pelagian writings implied throughout that nature and grace were in opposition. Even on those occasions when he admitted that there was some grace in nature itself, he countered them by maintaining that natural endowments were not to be confused with grace: "The capacity to have faith, as the capacity to love, belongs to man's nature; but to have faith, even as to have love, belongs to the grace of believers."[4]

That grace pertained to "the cure," not to "the constitution" of nature,[5] was the message the church received, received in shining, cadenced phrases that sank into consciousness and stuck in the subliminal mind. The features of Augustine's thought that modified, at times almost erased, the opposition, were lost on all but a few close students of his works. After him, there was little enough talk of the grace of nature in the Western church. The tendency toward opposing nature and grace, with what clearly seemed to have his great authority behind it, found ready growth in the crumbling structures of Rome and in the dark shadows of the barbarism of the centuries following. The church offered a gracious respite from the encircling chaos; grace resided within the confines of its communal life and all without seemed under the dominance of a nature

1

stripped of grace by Adam's fall. There were, of course, many positive discussions of creation and of the presence and power of the divine within it, but they were not linked with the doctrine of grace. Nature was conceived primarily as human nature and grace was understood as limited to the sphere of the religious life, to that which pertained almost entirely to ecclesiastical confines.

Augustine had well prepared the way for this development, and not only in his polemics against the Pelagians, but in his mature, magisterial works such as *The City of God.* "As soon as the first parents transgressed the commandment, divine grace forsook them";[6] it "deserted them."[7] Although he makes remarks that undercut the force of language like this, none is so readily accessible as the sharp, unequivocal phrases just quoted. For a multitude of his disciples, such sayings virtually had the force of Scripture.

The theology of nature and grace scattered in Augustine's writings is the foundation of the scholastic principle *gratia non tollit naturam sed perficit*: grace does not destroy nature, it perfects it. This principle was a powerful factor in theology, mitigating some of the worst results of the Pelagian controversy. Yet even it was frequently lost sight of, its mitigating force obscured. Nature and grace as opposed realities dominated the horizons of theological thought in instances too numerous to count. The consequences for Western Catholicism and so for Western culture were great. Theoretical thought and practical life were conditioned by it at their roots, and in due course it made for a derogation of nature more severe and inclusive than Augustine himself ever posed.

Beyond his anti-Pelagian writings stands Augustine's theology of creation. This theology, calmer and more considered than his tracts on nature and grace, comprises his most affirmative thought about the natural realm, which curiously is almost never considered in terms of grace. It is manifest though that the whole of creation derives from the divine generosity; the Spirit of God is intimately present in the structures of world, constantly enlivening, sustaining all things, whether small or great,[8] and is present with peculiar power in human life inasmuch as the divine image was not completely blotted out with the fall. The very search for God, Augustine everywhere implies, is of grace, though he does not explicitly term it so.[9] The absolute impossibility "for us to be unwilling to be happy," he says, is the ground of our striving for fulfillment in God. It is one of those "indescribable but amiable coercions of our nature."[10] This notion seems to bespeak of a grace of nature, though here again he does not term it so. He posits these "amiable coercions" throughout his writings. Predestination is itself one of them: "predestination is the preparation for grace, while grace is the donation itself."[11] The distinction between preparation for grace and grace itself, whether in relation to predestination or other "coercions" of our nature, is a good deal less clear than Augustine supposed. His adamant insistence on the distinction was born of his argument against Pelagius. His presuppositions regarding creation as essentially good in all its parts and as derivative from the generous action of God, blur the distinction more than he apparently realized. He never specifically inquired whether the gifts of creation were themselves of grace; had he done so, his answer would almost certainly have had to be in the affirmative. At least at one point he did link the two in passing,[12] but this was hardly consistent with the predominant sweep of his thought.

For Augustine, grace above all else is the grace of redemption. His theology of grace is developed almost entirely in terms of sin and the recalcitrant human will. The operation of grace is limited to human consciousness, to the realm of the spirit. Grace is inapplicable to the exterior circumstances of life, to its constitution; it is an interior reality, operating in the personal dimension of life and effectively nowhere else. He speaks frequently as though it were a matter strictly between the individual soul and God, that no exterior factors were at all relevant. It is not, he says in words that became normative for much of Western tradition, "by law and teaching uttering their lessons from without, but by a secret, wonderful, and ineffable power from within, that God works in men's hearts not only revelations of the truth, but also good dispositions of the will."[13] One wants to ask Augustine about the possible relation between the "ineffable power from within" and those things "uttering their lessons from without," whether the power from within is disparate from the things without, whether moreover interior grace could be recognized for what it is apart from factors exterior to the soul.

Augustine's thought is immensely complicated, throwing light on this issue, then on that, without ever demonstrating a fundamentally unified vision of reality as a whole. Indeed, it is hard to discern whether he really had any one such vision. He seems to have had visions of reality that conflicted, or at least dwelt together in his mind uneasily. The difficulty is probably less theoretical than psychological, though a number of his philosophical premises proved an impediment to a unified vision. In spite of his highly positive assessment of created reality, aspects of his own basic experience ran counter to it. The divine grace had rescued, wrenched him from a nature he perceived as vile. It was therefore one thing to glory in the order and beauty of the world, quite another to contemplate his own manner of being in the world. He could speak rapturously of "the settled order of things in Heaven . . . the boundless power of seeds, the beauty of light, the varieties of colors, sounds, tastes and scents,"[14] of the marvels of "the measure, order and form" in every nature.[15] He could even wax strong on the glories and wonders of human nature in its splendid cultural and technical attainments.[16] Yet when he turns to the religious and moral dimensions of life, he recoils. Human nature is stained, corrupt, sick; it is incapacitated by sin, ensnared by earthly affections and of itself helpless to perform any good whatsoever.

So alert as Augustine was to the wondrous variety of nature and as keenly interested as he often showed himself in the science of his time, he steered his readers away from both. "[I]t is not necessary to probe into the nature of things, as was done by those whom the Greeks call *physici*; nor need to be in alarm lest the Christian should be ignorant of the force and number of the elements. . . . It is enough for Christians to believe that the only cause of all created things is the goodness of the Creator."[17] While this appears in a handbook designed for those for whom such studies may have been beyond reach, the sentiment is everywhere present in his writings. "Men go on to search out the hidden powers of nature . . . which to know profits nothing."[18]

Augustine consistently affirmed the goodness of created reality, but he valued it primarily as that which invited his mind to seek God. Its changing forms were an inducement to look beyond them toward the unchangeable, to that which alone was real. His indebtedness to the Neo-Platonists and doubtless the residual influence of his years as a Manichee had so colored his understanding of nature that pockets of negativity toward it remained a powerful though obscured factor in his mind. The biblical doctrine of creation, with its intensely positive view of nature, was intentionally dominant and certainly a controlling feature of his thought. The negative tendencies however were present and always operative.

Even in the case of Psalm 24, where God is being praised for the glories of creation and the giving of the law, Augustine curiously confines himself to comments on the church. "The earth is the Lord's and the fullness thereof, the world and all that dwell therein" is said to represent the church, which embraces the whole world.[19] "The earth's form of beauty," he says in relation to Psalm 144, "is a sort of voice of the dumb earth," summoning the mind to worship God, to turn from that which is without to that which is within.[20] Created reality at best gives rise to an "enquiring which is itself a questioning." The truth is discerned in the interior life of the soul, "in the embracement of my inner man."[21] The world of the senses, for religious and moral purposes at least, was radically devalued, made wholly subsidiary to what he took to be an inner life of the mind that existed and functioned in mysterious independence of what was without.

The chief contribution of Augustine to the doctrine of grace lies of course in his emphatic emphasis on interiority. Grace is the gift of the Spirit to the inner man, "by whom there is formed in the mind a delight in, and love of, that supreme and unchangeable good, which is God, by which he may conceive an ardent desire to cleave to God."[22] But this emphasis, supported by his notion that the soul in some real sense existed separately from the body, provided the precise ground for the inadequacy of his point of view. It prevented him from appreciating, at the fundamental level, exterior reality as indispensibly ingredient both to the operations of the mind and to the experience of grace. In more than a little of his thought about grace one might gain the distinct impression that even the embodiment of grace in Christ was not strictly necessary. This is true not only in the case of his deliberations on predestinating grace—an obvious instance—but in his general tendency to assign little or no importance to outward forms and forces in his theology of grace as a whole.

Although he everywhere proclaims that the things that are made declare the glory and power of God, Augustine nowhere in his writings on grace makes provision for the principle that this proclamation entails. He was, it appears, content to speak of the goodness of created reality, insofar as it had any being at all, as reflecting the absolute goodness of the creator. It existed by divine donation but Augustine could not bring himself to own that it existed by grace. He could not of course consistently uphold the notion that grace was a purely inward reality, a matter between the soul and God. Scripture and tradition were clearly means of grace for him, as was the life of the church and the course of events in personal and political history. It is a curious fact that he who gave the Western church such an intensely corporate understanding of itself as the many in the one and devised the conception of the city of God as a social reality through and through, a body united in a common allegiance and love, at the same time set forth a view of grace that privatized it and virtually limited its operation to the conscious mind—to individuals who had reached sufficient awareness "to delight in, to love, and to cleave to God." Here again inconsistency inevitably arose when he came to speak of the grace of infant baptism,[23] to say nothing of his deliverances on the irresistibility of grace in respect to those elected to salvation.[24] Grace here is a coercive force, something operating without regard for consciousness.

Augustine's doctrine of love to some extent softened his sharp strictures on grace, yet the same tendency was at work in both. It is possible, indeed probable, that his deliverances on love were dearer to him, more essentially Augustinian, as it were, than his writings against the Pelagians. Certainly they form a more attractive feature of his thought. Written apart from the stress of controversy and considered first in this light and then in another over the years, his teachings on love show him at his calmest and most winsome.

Natural loves are not denied. The capacity to love is the cardinal gift of nature. Our loves are that which define us; what is loved constitutes the core of human reality for it is our loves that drive us "whithersoever we go."[25] All relationships, whether on the personal, social, or political level, are determined by love. Self-love to the point of exclusion of others and God, amounting to the drive for self-salvation, is a "darkened form" of the image of God.[26] The fundamental problem of the moral life is not that we are unloving. We love plenteously. The trouble is that we love the wrong things or love the right things for the wrong reasons. Our loves require radical conversion; they need to be reordered to God, toward the One to whom they were ordinated from the beginning. Our loves therefore form the precise sphere for the operation of grace. Redemptive grace enfolds them and redirects them to their right order.

Augustine does not normally use the specific language of grace in his discussions of love, speaking rather of the Spirit as the power that informs and transforms human loves. It is clear, however, that in his doctrine of love he is concerned above all else to uphold the gratuity of grace. If he had a favorite text it was Romans 5:5: "God's love has been poured into our hearts by the Holy Spirit that has been given to us." It occurs three times in a letter to Anastasius concerning the Pelagian problem, and many times in other letters and writings.[27] That "man has not whence to love God unless from God"[28] was his constant message.

The other side of the utter gratuity of grace is utter human humility. Thus another favorite text was 1 Corinthians 4:7: "What do you have that you did not receive." In keeping with Pauline intention, Augustine limited the applicability of this saying to the grace of redemption. It could have been extended however to the grace of creation as Pelagius apparently desired. Pelagians hold, Augustine scoffed, "that grace is the nature in which we were created, not the grace of Jesus Christ."[29] But "if righteousness comes of nature, Christ died in vain."[30] Nature therefore is one thing, grace another: no righteousness issues from nature and there is thus no grace in nature. Grace is purely and wholly found in the redeeming power of the Spirit of Christ. That humility could be induced only—perhaps we had better say primarily—through redemptive grace was a settled conviction of Augustine, something which made, I can only believe, for his misjudgment of Pelagius, that the whole Pelagian program was one of pride, a boasting in human prowess against the divine bestowal. Pelagius, if his teaching can be discerned in Augustine's rendering of it with any real accuracy, glorified human capacity not through pride but through gratitude, through grateful recognition of God's gifts in creation as well as in redemption. However inadequate his understanding of what redemption involved, Pelagius had a healthy regard for the wonders of human nature as gifts of God and did not want these primal gifts to be obviated. Yet at the same time he saw the necessity of an increment of grace for the purpose of redemption, though the increment he spoke of was very sparse in comparison with Augustine's conception. He no doubt had a deficient sense of the compelling power of the misdirected will, to use Augustinian language, but he had a keen appreciation of the mysterious yet gracious order in which we are set. Redemptive grace for him was a bonus, a gift additional to the splendid grace of nature, both constituting, most probably, one thing, not two.

That Pelagius was not always wrongheaded receives corroboration in his judgment that human beings were created mortal, that death was simply a natural consequence of living. It did not result from the fall as Augustine and tradition affirmed; it was a structural feature of life as such. Few theologians today would wish to deny this. His emphasis on sin as socially transmitted, as induced by familial and communal practice and attitude, is also congenial to modern theologians. Augustine was right in many instances, in more perhaps than Pelagius, but he was not always right. For one thing, he never sufficiently distinguished between finitude and sin, holding that many of the exigencies of finite nature were sinful. Pelagius's perception was more realistic on this score even though his estimate of the power of the will to accomplish the good was excessively optimistic. The old saying that his platform was salvation by education has point. It is not always clearly recognized however that for him the educator was God and the principles of the educative process were gifts of grace. Augustine's complaint that Pelagius glorified God as creator to the neglect of God as redeemer was not entirely just, revealing perhaps more about his own priorities than those of Pelagius. However inadequate his theology of grace, Pelagius was right in this much at least: if grace is not to be found in the very constitution of nature, the restitution of nature by grace is adventitious, something that can only make for a severe rift in Christian awareness.

Nothing said here of course is intended to scold Augustine. He was a pioneer in theology and his contributions to it, including the theology of nature and grace, are beyond telling. But as Karl Barth has noted, all theologians, however significant their contributions, leave behind them an evil legacy. The greater the theologian, the greater the evil left behind. Augustine's philosophical inheritance and his own personal proclivities barred him from bringing creation and redemption into a unified whole. His pronounced tendency to demean nature when considering it in the light of grace arrested the development in Western theology of a positive understanding of nature, and does so yet to an extent that can scarcely be exaggerated. His reaction to Pelagian teaching—and to him we owe almost everything we know about it—was both loss and gain for the church and, by derivation, for Western thought in general. It was a gain in depth and interiority but a loss in terms of breadth and in understanding that the human realm within was possible only upon the basis of the natural realm without.

The theological stance Augustine established in the Western church found its central formula not only under his aegis but in a phrase that echoed his very words: "grace does not destroy nature, it perfects it." While this formula had many good uses, as already suggested, and has many good uses yet, it nevertheless set nature and grace apart. Nature, the formula implies, is without grace until graced by redemption. Behind it lay Augustine's insistence that grace deserted the first parents upon their disobedience. The framers of the formula had no wish to posit nature or even human nature as a graceless void, certainly not Saint Thomas, in whose writings the formula finds explicit expression. For all of them creation derives from the free and gracious act of God; not only so, for God animates it, dwells in its every part by the power of his word. As Augustine himself put the matter, the word enlightens all rational minds and beasts, "down even to the minutest worm."[31] And if vestiges of the

Trinity remain in human nature and indeed throughout creation as a whole, as Augustine avers and tradition repeats, then creation is certainly not a graceless void. Yet however true this was for him and those who followed, grace was conceived as redemptive of nature, as other than nature, something coming upon it from without.

The tendency to divorce nature and grace took many twists and turns in Western thought. Augustine's influence marked the process throughout, often directly, sometimes only indirectly, but it was always a present and potent factor. My aim here is not to trace in any detail the impact of Augustine's theology on Western thought but to point to moments where it was either decisive or determinative.

The supreme instance perhaps of the impact of the Augustinian tradition is found in Luther's almost total concentration on the inner life of the soul. It is here where grace is operative; the world of nature is scarcely given a glance. The natural theology of the Scholastics is roundly denounced and even its very limited denotation of the gracious element within nature is rejected. "When Luther turned catechist and found himself obliged to teach the doctrine of creation, he brought it all under the same *pro me* which he had found in the gospel of grace, and he reduced the whole world of nature to a repository of goods for the service of man."[32] Luther's great influence, one crossing virtually all denominational barriers at many crucial points, needs no comment.

Less direct but still determinative was the influence of Augustinianism on René Descartes. I do not refer here to the high probability that his *cogito ergo sum* formula and the general perspective behind it, despite Descartes's disclaimer, were inspired by Augustine's deliberations in *De magistro* and elsewhere.[33] I refer rather to the basis in the Augustinian tradition for his bifurcation of the mental and the material realms. The split between mind and matter which found "clear and distinct" status in Descartes's thought was grounded in the split between nature and grace that dogged Western Catholicism from the time of Augustine. "Thinking substances" were altogether different, Descartes declared, from extension of whatever kind—matter, space, the human body itself. Extension was deemed mechanical, dumb, devoid of sense.[34] The separation he posited between mind and matter had a long and involved history, to be sure: the growth of science and the increasing control over natural forces, the discussions of the philosophers of nature who preceded him, and the deep residue of Neo-Platonism in Western tradition, attributable in no small part to Augustine himself, were formative factors of Descartes's dualism.

But there was also the specific impact of the Catholicism in which he was grounded and which owed its forms and spirit to Augustine as to no other patristic thinker. Descartes's bifurcation of mind and body was already implicit, almost explicit indeed, in the train of thought that Augustine set pacing in the latter part of the fourth century. Even though a great deal of his speculative and theoretical thought went far beyond received structures of belief, Descartes remained within the Catholic tradition and was guided by its general understanding of life and the world.

Through the agency of Cartesian philosophy and attendant forms of thought, the Augustinian tradition went on to make an impact on Immanuel Kant, who has influenced the course of Western theology more perhaps than any other philosopher since his time. That that influence is far from moribund, few could doubt. It remains a very potent factor in Protestant theology and in recent years it has become a determining force in Roman Catholic theology, with the shift from cosmological to historical and anthropological thinking in so much of it.

When Kant declared that nature in itself could not be known objectively, that it had no bearing on the matter of God's existence and that the moral realm alone provided an avenue for affirming God, the rift between the world without and the world within was greatly deepened. An echo of Descartes's dualism was heard in Kant, even though the Cartesian philosophy was not something to which he directly subscribed or which he highly regarded. While he had a much clearer grasp of the relation of mind and matter than Descartes, he lived in and breathed the dualistic atmosphere decreed by Cartesianism. It was similarly so with Locke and Hume who influenced him most directly. Owing to its rigor and to the temper of the times, Kant's thought had the effect of isolating the human, historical realm from the natural realm more forcibly than Descartes's.

In his inaugural dissertation, which appeared in 1770, Kant set forth the distinction, amounting to a virtual bifurcation, of the world of the senses and the world of the mind. The title of the piece indicates as much: *De mundi sensibilis atque intelligibilis forma and principiis*. Although his mature thought went far beyond the sharp distinction drawn here, the dualistic stance remained operative and was never wholly erased. Defenders of Kant have endeavored to show that his overall view is not truly dualistic, that in "the last analysis" he "does not divide the 'world,' ontologically speaking, into a realm of being and a realm of norms," and that this was done not by Kant himself but by the "Kantians" and the "Neo-Kantians."[35] Possibly this was the case. Yet the fact is that Kant was perceived by many, perhaps most, of his immediate followers to have posited a fundamental duality between the two realms. In terms therefore of the influence he exercised in subsequent history, there can be little doubt that the dualistic tendency in his thought, or what was perceived as such, proved dominant.

Theology and philosophy after Kant, particularly in Germany, found themselves increasingly locked in the human realm, with the natural realm as lifeless, valueless stuff for human control. Hegel, although he expended a vast amount of speculative energy in his work on the philosophy of nature, viewed the natural environment as the merest vehicle for the human spirit. Nature and all its objects had little bearing on the existence of God; the slightest, most fleeting thought of the human mind, even its meanest whim, provided a far greater testimony. The starry sky that gripped Kant's mind was described by Hegel as only a sort of "light-eruption, no more astonishing than a crowd of men or a mass of flies."[36] This proud disdain of the natural world lives on in the thought of more than a few theologians today. In company with it is an anthropocentricity of truly remarkable proportions, several instances of which we shall deal with later on at some length. At the moment, however, a few further glances at the movement of Western thought toward the bifurcation of human history and its setting in nature might prove useful.

Hegel's great contemporary, Friedrich Schleiermacher, was frequently accused of valuing the natural realm too highly, his stress on the divine immanence resembling, his critics alleged, the pantheism of Spinoza. Neither Spinoza nor Schleiermacher was a pantheist in the strict sense of the term, though both had quite positive things to say about nature. Schleiermacher's youthful work, *Speeches on Religion*, was replete with the romantic feeling for nature, something of which was retained in his mature and greatest work, *The Christian Faith*. The divine omnipotence, he says in the latter, "in all its livingness reveals itself everywhere in the world, as eternal omnipresent and omniscient, without any distinction more or less, without even a contrast in respect of dependence between one part and another."[37] The *Speeches* held that nature was the expression of the infinite and that religion was a sense and taste for the infinite. While there is a good deal of continuity between the earlier and later work, the status of nature is dramatically reduced in *The Christian Faith*, where he insists that the sole source of theology lies in the deliverances of the religious consciousness, in the pious feelings of the Christian community. Primary among the immediacies of religious consciousness is "the sense of absolute dependence," which entails a consciousness of the world, of the self as in some sense dependent on the world and of the world itself as a dependent reality. But despite this Schleiermacher holds that the doctrine of creation is secondary and derivative: the doctrine of preservation is prior in consciousness. One wants to ask however whether the consciousness of preservation does not involve consciousness of creation as that which is being preserved, that is, whether the divine does not preserve what it forms, whether indeed the two doctrines can be severed. But Schleiermacher would not have it so. Although his evaluation of nature was highly positive, he allowed it to have only an indirect bearing on theology. The deliverances of immediate consciousness were overwhelmingly those that pertained to the sphere of redemption. As with Augustine, he would not say that nature was of grace. His doctrine of preservation implies that it is, yet he formally limited grace to matters associated with the redeemer.[38]

For Schleiermacher the prescribed province of theology was an almost exclusive concentration on the realm of grace, on the impact of the person and work of Christ upon the believing community. His limitation of the concern of theology to what the religious consciousness delivered was taken up by the many theologians who venerated him and fell captive to his new theological approach. Thus Albrecht Ritschl, indebted to Kant, Schleiermacher, and Herman Lotze, declared that "theology has to do, not with natural objects, but with states and movements of man's spiritual life."[39] He considered nature as the enemy of freedom, redemption as the victory over its constraints, and history as the arena in which the battle was to be fought and won.[40] Ritschl drew the line between nature and grace decisively. The tendency in Augustinianism to make them oppositional becomes in Ritschlianism a division, with no loose ends. Metaphysics, conceived as interpretation of nature, has no place whatever in the concerns of theology.

Continuing the Ritschlian dichotomy, Wilhelm Herrmann declared that we can "no longer hope to find God by seeking Him in nature. It is only out of the life of history that God can come to meet us."[41] This utterance found many echoes in the following decades, as did his better known dictum that we "find God in nothing but Christ."[42]

Two more features in the development of Western thought enter into our concerns here, existentialism and Marxism. Both reflect and are dependent upon the theological tradition initiated by Augustine, though many other factors of course paved the way for them and shaped their historical specificities. In each the human realm is exalted, the natural realm disparaged; in each whatever meaning is to be found has its locus within the dimension of history, with nature as at best a backdrop for human activity.

Karl Löwith describes with great power the stance of these movements and their deep affinities.[43] Regarding existentialism, he notes that the "world" for Sartre, Heidegger, and Kierkegaard is a world without nature; it is the human world of selfhood and interhuman relations (and, we need to add, the agonizing lack of them). Heidegger reserves the lowest category of the merely "existent" for nature, into which human beings are "thrown," cast as aliens. We have no place in nature; human existence is a "metaphysical displacement." This understanding of the human situation is rightly linked with the loss of the pre-Copernician view of an ordered universe in which human beings could feel at home: a centerless, limitless universe throws us back on ourselves, as Pascal centuries before perceived, and with it concern for the inner life tends to become exclusive.[44]

But behind the modern view of the cosmos there was another ingredient of this "metaphysical displacement," and here again the Augustinian tradition was silently at work. Although Augustine had a firm sense of an ordered world, a deep undercurrent of his thought tended to obviate the notion that the world, however ordered, was a place in which human beings could be at home. Continuing the ancient idea of "the Platonists" that the soul was independent of the body, he held that the soul was somehow lost in the world and longed for its true home in the sphere of eternity. This long tradition, bequeathed to Western Catholicism in large part by Augustine, could not but have contributed to the sense of forlornness in the modern world, even though the development of scientific knowledge was its immediate background.

Augustine was also an inspirant of the existentialists' stance of deep dread of science and dismissal of its importance for human self-understanding. What was of moment in his thought, as in that of the existentialists, was not science but salvation, concern for the inner life of the soul. It is small wonder that among the ancients Augustine is often deemed one of the chief precursors of existentialism.

Kierkegaard implicitly dismissed the laws of the cosmos, the discoveries of both telescope and microscope, as having no relevance for understanding human existence, for "what is the use of explaining the whole physical universe or world history if one does not understand oneself."[45]

Concern for cosmic and world history is an escape from the self into illusory importance. The history of importance for the self is immediate history, the negativities of the age, its forlorness and brutal facticity.

It needs to be noted that this immediate history has a history, something that Kierkegaard did not take into account. The negative experience of the modern age began with the anxiety produced through the postulation of a universe of indefinite limits, one that seemed to leave the human enterprise on the edge of nothingness. Existentialism is therefore concerned not solely with "personal history" but with the aggravating forces of history that condition and shape human existence. Although it is true that existentialists tend to decry interest in world history as such, they have been peculiarly aware of the weight of modern humanity's historical inheritance and have effectively focused attention upon it, however limited their view of it or however ahistorical many of their deliverances were.

Kierkegaard's notorious disregard for the history of Jesus' life is a case in point.[46] Still for him, the eternal paradoxically entered time, altering time for all time. Theologians after him were similarly dismissive of the personal history of Jesus, but were keen to set forth the radical alteration that occurred in history through his life and death and to concern themselves with its consequences and possibilities for all subsequent history. Thus history for them became the realm of whatever grace there was. All without was menacing, dark and intractable. But although nature was verbally denied, dismissed as irrelevant to existence, in its threatening immensity it was a prime factor in existential self-understanding.

Existentialism, heavily indebted to Kant's "Copernician revolution," made for a continuing and deepening split between human consciousness and the nature out of which consciousness arises. Kant himself marveled reverently before "the starry sky above" and "the moral law within," and he did so perhaps equally. His existentialist heirs, however, evinced little or no reverence for the heavens. Instead of reverence there was resentment, dread, and dismissal. The personal dimension of life was torn out of its cosmic dimension; history was abstracted from nature. The marvel of it is that there was no recognition, or very little recognition, that such an abstraction was the merest chimera of the mind.

Another factor making for modern theology's narrow concentration on history is the powerful impetus of Marxism. Few movements have exercised such widespread and telling influence on theological self-criticism and construction in the modern period as the challenge of socialistic philosophy, principally that initiated by Karl Marx. It hardly needs to be said that Marx shared the lack of concern for nature evinced in the thought of Hegel, his mentor. The Hegelian emphasis on the realm of the human spirit became the Marxist emphasis on the realm of human productivity. The world that is natural to human beings, Marx held, is not the world of nature but the world of history because man produces the latter by means of his own labor.[47] Nature is the precondition of human activity, of interest only in so far as it could be humanly seized and utilized. The materialism of which Marx spoke with unremitting passion was not the material universe but the historically determined conditions of labor and production. The "means of life" and the visionary promise of an "earthly kingdom of freedom" form the driving motifs of Marx's philosophy. Human beings are what they are because of their history, the modes of production that have determined their activity. Concern with the "world" is concern for history and how to change it.[48]

Although Marx's scheme and program had their immediate matrix in the industrial revolution and were rendered historical possibilities in terms of it, Western Christianity prepared the way for their development. Marxism is cast in the peculiarly Western mode of thought with its anthropocentric focus on history and with nature as little more than a tool for human hands. The split between nature and grace in the Western church and its secularized versions in European philosophical thought were powerful intellectual forces in the formation of Marx's mind. The industrial revolution, apart from which Marxism could not have arisen, was itself derivative from the divorce between science and theology, behind which was the separation of nature and grace in ecclesiastical tradition.

Though deeply deviant and powerfully shaped by the spirit and forms of the modern period, Marxism was spun within the vast, intricate web of Western Catholicism and its corrective footnotes in Protestantism. Augustine therefore was inevitably a factor in its emergence. Moreover, his *City of God*, the first great philosophy of history (best characterized perhaps as a theology of history, though Augustine would not have called it this), was a precursor to Marx's scheme, which is as "religious" in cast as it is political, if not more so. Marx devised a full-blown philosophy of history with salvation at its center. Although salvation was conceived in purely temporal terms, with "grace" as the dialectical forces of history and "sin" as economic oppression, the goal of the scheme is not simply socialistic, it is salvific. It is of course not possible to determine to what

15

extent Augustine's great treatise influenced him. On the one hand, the influence was no doubt mainly negative in that Marx denied Augustine's chief interpretative categories; on the other, there was the broad sweep of thought, inclusive and visionary, that marked the *City of God* and that was the shade behind all those philosophies of history in Western thought that helped to shape the Marxist gospel.

Someone has said that of all modern figures who have influenced the course of theology, Marx ranks higher than any other, with the possible exception of Freud. It has been said further that these two thinkers have contributed more to theological orientation and methodology than any theologian writing since their time. That there is point in this few would contest. I do not however want to press the point here but to observe in passing that socialistic philosophy, depth psychology, psychoanalysis, and allied disciplines have served to rivet our attention to ourselves and our historical situation. The impact they have had on theology, often in combination though rarely without significant adjustment, has been quite varied, but one thing has commonly resulted: an affirmation of the split between nature and history, the natural and the personal, and a concentration on the latter as the sole arena of authentic theological concern.

A number of theologians of our epoch have, to be sure, moved in a counter direction, emphasizing the natural at the expense of the historical dimension of life. Some few of them reduce history, as nearly as possible, to a natural occurrence. This theological naturalism finds its basis in what is taken to be the implications of natural science. Rigorously reductionistic and materialistic schemes that effectively claim that human forms of behavior and so human history are simply material systems—for example, that of B. F. Skinner—are rarely espoused by theologians who see the necessity of making provision for human purpose and its consequences in history. In its nonreductive interpretations, theological naturalism has made important contributions to Christian thought, helping to generate a renewed regard for nature, however limited in extent. The dominant trend in theology has been overwhelmingly in the opposite direction. Although the modern ecological movement is tiptoeing about in some theological quarters and disturbing the dogmatic slumbers of an increasing number of Christian thinkers, the line most often taken is that best drawn by Wolfhart Pannenberg, who holds that for people of the modern world, "there is no longer any direct way from the facts of nature to the idea of God . . . the world cannot be the point of departure for the grounding of religious assertions."[49] According to Pannenberg and those of like mind, anthropology and history provide the ground in which theology has to dig. While it is true that theology must do much if not most of its digging here, the question that is arising more and more often is whether it must not dig deeper, finding its grounding in that which provides the ground of history itself.[50]

CHAPTER 2

Irenaeus and the East

AUGUSTINE WAS CLOSEFISTED with the term *grace,* jealously reserving it for the realm of redemption. The Greek fathers, in marked contrast, were generous with it, declaring that grace was everywhere and that everything was a work of grace. They did not look upon the creative action of God and the grace of redemption as in any sense separable; grace was unitary, continuous, and universal. As a result, the spirituality and consciousness of the East is less constricted and considerably more unified than that of the West, so largely fashioned in the cauldron of conflicts that resided in the mind of Augustine of Hippo.

It is of course easy to exaggerate the differences between the two traditions. The differences however are far from small, particularly perhaps in regard to the formal understanding of the relation of nature and grace. I want to examine some of the differences in what follows and to point to some of the similarities as well. Since Irenaeus of Lyons is one of the most influential of early Eastern theologians, his thought will be treated in some detail, followed by a number of general observations on the Eastern tradition as it bears on nature and grace.

The immediate background of Irenaeus's writings is the depredation of the created order by the Gnostics, a fact that conditions both the approach and the result of his theology. Had he been writing against something like Pelagianism rather than Gnosticism, his thought would no doubt have taken a different turn. It is not likely however that he would have gone to the lengths Augustine felt constrained to go. Not only did he stand in an earlier and more fluid tradition, he was, if his character is reflected at all well in his writings, a good deal more even-tempered, less conflicted, and more kindly disposed by nature toward the human condition than Augustine. Though he does not present us a systematic theology, he does give us a system of doctrine, one that is coherent and more or less consistent. If it lacks the depths and imaginative leaps of

Augustine's thought, the brilliance and philosophical acuity of Origen's, and the range of the theology of both these great thinkers, it has its own distinctive character, presenting a vision of Christian experience and understanding that has about it a wholeness that both affirms life and goes a long way toward supplying the theological grounds for the affirmation.

The root doctrine of Christian faith for Irenaeus is that God is the creator of everything that is; nothing else makes sense apart from this. The Gnostic writers he opposed, mainly Valentinus and Marcion, were undercutting, he believed, the very foundation of faith by their denial that the creator was not ultimate but a secondary deity, a demiurge who created a world less than good, and that the saving deity manifested in Christ was higher and other than the deity who created. "It is proper," he says early on in *Against Heresies*, a work written between 182 and 188, "that I should begin with the first and most important head, that is, God the Creator, who made the heavens and the earth" and "to demonstrate that there is nothing either above Him or after Him . . . since He is the only God, the only Lord, the only Creator, the only Father, alone containing all things, and Himself commanding all things into existence."[1] That the world is called into being by God, loved by God, and continually sustained by God is for Irenaeus the *sine qua non* of everything Christians believe and hope.

The idea of God that Irenaeus entertains is largely biblical, though certain philosophical doctrines current in his time have a place in his thought, such as the divine self-sufficiency, immutability, and impassibility. He does not show a great deal of interest in philosophical doctrines, however, and tends to shy away from them. He knows the power of philosophy through Justin Martyr and others as well, and at one point at least gives guarded praise to Plato, who proved "to be more religious" than the Gnostics in allowing that the same God who was both just and good was the maker and framer of the universe.[2] The philosophical doctrines that he makes use of are either those already appropriated in the tradition or in his hands made to bend to a scriptural interpretation. Thus impassibility is not allowed to deny the creator pity for the creatures or to interfere in any real way with the suffering of Christ.[3]

Irenaeus does not spend much time speculating about the origins of the world, holding that the Gnostics had been led into grievous error by their fits of speculation. "[W]hat is true, sure and incontrovertible" about the origins of the world "belongs only to God."[4] In regard to this and many other matters, we should have recourse to the Scriptures, "being most

19

properly assured that the Scriptures are indeed perfect, since they were spoken by the Word of God and His Spirit."[5] It is enough to have the knowledge of faith that the world exists through the grace of the one and the same God disclosed to Abraham, Moses, and the prophets and who is the God and Father of Jesus Christ.[6]

God creates out of complete freedom, Irenaeus holds. God is constrained by nothing outside of the divine will of love. God neither needs the world nor is God's tranquility disturbed by the world. Every aspect of the world, from the meanest of entities to the highest, needs God, without whom the world would have no tranquility at all and would fall into the nothingness out of which it was called. Creation derives from the divine generosity, from, we might say, absolute grace. The need the world has for God means that it exists by grace, is sustained by grace, and is furthered by grace. In short, for Irenaeus, its every part and every prospect are of grace.[7]

That God is present to the world at every point and that it lives by the divine life are not, Irenaeus insists, to be accounted strange since the world is the expression of the divine will and the object of God's love. God is present in the world by the divine "two hands," the Son and the Spirit, frequently designated Word and Wisdom.[8] Occasionally Irenaeus speaks of the Word as mediator between God and the world, but this is not his most characteristic usage. His conception of the Word, together with that of the Spirit, is that it is the very presence and action of God in the world. The relation of God and the Logos is best seen in such statements as these: "God being all Mind, and all Logos, both speaks exactly what He thinks, and thinks exactly what He speaks. For His thought is Logos, and Logos is Mind, and Mind comprehending all things is the Father Himself."[9] God is not a compound being, "as if God were one thing, and the original Mind another" and "so again, with respect to Logos."[10] The Mind and Spirit were "anterior to all creation."[11] In the creation of the world they were not creative agents of God so much as God's own creativity in action.

The world in a special and direct sense is of the Word's making. It belongs to the Word. The Spirit or Wisdom is cited along with the Word from time to time but frequently the Word is mentioned alone, the function of the Spirit being assumed or perhaps subsumed under the Word's. The world belongs to the Word in a peculiar sense because its structures in every case are those given to it by the Word. And not only so, for the Word's presence in the world's structures is a veritable indwelling, even a "mingling."[12]

In Irenaeus's usage, Word and Christ tend to be interchangeable, as for Justin Martyr before him. Though he speaks most often of the Logos as the creative power of God in self-expression, he can speak of Christ as the Son or Word who fashions the world with the Spirit. Christ ceased to be a title with Paul and became a name only to become another title, a title ascribable to the eternal creative energy of God, one still retaining, however, its salvific and historical association with Jesus as the Christ. In Irenaeus's terms then the world was created by Christ and moreover it looks toward Christ. In the incarnation Christ comes to his own in the most literal sense. He has created the world in order to enter it, to be embodied within it. His coming into the world was predestined by God from the beginning.[13]

Yet Irenaeus's primary focus of attention in the whole creative process is the creation of Adam. Adam was created in order that his creator might enter him and move him toward the end for which he was formed. That end is Christ, the self-expression and perfect image of God. In creation Adam is given a capacity to receive the divine life; he is essentially *capax dei*, "a vessel open to God," who finds his life in receiving from him who is life itself. This is the context in which Irenaeus's famous line "the glory of God is a living man" is set.[14] Adam, as first and representative man, was thus made to become the image and likeness of the creative Word of God.[15]

The first Adam was deflected from his destiny, as were his descendants through him, by the machinations of Satan, a fallen angel. Irenaeus takes Satan and his power as utterly real, as much so as his adversaries the Gnostics, with however this decisive difference: the evil power was subject to God and had his dominion only by God's leave. According to Irenaeus, God created Adam and his seed to be higher than the angels. Satan was therefore jealous of Adam and undertook to bring him down to ruin. Adam was a child, was immature, that is, was without the capacity of adult judgment, and was therefore easily deceived by Satan into denying God and attempting to rely on his own resources.[16] This idea does not accord well with Irenaeus's insistence that Adam's fall was occasioned by the misuse of his freedom, a freedom that seems to be pretty adult, but to this I will turn in a moment. The point to be made here is that despite Adam's betrayal of God in Eden, the creator never ceased to be with him

21

in all the dispensations of his life and so in all the dispensations of the history of his descendants.[17]

Irenaeus is very tender toward Adam, insisting that his salvation was not only possible, but assured.[18] Adam moreover was not cursed; the curse fell upon the ground or, as Irenaeus sometimes put it, the Serpent,[19] "that it might fall upon man with a mitigated rebuke."[20] And by degrees, little by little God "took compassion upon man."[21] Death itself bespeaks of grace for Irenaeus, for through his pity, God interposed death on man "so that his sin would not be interminable and irredeemable" and so that he might cease "to live to sin, and dying to it, might begin to live to God."[22] Going further perhaps, Irenaeus suggests that Adam's very bondage to Satan was of grace in that it engendered expectation and hope for deliverance.[23]

These points of view might indicate an uncommonly optimistic perspective on the fall of man. They tell however only half the story, if that much. Irenaeus's thought has a severity about it that is not always noted in treatments of his doctrine of humankind. Adam is, for Irenaeus, in the grip of the evil one; he is bound, captive to Satan.[24] The power of Satan over him is such that all life was taken from him, all life understood as true life in communion with God. Since Adam, humanity *is* fallen, thrust into the condition of sin, defeated and with no power whatever to undo the defeat.[25] Although Satan has license from God to prey upon Adam and his seed, he yet has the power to struggle with God and to win the battle for the souls of many. He must be decisively defeated at a great cost before his hold on Adam is broken and before he himself is bound eternally in hell.[26]

The condemnation of Adam and Eve and their descendants derives in Irenaeus's thought from two things, as we have noted. First, there is their childlike innocence, the vulnerability born of their immaturity. As creatures not yet fully formed, they were seduced by the wily and wicked intelligence of Satan. The immaturity of Adam and Eve is an Irenaean concept greatly esteemed by many modern theologians, emphasized sometimes to the exclusion of another and perhaps more prominent aspect of Irenaeus's thought: free will and its decisive abuse. However childlike the first parents were for Irenaeus, they were sufficiently developed to exercise deliberate choice. The power of choice belongs to human beings by creation. Indeed, free will is a distinctive mark of the image of God in us.[27] Disobedience, which brings separation from God and so death, is *allowing* Satan to have his way, is falling by deliberate act under his dominion. Punishment for falling is swift. Although not directly meted out by God and a natural consequence of an unnatural condition, it implacably falls on the disobedient one and all, because they are destitute of all that is good.[28]

But Irenaeus cannot rest with a picture of such bleakness. Even if it entails something like contradiction, he will modify the devastation of the fall, although never for a moment denying that it was devastating in its effect upon the whole range of human life. As noted already, he will not have fallen Adam and Eve bereft of God. They remain ordinated toward the Son and the Spirit.[29] They have life, even if not true life, by the gift of God. Their very flesh is never destitute of the constitutive wisdom and power of God. They can follow the divine commandments since a small seed of righteousness remained in them and, above all else, they retain the capacity to receive God.[30]

While he does not do so invariably, Irenaeus makes a distinction between the image and the likeness of God.[31] The distinction was a happy one for it suited his overall purpose well. What Adam lost in the fall was not the *imago Dei*. By creation he was the image of God and nothing could alter this most fundamental fact of his being. But through disobedience he lost something that belonged to him by nature, and in his sin he became unnatural. He lost the *similitudo Dei*, lost the freedom to be like God, and with this lost incorruptibility and immortality, that which essentially denoted likeness to God. The image of God is therefore the capacity for God; the likeness is the capacity fulfilled through a renewed participation in the life of God. Such a participation was possible only through an utterly gratuitous act of God. It awaited the gift of the one in whom the image and likeness were altogether coincident, the embodiment of the Word in the second Adam.

Although his interest is confined for the most part to biblical history, Irenaeus can be generous in his estimate of those outside the stream of that history. Christ as second Adam comes for all people, not only those alive at the time, but for all "who from the beginning, according to their capacity, in their generation have both feared and loved God, and practiced justice and piety towards their neighbors, and earnestly desired to see Christ, and to hear His voice."[32] By desiring to see and hear Christ, he means apparently a longing for salvation and for the salvific Word. Irenaeus can sometimes be less generous, gingerly opining in one instance that certain of the Gentiles "being moved, but though slightly, by His providence, were nevertheless convinced that they should call the Maker

23

of the universe the Father."[33] Yet he affirms that that creation everywhere witnesses to the power and wisdom of the creator and that it is there for all to see.[34]

But Irenaeus does not dwell on this matter very long. His chief concern is with the people of the two covenants, whose descedants are to be gathered into the one faith of Abraham. Central in the first covenant is the law of Moses, for which Irenaeus has a profound regard and love, especially the moral as distinguished from the ceremonial aspect, though the latter too had its uses in his view. The law, he says, provided the means for man to have "the friendship of God" and "made man glorious."[35] Before Moses the righteous forebears had "the meaning of the Decalogue in their hearts," but this primitive righteousness died in Egypt. The law was thus given for a people in bondage, for the unruly in the desert. Yet it was graciously promulgated and graciously suited to their condition, providing means for the confutation of Satan and for bringing the people into outward conformity to righteousness. The Word of God revealed the law to Moses.[36] As such, it was a signal act of grace.

Irenaeus staunchly defends the integrity of the law. While it is anticipatory of the gospel, Christ does not bring a higher law down from heaven. The great commandment was given to the Jews. It is not abrogated in the gospel; it is renewed and fulfilled. Christ threw no blame on the law. He threw blame on those who repeated the words of the law and were without the love it called for. Christ is "the end of the law because He is its final cause."[37]

The whole of the first covenant, and not only the law, was for Irenaeus the mark of God's continuing graciousness to Adam's descendants and a ceaseless endeavor to bring them to sufficient maturity to recognize and accept the salvation prepared for them in Christ before the foundation of the world. The first covenant writings, without exception, bear witness to Christ, Irenaeus says, following a tradition he inherited and strengthened in the effort to claim the entire biblical dispensation for Christianity. They signify Christ and are types of the future because "one and the same householder produced both covenants, Jesus Christ our Lord." Christ spoke with Abraham and Moses, and with the prophets, who knew beforehand of Christ's advent.[38]

While Irenaeus highly valued the old covenant, he was as hard on the Jews of the time of Jesus as Justin was before him. The "Jews" were slayers of the Lord, and the Lord took eternal life away from them. Apart from the Jews' rejection of Jesus, there would have been no new and more glorious covenant. We were saved by "the blindness of the Jews."[39] As unattractive and unfair as this judgment might appear to us, by Irenaeus's time it was already a fixed feature in Christian thought, one that in the long reaches of history produced many sad and tragic episodes of discrimination and persecution.

However questionable his attitude was at this point, Irenaeus looked for signs of grace in all aspects of the ancient covenant and found them in abundance. He found grace also at work in the political sphere. While he is only a little less negative about the social and political order than Paul, he tends to take the dictum that "the heart of the king is in the hands of God" (Prov. 21:1) somewhat further. The Gnostics maintained that the "higher powers" to which Paul had enjoined the obedience of Christians were angelic powers, "invisible rulers," not actual human authorities. What Paul meant, Irenaeus declares, is manifest in his saying that tribute is to be paid to those who are God's ministers (Rom. 13:6). The kingdoms of the world were not handed over to Satan, contrary to Satan's assertion at the temptation of Christ. The Word spoke by Solomon: "By me kings do reign, and princes administer justice. By me chiefs are raised up and by me kings rule the earth" (Prov. 8:15–16). Magistrates therefore, "having laws as a clothing of righteousness whenever they act in a just and legitimate manner, shall not be called into question." If they subvert justice, the just judgment of God comes upon them as upon all. Earthly rule has been appointed for the benefit of the nations "so that under the fear of human rule, men may not eat each other up like fishes."[40] The restraint of evil is not however the sole function of the state. The authorities of the state minister positively to the well-ordering of life and to the good of those from whom they exact tribute. Their service is by God's power and will of love.

Irenaeus of course is interested in demonstrating that the Christian mission is consistent with Roman authority—and his teaching here is to a degree self-serving. But this does not obviate the force of his dicta that governments promote human welfare and that benefits derived from just laws and just administration of them are expressive, in some sort at least, of divine grace—in some sort, because for Irenaeus the world outside of the covenanted realm of grace is a world of vast darkness.

Freedom there is severely truncated. Although the power to will and to choose remains to human beings, they are totally without real freedom, the freedom that makes for salvation—the freedom which is the grace of Christ, and which is the ability to live to and in God. Apart from the grace of Christ, bondage prevails universally. Only through Christ and Christ's body, the church, is renewal, the power to grow toward the likeness of God, available. The gift of saving faith "has been entrusted to the Church, as breath was to the first created man, for this purpose, that all members receiving it might be vivified . . . those who are not partakers of it, who do not join themselves to the Church, defraud themselves of life." Then follows the well-known statement: "For where the Church is, there is the Spirit of God; and where the Spirit of God is, there is the Church, and every kind of grace."[41] Deliverances of this kind do not easily accord with Irenaeus's rather more universalistic notions about the operation of grace. The two exist side by side in unresolved tension, somewhat as in Augustine.

Irenaeus, however, does not sound the note of predestination in his doctrine of hell, insisting always that eternal punishment awaits those who in the midst of life separate themselves from God. A habitation fit for them is prepared by the Word, where they are destitute of all life and are in never-ending darkness.[42] While he mentions the eternal fire of hell, his preferred metaphors are darkness and loss. His use of the darkness of hell has special reference to apostasy, to those within the church who were led astray by the heretical Gnostics, but it is set within the broad stream of human history.

In regard to salvation, Irenaeus holds that all that is truly human is salvable. Contrary to his Gnostic opponents, he accords a very high value to the material conditions of life. "[V]ain in every respect," he says, "are they who despise the entire dispensation of God, and disallow the salvation of the flesh, and treat with contempt its regeneration, maintaining that it is not capable of incorruption." The context of this declaration is the Eucharist. The manufactured bread and wine, he says, receive the Word of God, and from these the substance of our flesh is increased and supported. How then can it be said "that the flesh is incapable of receiving the gift of God? . . . What remains to prevent the flesh from participating in corruption?"[43]

Behind the Eucharist lies of course the manifestation of the Word in the flesh. In Jesus "man, not just a part of man," was formed into the likeness of God. Unless the flesh were to be saved, the Word would not have taken upon himself the same substance as man. Christ, the perfect human, consists in the "commingling" and union of both the soul and the fleshly nature, a work performed by "the Hands of the Father, that is, by the Son and the Holy Spirit."[44]

26

Something of a problem emerges for Irenaeus owing to Paul's assertion that "flesh and blood cannot inherit the kingdom of God" (1 Cor. 15:50). If we must speak strictly, Irenaeus says, we have to admit that "the flesh does not inherit, but is inherited" by the Spirit and is translated into the kingdom. As the flesh "is capable of corruption, so it is capable of incorruption; and as it is capable of death, so it is also of life." Flesh and blood in Paul, he says, apply to the carnal deeds of the flesh, which pervert man and deprive him of life. It is essential always to remember that man is redeemed by the flesh of the Lord and reestablished by his blood.[45]

Just how high a value Irenaeus placed on the material realm is found in a very forceful way in his eschatological vision, one of the most wholistic in early Christian literature. A few lines will be sufficient to denote its basic features. For Irenaeus neither the "substance nor the essence" of the creation is to be annihilated since he who established it is "faithful and true." Only "the fashion of the world" passes away, that is, only those things among which transgression has occurred. The "fashion of the world" is temporary; when man is renewed in Christ, the second Adam, he becomes incorruptible, precluding even the possibility of becoming old. At the end there shall be a new heaven and a new earth, in which the flesh shall remain, "always holding fresh converse with God."[46] The creation is to be freed from the bondage of corruption, "confirmed and incorporated" with the Son and to be brought to "perfection," the first-begotten Word descending to the creature he has formed and containing it, while at the same time the creature contains the Word and ascends to Him, "passing beyond the angels." It is to be made finally and fully after the image and likeness of God.[47]

In the consummation, nature, shorn of its curse, will serve humanity completely. As Adam had dominion over the earth at the beginning, so will his descendants at the end. Animals will be in subjection to them and will revert to the food originally given by God. The lion will feed on straw and the new earth will fructify with vast abundance. Irenaeus declares that these things are not to be interpreted allegorically of celestial things. The earth itself will be transformed. Even the earthly Jerusalem will be rebuilt after the pattern of the Jerusalem above.[48]

The question arises whether for Irenaeus the consummation was to be a restoration of the original creation, a completion of it, or the creation of something new on the basis of it. The answer is yes on all three counts. In instance after instance he speaks of the restoration of the first creation, first in Christ as the new Adam who recapitulates all things in himself, and then as that which duplicates the conditions of Eden. But the term *restoration* is not strong enough to convey Irenaeus's full meaning. In his view, original creation was necessarily imperfect. Only the uncreated is perfect; the created is deficient in being.[49] In redemption God comes in the perfection of his Word and unites himself with a creature of the earth, Jesus of Nazareth. The enfleshed Word prepares the seed of Adam for the consummation, at which time God, while remaining infinitely transcendent, will fill all things with his own life. Creation is therefore brought to completion, to the fullest perfection God wills to bring it. Irenaeus's assertion that the world is to be perfected does not mean that it is to attain perfection in the same sense as the uncreated God eternally possesses it. The consummation is to be a new *creation,* forever the gift and work of God's grace, and forever subject to his rule. That which is perfectly subjected is not identical with that which is perfect in itself. And the new creation is defined as that which is to be perfectly subject to the perfect will of God.[50] It is clear from this that the consummation is to entail novelty and is more than the restoration of original creation. The second creation is to be more glorious than the first.[51]

"Creation is suited to man," Irenaeus says, "for man was not made for its sake, but creation for the sake of man." The "things of time" were created so that man could "grow out of immaturity" and be formed into the likeness of God.[52] Viewed in the light of statements like these, Irenaeus's writings are markedly human-centered. The redemption of the human race and its restoration to original grace seem to be the first and final preoccupation of God, something requiring all the divine effort and thought. The anthropocentric strand in Irenaeus is based of course on the biblical witness and on the incarnation as the revelation of the divine concern for the welfare of human beings. The mercy, not the majesty, of God, he holds, is revealed in the incarnation.[53] The majesty of God is revealed in the creation. Irenaeus's constant stress on God as creator, as transcendent and gloriously distinct from creation, provides a strong theocentric note, a countervailing force to the anthropocentricity so evident in much of his theology. Anyhow, the matter of human-centeredness for him is closely tied to Christ-centeredness. It is Christocentrism that is the most marked feature of his writings as a whole. Redemption is certainly for our sake, as is consummation, yet like the difference between the perfecter and the perfected, there is the difference between the redeemer and the redeemed, the agent of consummation, and those to be drawn into the consummation. The prime theological concern of Irenaeus was the Word of God, the Word who created the world. Since the Word was predestined to be incarnate before the world was created and was predestined to sum up all things before there was ever a human being on earth, Irenaeus might better have said that creation was for Christ, not the human race.

Although he implies this at many points, so far as I am able to determine, he never says it directly.[54] With his conviction of the deep and enduring tie of Adam with Christ, he might have found it artificial to say that creation was for the sake of Christ without at the same time saying that Christ was for the sake of Adam and his seed.

Despite Irenaeus's high evaluation of nature and firm conviction that the created order witnesses to the power and glory of God, only a fragment of his attention is turned toward the created order. Most of it is turned toward history, the salvation of Adam by Christ. Nature after all was cursed, not Adam. The redemption of nature was dependent on Adam's. Not only is nature secondary to history in Irenaeus's interests, he finds its fundamental value in its service to humankind. While he posits the creator's love for creation, which perforce lends it its value, as this works out in his theology, the creator loves the creation for humanity's sake. The center of the whole is for the sake of Adam and his seed, those whose destiny through the second Adam is conceived as higher than that of the angels.

Yet it is manifest that the doctrine of absolute creation and the good of every created entity is the bedrock of his theology. It is only on the basis of creation out of grace that the humanity of Jesus, body and soul, could be a fitting instrument for receiving the life of God and for restoring the race to communion with God.[55] It seems clear too that belief in the "maker and framer of all things" had so gripped Irenaeus's mind that he could scarcely write a word without having it in view. The pervasive threat of Gnosticism had more than a little to do with this, but he must have had already a marked predisposition toward affirming the centrality of creation in Christian faith, if not any developed doctrine about it. Even so, if creation is central for him it is because the human race is central in creation and because Christ is central in both.

In regard to created entities in themselves, Irenaeus evinces minimal interest. Only rarely do creaturely things come into his purview. It is true that he speaks of the Word "through whom the wood fructifies, and the fountains gush forth and the earth gives forth its fruit,"[56] and of the rising of the Nile, the formation of rain, lightning, gatherings of clouds, vapors, and the like.[57] He speaks also of light and darkness, the bread and the wine of the Eucharist, but all of this is directed toward the establishment and defense of his doctrine of salvation. Cosmic interests, although present, are wholly subsidiary to soteriology.

Eastern theologians writing after Irenaeus continued the patterns of thought he laid down so effectively. Differences in emphasis appear but the principal thrust remains the same. "The river of grace flows everywhere," fulfilling all created things, "unintelligent and intelligent."[58] Grace is in effect God in relation to the world, the divine self-impartation as creator, redeemer, and fulfiller. "[T]he beneficence of God is everywhere beforehand," John Chrysostom says, specifically categorizing creation, the law of nature, the law of Moses, and the law of conscience as works of grace.[59] The fall into sin did not result in gracelessness; it resulted in a diminution of the effect of grace. Human ability to appropriate grace was weakened but in itself grace remained always and ever what it was. The effect of original grace, the grace of creation, was impaired by the fall. But from the beginning God purposed a special grace to reclaim humankind. The grace of redemption is not considered different from that power which was everywhere gracious. It is however generally held to be superior in degree and intensity. This superiority for some writers derives from the degree of human openness to its impact; for others the grace of Christ brings about a "recreation" which is "more divine and higher than what was before."[60] Still for all, redemption is a furtherance of the grace of God in creation. "God brings back," as Gregory of Nyssa declares, "His own creation to the original grace."[61]

The Eastern theologians also continue Irenaeus's relatively generous estimate of human freedom. They allow no compulsion contrary to the free will given in the grace of creation. "God knows all beforehand but does not determine all . . . does not compel to virtue by force. . . . Virtue is given by God in our very nature, and He Himself is the beginning and true cause of every good," John of Damascus says, yet "it is in our power either to abide in virtue or to forsake virtue."[62] Vice is the departure from good; virtue is abiding in that which accords with our true nature. That sin is a departure from the good was a doctrine as dear to Augustine as to the Eastern theologians. And in some instances he was as certain as they that grace was essentially persuasive, a "wooing" of the Spirit, though he did not allow this idea to determine the main thrust of his theology of grace.

Augustine would of course approve of Basil's doctrine that the Spirit everywhere pervades creation, "flowing, pouring into, penetrating and enlightening."[63] He himself says as much. The difference of course is that for Basil and the theologians of the East, the natural order is explicitly of grace and is evaluated as a work of grace, while for Augustine grace is largely restricted to the process of salvation.

A further significant difference between Augustine's perspective and that of the theologians of the East concerns the nature of Adam's fall. In the East, Adam is injured by the fall but he does not fall flat on his face; he stumbles, falters badly, and loses his direction. He is never forsaken by God or deserted by grace. God continues in providential care of Adam and his offsprings, punishing, prodding, preparing them for the fullness of grace and glory. And beyond Adam, creation itself is never for a moment without grace. As Irenaeus himself put it, "God performed on it all kinds of healing."[64]

The Western perspective on the fall and on grace, according to Philip Sherrard, ruptured the organic links between man and nature and led to "the loss of a sense of the divine in nature . . . , a loss of the sense that the universe has a sacred quality . . . , that creation actually participates in the divine, and is an actual mode of existence or embodiment of the living, ever-present God."[65] Sherrard, an Orthodox theologian and philosopher, goes on to make several other important points about the differences between the Eastern and Western views. In the East, he says, nature is not generally looked upon as something God acts upon from without; it is that through which God expresses the divine life from within. While the difference between the uncreated and the created is maintained (as in Irenaeus), the transcendent, spiritual creator is expressed in the material of creation, hence there is no ultimate dichotomy between them. Through the idea of nature as intrinsically sacred and as embodying the divine, Eastern thought posits a truly and fully sacramental idea of creation, something impeded in the West by the influences of the Augustinian tradition.[66]

Going further perhaps than the Eastern fathers themselves thought to do, though in keeping with the tenor of their theology, Sherrard declares that in creation God becomes God's own image. He is certainly right however to claim that for them creation is the realm in which God's "dynamic, pulsating energies are made manifest," and that for them the difference between the activity of the Spirit in nature and outside nature (meaning, one supposes, in history or in humanity) "is one of degree only, not of kind" or a difference in mode of operation. "Like the Eucharist," Sherrard holds, "nature is a revelation not merely of the truth about God but of God Himself. The created world is God's sacrament of Himself to Himself in His creatures: it is the means whereby He is what He is." For all that, if there were no creation, "then God would be other than He is; and if the creation were not sacramental, then God would not be its creator and there would be no question of a sacrament anywhere."[67]

This account of Eastern thought and its difference from that of the West is penetrating and convincing. I do think however that in certain instances it exaggerates the differences or, perhaps better said, it neglects to bring into focus the similarities between the two traditions, which after all are far greater than the differences. When the similarities are brought into prominence, an exercise upon which more energy might be expended than often is the case, it might even be seen that Augustine, despite the negative strands of his thought, is the bridge theologian between East and West. It might at least be claimed that in the light of the manifold dimensions of his thought, few other theologians deserve the title more than he. Gregory of Nazianzus is a possible claimant, but his thought lacks the range and deep linkage of Eastern and Western interests found in Augustine's. But however this may be, it needs to be noted that the disparity between East and West, pronounced as it is in many instances, does not dissolve the fundamental unities.

A case in point and far from a minor one is the pervasive negativity toward nature in both traditions. Underneath the doctrinal affirmation of the world as good and as embodying the grace of God in all its parts, there was in the East no less than in the West a strong feeling that the "Platonists" were right in asserting that knowledge of nature was not knowledge of reality. The unchangeable was alone real and it was possible to have real knowledge of the unchangeable alone. The observation of nature gave rise merely to knowledge of certain movements, not to that which abides.[68] Knowledge of motion, according to Basil, "is useless to us." Moses did not trouble about it.[69] Inquiries into nature are, these writers held, like writing on water or drawing water in a sieve. And speaking of the role of the priest, Gregory Nazianzus holds that it is to provide the soul wings, to rescue it from the world and give it to God.[70]

The Eastern fathers did not advocate scientific inquiry regarding the ways of nature any more than Augustine. Nature was of grace for them and was theologically significant as revelatory of God, as even in some sense embodying God. At the same time it was considered a snare and a delusion, something to be eschewed, renounced in the interest of salvation. The study of natural phenomena, much as they might be admired and even loved as created and indwelt by God, could not advance anyone toward truth. Nature was highly valued in the context of a grand doctrinal scheme but practically, that is, in terms of understanding it in its details and the cumulative results of those details, it was of no value to religion.[71] In the light of the affirmation that God was present and active in even the most minute facet of created reality, it might not be an unreasonable expectation to find the Fathers urging a tireless endeavor to search out the secrets of nature in the belief that the knowledge of God might in some way be furthered. The affirmation however clashed with a philosophical devaluation of nature that ran deep in consciousness and that effectively blocked detailed consideration of nature as a serious enterprise. Nature was glorious in idea; it was demeaned in fact.

The differences in perspective concerning the nature of Adam's fall between East and West, of which due note has been taken, do not outweigh the unities. To claim that the "fall is to Irenaeus hardly more than an intermezzo, needful to set off the work of salvation that God has carried out in Christ," that it was "an almost harmless intermezzo of no essential importance," that its consequences "were not after all, so dreadful"[72] is to ignore much of the evidence. The act of disobedience for Irenaeus occasioned incalculable loss, loss of likeness to God and loss of immortality. However kindly disposed God remained to Adam after the fall, his sin had devastating consequences for him and for his seed. To make light of Irenaeus's view of the ravages of the fall is to misconceive half of what he says about it. If the loss of immortality is not dreadful, what is? The fall into corruption has behind it so severe an impairment of human nature that Irenaeus can liken it to death to God. Though their interpretations of Adam's life before and after the fall are markedly different in emphasis, Augustine and Irenaeus are at one in their insistence on the actual occurrence of the fall and the spoliation it occasioned. It was decisively determinative for each of them. The differences in interpretation, though not insignificant, are minor in comparison with this fundamental unanimity. While the fall was determinative for both, for neither was it definitive, even though Augustine sometimes implied as much in his darker moments.

The general view of the Eastern fathers about the fall is more or less Irenaean. This is to say that they take the fall into disobedience with as much seriousness as the Western theologians, including Augustine himself, even though they mitigate its effects. As a consequence their theology is primarily a theology of the grace of redemption. Although the theology of the grace of creation is more prominent in the East and is more clearly linked with the grace of redemption than in the Western tradition, for both redemption occupies so pivotal a position that creation is either pushed into the background or made to serve as a preamble to redemption. There are of course notable exceptions to this tendency. Irenaeus is himself a partial exception. Despite however his great emphasis on God as creator, the redemption of Adam and his seed was the pivot around which his thought revolved. That this was not his sole preoccupation is something for which we ought to be grateful, for apart from his emphasis on creation, his theology would have been far less arresting. As it evolved, Irenaeus bequeathed to the Eastern church much of its theological direction and the shaping power of its spirituality.

In its inclusiveness and generosity, the thought and spirituality of the Eastern church is immensely appealing. A number of Western writers hold that Eastern "charitology" is "fluid and undefined."[73] In the light of Western standards, this is so. One wonders, however, whether the Western passion for precise distinctions and definitions, beginning with Augustine and reaching its height in scholasticism, did not overreach itself; whether it is preferable to the modest, descriptive approach of the East. Given the infinite mystery of divine grace and the almost infinite mystery of human freedom and receptivity to grace, precision and clarity in regard to the relation between the two seem quite out of place, if not quite impossible. The strident search of the scholastic mind for "clear and distinct ideas" about such matters prepared the way for Descartes's efforts and their far from happy consequences. No doubt something was gained through the labors of the scholastic theologians in defining and codifying grace. To disparage them so absurdly as Luther and later Colet were to do was unfair and in part unfounded. Still their disparagement had point. It will not do simply to assert that the Scholastics did not know what they were talking about. The subtlety of their distinctions spoke to special requirements of the church of their times. Taking into account the intellectual and theological climate in which the Scholastics lived and wrote, something that had been gathering force for centuries, they did what they had to do. But while they performed their task in accordance with their lights, there can scarcely be much doubt that they carried the enterprise of definitions and distinctions to an unwonted extent. The theological mind found satisfaction in the endeavor, but one wonders how much the ordinary worshiper or the theological enterprise was furthered by it.

Although the doctrine of grace was treated far more elaborately and systematically in the West than in the East, in the end no fundamental advance was made in respect to the central issue of grace in relation to freedom. As to the question of nature and grace, the more expanded and intricate the distinctions and definitions became, the more entrenched the theological gap between nature and grace tended to become. The grace of the ecclesiastical sacraments was plumbed to great depths with many refining definitions, but all the while the sacramental character of creation as a whole received scant attention. The descriptive theology of the Eastern fathers, which almost invariably set nature within the context of grace, has about it a cogency and a consistency exceeding that generally found in Western theology.

The drift and direction of Eastern theology's understanding of nature and grace are things from which Western theology can learn and is learning much. It should not be supposed, however, that the solution to the problem of nature and grace is to be found in Irenaeus or his theological heirs in the East. They provide invaluable signposts, signposts that have directed and deepened the life and worship of the Eastern church intensively and extensively, and in some measure, the Western church as well. But we need to go beyond them toward a much greater awareness of the context of history in nature, nature as we have come to understand it today through the deliverances of the scientific enterprise, and history as we have come to view it through the critical method. The problem of nature and grace is particularly acute for Western theology, owing not only to our intellectual and historical inheritance but to our experience of the explosion of knowledge about reality which our sciences have given us and with which we must reckon.

The chapters that follow will show that Irenaean and Augustinian influences are very much alive in modern theology in the Western world. The theologians considered all work within these traditions in one fashion or another, trying at the same time to deal with aspects of the pressing problems given in the cultural and social situation of the times. All are Western writers for two reasons: first, mentioned already, the matter of nature and grace is especially acute in the West; second, the Western tradition is the one in which I stand and for which I have a greater fear, that is, fear that its conception of nature and grace may continue in its dichotomizing tendencies to its great loss, may indeed fail to reach the level of thought about the relation of nature and grace traditionally demonstrated in the East. There are clear signs however that many thinkers are prying at the fingers of the fist that holds Western theology in history and in isolation from nature. Release may be in the offing, but a great deal more prying at the fingers of the fist must be done owing to the fact that the grip has so long been tightening.

The next chapter deals with the thought of a modern Protestant theologian, Paul Tillich. The jump from Irenaeus to Tillich is not so abrupt as might first appear. The problems Irenaeus struggled with are not unlike those Tillich confronted, though the context has changed drastically. With Tillich we are thoroughly immersed in the modern historical consciousness, something unimaginable for Irenaeus. Yet they shared a most fundamental theological concern: how to conceive of created reality in relation to redeemed reality; how the great appearances of nature were to be seen in the light of the grace of God. The results of their deliberations, despite great and expected differences, are not altogether dissimilar.

CHAPTER 3

Tillich and the Multidimensional Unity of Life

IN THE THIRD VOLUME of his *Systematic Theology*, Tillich remarks that although the religious significance of the inorganic is immense, it is rarely considered by theology. For that matter, he goes on to say, the quantitatively overwhelming realm of the inorganic has had a strong antireligious impact on many people in the ancient and modern worlds. As a result, a "theology of the inorganic is lacking."[1] He attempts to sketch such a theology under the general category of "the multidimensional unity of life." This part of the system makes a significant contribution to the theology of nature and to some extent also to the theology of grace. The principles Tillich sets forth, moreover, are applicable at certain crucial points to the issue of the relation of nature and grace. Before turning directly to them, a few comments about his general attitude toward nature and attendant matters might be useful.

Tillich remarks that he was always at odds with the Ritschlian theology which posits an infinite gap between nature and personality and assigns to Jesus the function of liberating personal life from bondage to the nature within and beside us. He notes too his opposition to the strand of Calvinism which looks on nature as something to be controlled morally and technically, and affirms his own view that mystical participation in nature is possible and real, that the finite is capable of the infinite and that nature is the finite expression of the infinite ground of all things.[2] In his attempt to construct a basis for a Protestant rediscovery of the sacramental principle, he says that the power of nature must be found in a sphere prior to the cleavage of the world into subjectivity and objectivity, prior to the Cartesian duality. When adapted to sacramental use in Christianity, nature must be understood historically, that is, included in the history of salvation. Thus understood, natural objects can become the bearers of transcendent power and meaning. "Nature is not the enemy of salvation," he declares, "rather nature is a bearer and an object of salvation."[3]

Although Tillich does not believe that a natural theology is possible since there is no revelation in nature, only revelation *through* nature, he does accept the *analogia entis* between the finite and the infinite. All knowledge of God is analogous or symbolic, hence without recourse to analogy nothing could be said about God. It is necessary to use material drawn from the finite realm in order to give content to the cognitive function in revelation. He does not hold that the infinite can be abstracted from the finite, but simply that analogies or symbols drawn from the finite have to be used to speak of the infinite.[4]

Tillich has one of the most complete doctrines of reason in modern theological literature. It is of profound interest and is basic to understanding his system as a whole. Here, however, I need point only to several of its features in relation to his doctrine of revelation, which is key to the method of correlation that informs the system throughout.

The rational structure of the universe and of the human mind, Tillich says, is *logos*. Otherwise it would not be possible for the mind to grasp and transform reality. Ontological reason, as an expression of the universal *logos*, is identical with revelation; it is the self-manifestation of the divine *logos*. While in human beings reason is subject to sin and error, to the destructive forces and forms of existence, there is yet an ontological aspect to human reason. Reason in us therefore has both an essential quality and an existential actuality. It is never completely severed from its ontological ground or unity with the *logos* of being. This is its essential quality. Although finite or existential reason is separated from its ground in the infinite, it is yet "aware" of the infinite and of its own essential structure. In realizing its finitude, it becomes aware of infinitude. The very contradiction between finitude and infinitude points to their unity; if there were no unity between them the awareness of finitude could not arise.[5]

Despite the twists and turns, the lapses and sin-infected character of reason in concrete existence, and in part because of them, reason calls for or seeks revelation. It seeks its own infinite ground, its essential unity with the universal *logos* of being. Reason does not resist revelation; it asks for it because revelation is itself the reintegration of reason.[6]

Revelation for Tillich is in every case the manifestation of the mystery of being, that is, of the essentially mysterious which does not lose its mysterious character when it is revealed. The divine reveals itself precisely as infinite mystery; it does so within the context of ordinary experience, but revelation transcends the basic condition of finite rationality, the subject-object structure, and makes for the wholeness of the human mind, uniting its existential actuality and its essential ground.[7] Since "everything participates in being-itself," everything can become a medium of revelation. "There is no reality, thing, or event which cannot become a bearer of the mystery of being and enter into a revelatory correlation."[8]

These principles, preliminary as they are, will serve as a background for an account of Tillich's theology of life. They demonstrate a positive response to nature, a recognition of its theological significance and ways in which it is related to revelation. These features become even more pronounced in his deliberations on "the multidimensional unity of life," which in some instances seem to go beyond the implications of his "method of correlation," namely, reason (human moral and intellectual life) *raises* questions only and must await answers from revelation.

Remarking that the choice of metaphors reflects one's vision of reality, Tillich rejects the metaphor *levels* of life, together with correlative concepts such as *grades,* in favor of *dimensions.* To speak of levels is to presuppose a hierarchical order in which every genus and species of things, and through them every individual reality, have their place; it is to exclude organic movement from one realm to another and to base the relation of God to human beings on two levels, the supernatural and the natural. Although the metaphor of *dimension* is also spatial, it allows for movement from one realm of being to another, for the higher to be implicit in the lower and the lower in the higher. Depth does not interfere with breadth, since all dimensions meet at the same point and cross without disturbing each other. The replacement of the old metaphor by the new represents an encounter with reality in which the unity of life is seen above its conflicts. These conflicts are not denied but are seen as the consequences of the ambiguity of all life processes. They are not derived from a hierarchy of levels and are conquerable without the destruction of one dimension by another.[9]

In the dimensions of life, Tillich observes, the inorganic has preferred position insofar as it is the first condition for the actualization of every other dimension. All others "would dissolve were the basic condition provided by the constellation of inorganic structures to disappear."[10] With regard to relation between the inorganic and the organic, he points out that the various philosophies of life have rightly made organic life the basic meaning of "life" because, in a way more obvious than in the inorganic, organic life embraces several dimensions, despite the indefiniteness of the transition between them. I am glad to note that he goes on to emphasize that the dimension of the organic is potentially present in the inorganic, even though its actual appearance depends on conditions that biology and biochemistry seek to describe. Potentially, self-awareness is present in every dimension but it appears only under the dimension of animal being. The endeavor to pursue self-awareness back into the vegetative dimension cannot be verified and owing to this it seems wiser, Tillich says, to limit inner awareness to those dimensions in which it can be made highly probable in terms of analogy and emotionally certain in terms of participation, namely, the higher animals.[11]

Inner awareness, the psychological realm, is characterized by "self-related, self-preserving, self-increasing and self-continuing *Gestalten*" or living wholes. Within it, under special conditions, another dimension actualizes itself, that of the personal-communal or the "spirit." So far as we know, this has occurred only in human beings; the term *spirit* therefore designates "the particularly human dimension of life." As the power of life, spirit is not identical with the inorganic substratum which is animated by it. Rather, spirit is the power of animation itself; it is not something added to the organic system.[12]

A new understanding of the term *spirit* as a dimension of life, Tillich holds, is a theological necessity. In the attempt to provide one, he delivers himself of a number of semantic considerations into which I need not enter here. It is enough to note his conclusion: spirit is "the unity and power of meaning." Spirit includes mind but is not limited to it. Mind expresses the consciousness of a living being in relation to its surroundings and itself. It entails awareness, perception, intention and appears in the dimension of animality as soon as self-awareness appears. In rudimental and developed form, it includes intelligence, will, and directed action. Spirit includes not only mind but reason in the sense of *logos* as the principle of forms by which reality in one of its dimensions, and mind in all of its directions, is structured. "There is reason in the movement of an electron, and there is reason in the first words of a child—and in the structure of every expression of the spirit." But spirit as a dimension of life includes even more: it includes *eros*, passion, imagination. Without *logos*, however, spirit could not express anything. Reasoning, whether technical or ontological, is one of the potentialities of the human spirit in the cognitive sphere.[13]

The dimension of the spirit also and crucially includes the moral sphere. Morality, as Tillich understands it, is the means for actualizing the personal self; it is the function of life by which the dimension of the spirit comes into being. Although complete centeredness in human beings is essentially given, it is not effectively operative until it is actualized in the moral act. The moral act is not an act in which some divine or human law is obeyed but "an act in which life integrates itself in the dimension of the spirit, and this means as personality within a community." Morality is the totality of those acts in which the centered self constitutes itself a person, in which a potentially personal life becomes an actual person. Those acts occur continuously in personal-communal life; thus the constitution of the person as person never comes to an end during the whole life process.[14] It is a continual becoming.

Morality as a dimension of spirit making for the actualization of the centered self liberates the person from bondage to the environment on which every being in the preceding dimensions is dependent. Theories which try to explain human behavior solely in terms of its environment reduce it to the dimension of "the organic-psychological" and deprive it of spirit, thus making it impossible to explain how anyone can have a theory which claims to be true, "of which the environmental theory is itself an instance."

Human beings have freedom not only from their immediate environment, they have norms which enable them to determine the moral act through freedom. These norms express the essential structures of reality, of self and world. Human beings are able to respond to them or to refuse to respond to them. If we refuse, we give way to the forces of moral disintegration; we act against the spirit in the power of the spirit. For we can never get rid of ourselves as spirit. We constitute ourselves as completely centered selves even in our "anti-essential, antimoral actions," because "these actions express moral centeredness even while they tend to dissolve the moral center,"[15] Tillich says incisively.

The self-integration of person as person occurs only in a community, within the continuous encounter of centered self with centered self. The moral constitution of self in the dimension of the spirit begins in the encounter with others whose centeredness limits one's own, and this experience of limit is the experience of the ought-to-be, the moral imperative. A living being with the human psychosomatic structure, completely outside any human community, could not actualize its potential spirit. "It would be driven in all directions, limited only by its finitude, but it would not experience the ought-to-be."[16]

The last and all-embracing dimension of life is the historical dimension, which comes to its full actualization only in human beings in whom, as bearers of the spirit, the conditions for it are present. The historical dimension however is manifest in all of life, though under the predominance of other dimensions. The specific characteristic of historical life is the creation of the new. Although the creation of the new is present in all life, even if subdued, it is particularly marked in historical life, "for history is the dimension under which the new is being created."[17] Tillich might have added that nature is the dimension through which history arises and that the creation of the new in history is grounded in the "new" emergence of the historical dimension from the creative forces within nature.

Actualization of a dimension of life is a historical event, Tillich holds, within the history of the universe. Such an event, however, cannot be localized at a definite point of time and space. During the long periods of transition, "the dimensions, metaphorically speaking, struggle with each other in the same realm." This is obviously so in the transition of the inorganic to the organic, the vegetative to the animal, the biological to the psychological, and the psychological to the dimension of the spirit. The sharp division between those beings who have language and those that do not have it is marked by the same struggle, and the struggle goes on with every human being "as a lasting problem for the basis of the predominance of the spirit." A human being cannot *not* be a human being just as an animal cannot *not* be an animal. The human being, however, "can partly miss that creative act in which the dominance of the psychological is overcome by the dominance of the spirit."[18]

Tillich rejects the doctrine that at a precise moment of the evolutionary process God in a special act added an "immortal soul" to a human body, otherwise complete, with this soul as bearer of the spirit. In addition to its supernaturalistic suggestion, such a doctrine "disrupts the multidimensional unity of life, especially the unity of the psychological and the spirit, thus making the dynamics of the human personality completely incomprehensible."[19]

Under the principle of the multidimensional unity of life, the spirit cannot be separated from the conditioning psychological realm. Every act of the spirit arises out of psychological factors. It "presupposes given psychological material and, at the same time, constitutes a leap which is possible only for a totally centered self, that is to say, one that is free." If a dualistic contrast of the spirit with the psychological is inadmissible, so is any attempt to dissolve the spirit into the psychological forms out of which it arises. Psychologistic and biologistic monism must be denied along with dualism.[20]

The principle of the unity of life also prevents the inorganic realm from being described in exclusively quantitative terms. "No-thing in nature is merely a thing—if 'thing' here means that which is altogether conditioned, an object without any kind of 'being in itself' or centeredness," an object with "no element of subjectivity."[21] *Through a recognition of some such view as this,* Tillich holds, *a decisive step can be taken toward overcoming the gap between the inorganic and the organic,* something as dear to him as to Whitehead himself. "Just like every other dimension, the inorganic belongs to life, and it shows the integratedness and the possible disintegration of life in general."[22]

In Tillich's view provision must be made for the distinction between lower and higher forms of life. This distinction is justified, he holds, if the term *highest,* in the case of human beings, is not confused with the *most perfect.* A lower being can be more perfect than a higher if perfection is understood as the actualization of potentialities. Human beings cannot only fail to actualize their potentiality, they can deny and distort it. In spite of this, human beings constitute the highest category of being under two criteria: "the definiteness of the center" and "the amount of content united by it." These criteria determine the establishment of the animal dimension above the vegetative, inner awareness above the biological, and spirit above them all. "Man's center is definite and the structure of its content is all-embracing." "In contrast to all other beings, man does not have only an environment; he has a world, the structured unity of all possible content."[23]

In human beings growth and decay, life and death are consciously experienced. In every life process the conditions of life are the conditions of death. "The same cellular constitution which gives a being the power of life drives toward the extinction of this power."[24] Human beings alone are fully aware of this fundamental character of all life and its ambiguous quality. This awareness is an aspect of human transcendence over these forces, even though as completely subject to them as lower forms of life.

Growth of an individual life always takes place within the context of all life. One life form encounters another, with both creative and destructive consequences. "Life grows by suppressing or consuming other life. Life lives on life." A "phenomenology of encounters" could be written, Tillich says, which would show how the growth of life at every step includes conflict with other life. A life and death struggle is going on in all of what we call nature, and owing to the multidimensional unity of life, "it is going on also between men, within man, and in the history of mankind. It is a universal structure of life."[25] In these succinct deliberations, Tillich points to some basic realities in our situation, even though somewhat grimly put.

Concerning the fulfillment of the potentialities of the universe of being, he says that the unfulfilled potentialities of matter, for example, in the atom, are actualized in the human world. They are not actualized in the atoms, molecules, crystals, plants, and animals in themselves; they are actualized only in the spiritual dimension. The dimension of the spirit, as mentioned above, includes all other dimensions—"everything visible in the whole of the universe."[26] The spirit reaches into the physical and biological realms by the very fact that its basis is the dimension of self-awareness.[27]

The realm of history, as I have noted, arises only with the dimension of spirit. The dimensions of history are present in other realms of life other than the human, but in an anticipatory way. Even in the inorganic, and certainly in the organic realm, there is *telos*, an "inner aim" which is quasi-historical, "though not part of history proper." History in the prehuman realms, he speculates, lacks ultimacy. The experience of ultimacy and the ability to produce embodiments and symbols of the ultimate are possible only with the emergence of the dimension of the spirit.[28] In history the potentialities of the inorganic become actual; the actualized historical realm includes the actualized inorganic realm, but the reverse is not true. The relation between the two is not a simple polarity. Historical humanity is new, but is prepared for in prehistorical humanity, answering in part to an issue raised above. And again, "the point of transition from the one to the other is essentially indefinite."[29]

Human beings as bearers of the spirit are open to the Spirit of God. But in order to be present to the human spirit, the Spirit of God must be present in all the dimensions which are actualized in human beings, and this means all the dimensions of the universe.[30] Because of the multidimensional unity of life, all dimensions, as they are effective in human life, participate in the Spirit of God. This refers directly to the dimension of self-awareness and indirectly to the organic and inorganic realms. Here Tillich points once more to the biological and psychological basis of spiritual life.[31]

In the symbol of the Kingdom of God he sees the hope of the fulfillment of all life. It is a kingdom not only of human beings but also involves the fulfillment of life under all dimensions.[32] The kingdom "is the non-fragmentary, total and complete conquest of the ambiguities of life—and this under all dimensions of life, or, to use another metaphor, in all degrees of being."[33] Nothing positive in being is excluded from it, and since there is nothing merely negative, nothing that has being can be ultimately excluded.[34] This entry qualifies the pessimistic viewpoint Tillich draws in picturing the conflicts within the structures of life. For him, hope for fulfillment in the Kingdom of God is the one ground of optimism.

Without attempting to be anything like exhaustive, I have tried to indicate some of the main features of what Tillich in one place has called his understanding of life from a philosophical point of view.[35] In the same place he expresses his indebtedness to a number of earlier thinkers, most notably to Schelling and Hegel. He calls his effort in his systematics "precarious and dangerous" but makes it clear that such an effort is essential, with whatever inconsistencies it might entail. It is so, he says, because much theology of this century has tried to remove God from nature, and when this happens, God gradually disappears to us because we ourselves are nature. "If God has nothing to do with nature," he goes on to say, "he finally has nothing to do with our total being."[36] A little later on he quotes Aquinas's remark that "he who knows anything, knows something about God," and himself remarks that "whatever we know in any realm bears witness to its creative ground." Since moreover science deals with "the *logos* of being, the inner structure of reality, . . . the witness of science is witness to God,"[37] here again tempering perhaps a strict interpretation of his method of correlation.

The doctrine of the multidimensional unity of life, although not worked out fully until the final volume of the *Systematics*, is germane to the system as a whole. Very early on Tillich speaks of human beings as participating in all levels of life, as "the microcosmos of the macrocosmos."[38] "What happens in the microcosmos," he says a little later, "happens by mutual participation in the macrocosmos, for being itself is one."[39] He notes too that without the world, the self would be an empty form; self-consciousness would have no content. We participate in the universe as a whole because the universal structures, forms, and laws are open to us; through these we participate in the remotest star and the remotest past. "This is the ontological basis for the assertion that knowledge is union and that it is rooted in *eros* which reunites elements which essentially belong together."[40]

While we participate in our environment and in the universe itself, our participation is always limited even though potentially there are no limits that we could not transcend. Full participation is only at the level of life which is our own. The person "has communion only with persons," for communion is participation in another completely centered and individual self. This communion is not something an individual might or might not have. "Participation is essential for the individual, not accidental. No individual exists without participation, and no personal being exists without communal being."[41]

In the second volume of the *Systematics*, the doctrine of the unity of life is as dominant as it is in the first, perhaps taking on even greater range. "[T]he universe," Tillich says, "participates in every act of human freedom" through union with "the deciding center" in human beings. Further, there are analogies to freedom in all parts of the universe itself. "From the atomic structures to the most highly developed animals, there are total and centered reactions which can be called 'spontaneous' in the dimension of organic life." Since "[m]an reaches into nature, as nature reaches into man," nature shows analogies to human good and evil doing. "This makes it possible and necessary to use the term 'fallen world' and to apply the concept of existence (in contrast to essence) to the universe as well as to man."[42] Indeed, "[m]an cannot claim that the infinite has entered the finite to overcome its existential estrangement in mankind alone," for the function of Jesus as the Christ "is not only to save individuals and to transform man's historical existence but to renew the universe."[43] This is so because the "interdependence of everything with everything else in the totality of being includes a participation of nature in history and demands a participation of the universe in salvation."[44] And this final entry in this connection from the second volume: "The Christ is God-for-us! But God is not only for us, he is for everything created."[45]

The God of whom Tillich speaks is the God of grace. The term *grace*, he says, "qualifies all relations between God and man in such a way that they are freely inaugurated by God and in no way dependent on the creature."[46] He describes two basic forms of grace: (1) the grace which characterizes God's creativity, and (2) the grace of God's saving activity. The first provides participation of everything in being and the second gives fulfillment to that which is separated from the source of fulfillment. It is possible, he goes on to say, to distinguish a third form of grace, which belongs to creative grace on the one hand and to saving grace on the other, and which might be termed "providential grace." Its aim is the fulfillment of the creature in spite of resistance. In Augustine's term it is *gratia praeveniens,* "prevenient grace," which prepares for saving grace through the processes of nature and history.[47]

At this point we find the fullest discussion of the doctrine of grace in Tillich's system. There are however illuminating but scattered references to it in his other works and throughout the system,[48] indicating that Tillich, like most of us, thinks in spurts, not complete consistency. In one place in the final volume we find a particularly significant statement, a very "Tillichian" one: "Theologically speaking, Spirit, love, and grace are one and the same reality in different aspects. Spirit is the creative power; love is the creation; grace is the effective presence of love in man."[49] While he does not speak extensively about grace, it can be argued that his entire theology is a theology of grace. "Grace," he says, "is the impact of the Spiritual Presence,"[50] thus wherever we read Spiritual Presence, divine life or divine spirit, we could read grace or at least interpret these designations in terms of grace. One thing however that Tillich has made clear is the utter gratuity of grace. Grace means that the Spiritual Presence cannot be produced but is given.[51] From beginning to end, he is always anxious to set forth grace or the impact of the divine as unexacted gift. And while he does not link his doctrine of the unity of life specifically with grace, he has provided obvious parallels to it, giving a schema that helps to clarify theologically the relation of nature and grace.

"As Spirit he [God] is as near to the creative darkness of the unconscious as he is to the critical light of cognitive reason."[52] Because this is the case, the Spirit is active in the inorganic realm as well as the organic; no aspect of nature is excluded from the divine grace. While "there is no direct impact of the Spiritual Presence on life in the dimensions of the inorganic, of the organic, and of self-awareness,"[53] there is indirect and limited influence upon all the dimensions of life. Impact on the psychological self implies "effects on biological self-integration and the physiological and chemical processes out of which it arises." This is not to be understood however as a chain of causes and effects, beginning with the impact of the Spirit on the human spirit and then causing changes in other realms through the human spirit. "The multidimensional unity of life means that the impact of the Spiritual Presence on the human spirit is *at the same time* an impact on the *psyche,* the cells and the physical elements which constitute man." This marks an immense advance on traditional notions of grace. Still, Tillich holds, "this presence is restricted to those beings in whom the dimension of the spirit has appeared. Although qualitatively it refers to all realms, quantitatively it is limited to man."[54]

While this is a fine distinction, instead of putting it this way, Tillich might better have said that while the Spirit is *discerned* in the human dimension, it is nevertheless present to all other dimensions of life in the objective sense. The assignment of limits to the divine presence is a precarious procedure, speculative, I should think, at best. Is it not possible to conceive of a certain "communion" of the divine with lower forms of life? If knowledge is communion, as Tillich insists, and God's knowledge is exhaustive of every detail of creation, God might well be conceived not only to be related to, say, a worm, in the sense that the divine life is related to all finite forms, but to have a relation with it. Certainly God could delight in it no less than Darwin delighted in those in his backyard.[55] Worms burrow through the ground and produce topsoil that makes growth possible. They do so with the utmost consistency, in accordance with, we have to say, the *logos* of being. We can recognize this and even, as in the case of Darwin, develop not only respect but an affectionate regard for them. Is it not necessary to say that the infinite Spirit's relation to them infinitely exceeds that of the finite spirit and quite possibly, perhaps probably, entails a certain communion with them and with every particle of being? If God loves the whole creation wholly, that is, loves it wholly in its minutest aspect and not simply as a whole, would God not have not merely a relation *to* but *with* all things? This is speculative, no doubt, but it is no less speculative than assigning *limits* to the divine presence.

This speculation is far from trivial; it is posed as a possible limit to the anthropocentricity that Tillich does much to overcome but in the end falls subject to. It may be that this anthropocentricity is inevitable, some form of it doubtlessly is, but it requires modification in the light of our rapidly expanding knowledge of universal reality. This knowledge is our knowledge and is therefore ineluctably centered in the human sphere. It greatly transcends the human sphere however and creates the conditions for a new or at least greatly increased level of human self-transcendence, one that might enable us to locate ourselves a little less centrally in creation. "In maintaining that the fulfilment of creation in the actualization of finite freedom, we affirm implicitly," Tillich says, "that man is the *telos* of creation."[56] In another connection he puts the matter somewhat differently: "Creation has no purpose beyond itself"; the concept "purpose of creation" should be replaced by "the *telos* of creativity."[57] This way of expressing the issue is more theocentric, as Tillich acknowledges, but it also positions human beings in the context of reality as a whole and God's inner aim of fulfilling the whole as such, with humanity included but not the "purpose" of creation and therefore not necessarily its center. The second way of looking at it accords well with his view that God is essentially creative, "is creative because he is God," and that the doctrine of creation is the basic description of God's relation to the world.[58]

The doctrine of the divine creativity, as we have seen, occupies a pivotal place in Tillich's thought. From one standpoint it might be said to occupy the principal position but from another "the new being" in Christ might be said to take that position. It is clear that he wants to maintain the unity of creation and redemption and that he sees a basic reciprocity between them. Redemption, however, is conceived as part of the divine creativity. Jesus as the Christ is the central or at least a central manifestation of the creative grace of God. His appearance has as its aim the fulfillment of history and through history the fulfillment of creation. Fulfillment is not meant to be understood as restoration, though it is included. Jesus as the Christ is a "new creation" because in him estrangement between God and human beings and the world is overcome, which creates possibilities for the emergence of the new in manifold forms. But he came precisely for creation, to further, we might say, the creative process, directing it toward its *telos* in God. Creation, under these terms, is not for Christ, even though he was eternally purposed; rather, Christ is for creation. This formula may not do full justice to the intricacies of Tillich's thought, but it seems warranted by his affirmation that God is essentially creative and that divine creativity is its own end.

A good many theologians today have difficulty with this line of thought and tend to reject it out of hand, not only the conclusions but the teleological method itself, in the interests of eschatology. Tillich might well have taken the eschatological frame of the Scriptures more to heart. Were he living today, it is possible, though just barely, that he would do so. This is not however the point. The point is that with all his blind spots, his idealism and all the rest, he saw some things—many things indeed—with remarkable clarity and set them down with uncommon precision. The utter centrality of the divine creativity is, in my view, certainly among them. The divine life and the divine creativity are one and the same, and all divine "acts," all salvific forms, all revelation, all spiritual presence, all grace derive from the creative love of God, "the power of being." Jesus as "the new being" historically expresses the same

49

"power of being." He is for creation as historically expressed, even though that which he expresses, the eternal Logos, is one with God in creativity.

Tillich recognized the painful problem of pluralism as acutely as anybody in his generation and faced it more courageously perhaps than anybody else. The problem of pluralism for the Christian is focused of course on Christian claims for Christ. In a basic sense Tillich resolved the problem by considering Christ as part of the divine creative action, an action universal in scope but centrally manifest in Jesus as the Christ. But he found it necessary to sharpen this resolution, not without difficulty and a measure of ambiguity. It seems certain that he wanted both to claim a certain finality for Christ and to distance himself from traditional dogmatic formulations of that finality. Jesus-centered religion and theology were idolatrous in his view. Jesus, he held, can be the religious and theological object as the Christ and only as the Christ. A revelation is final only if "it has the power of negating itself." And this is precisely what occurred in the case of Jesus as the Christ. He is "the Christ as the one who sacrifices what is merely 'Jesus' in him." The decisive trait in his picture in the Gospels is the "continuous self-surrender of Jesus who is Jesus to Jesus who is the Christ." The claim of anything finite to be final in its own right is demonic and heteronomous. Jesus made no claims for himself and only so is he the Christ. But as the Christ he is the final and universally valid revelation. "Christianity itself is neither final nor universal," but in witnessing to the Christ it witnesses to final revelation. In the face of ecclesiastical or orthodox self-affirmations, the so-called liberal theology was right in denying that one religion can claim finality, or even superiority over others. A Christianity that does not assert that Jesus of Nazareth is sacrificed to Jesus as the Christ is merely one more religion among others. "It has," Tillich says, "no justifiable claim to finality."[59]

Although not relinquishing the claim for the finality of revelation in Jesus as the Christ, Tillich sought to reduce the claims of Christianity to finality and thus to open it up to values resident in other religions. Years after the above was written he found it necessary to make modifications, though modest, of his claim for the Christ, and under the influence of Mircea Eliade to give close attention to the claims of non-Christian groups. He even went so far as to say that if he had it to do all over again, he would devote himself to the systematic study of the religions of the world in the belief that theology in this age had to move on from an apologetic consideration of secularization to a new method and form, addressing itself specifically to the plurality of religious claims.[60]

In respect to the universal claim for the revelation through Jesus as the Christ, Tillich toward the end of his life showed himself more tentative than he had been in the system. Outlining the systematic presuppositions for a theology of religions, he noted that one of these should be the assumption that there may be, and he stresses the word *may* here, a central event in the history of religions which unites the positive results of the developments in the religions of the world and which "makes possible a concrete theology that has universalistic significance."[61] It seems clear that he still wants to claim finality for the Christ and perhaps implicitly does so, but it is now a tempered, somewhat qualified claim, one open at least to further questioning and future possibilities. He is of course adamantly opposed to any view that makes Jesus of Nazareth "the exclusive place where the word or revelation can be heard" and insists that the Holy is or may be universally manifest within finite forms, which he calls the sacramental basis of all religions. This fundamental perspective gives point to the view that his theology is first and last a theology of grace and along with this a theology of nature, with history as the realm in which both grace and nature are experienced and known.

As we have seen, he is certain that no natural theology is possible since for him nature in and of itself reveals nothing of God to human beings. There is revelation by God *through* nature but not *in* nature, rather like the idea that there is revelation through Jesus as the Christ rather than in him, which seems a mark of his Christology generally. But in posing a natural capacity in human beings for the reception of revelation, he has, as one of his critics asserts, moved precariously close to natural theology, if in actual fact he does not have one.[62] Tillich would reply to this, one might suppose, by saying that the *capax infiniti* is itself of grace, that is, traceable to the impact of the infinite or Spiritual Presence upon the finite mind. Since for him all knowledge of God is from God, he would have to make some such reply. But how different is this view from the old natural theology? That theology posed a certain independence of nature from the divine, but as created it was in grace and therefore retained elements or vestiges of the gracious hand of its Creator. There was thus that in nature which yielded some sort of knowledge of God. Tillich is saying something similar but on different grounds. The relation between God and the world and so of God and humankind is conceived to be much more intimate and immediate. The *vestigia Dei* doctrine in the hands of some of its interpreters implied that God was remote from creation; Tillich's theory entails the constant impact of God upon all finite reality. The finite is never without its infinite ground, for the infinite is related to the finite in its every aspect. The infinite is implicated in the finite even while infinitely transcending it.

I am not concerned to support or dispute the charge that Tillich has a covert natural theology. The charge specifically in view is made by a theologian who holds that "Christian theology bases its knowledge of God entirely on his self-revelation in Jesus Christ. Thus it cannot speak of God apart from what he has revealed himself to be in Jesus Christ."[63] For such a theologian theology is kerygmatic theology simply, and any suggestion of apologetical theology such as Tillich's is already ruled out of court. This aside then, the question I want to raise concerns the dogma, long established in Protestantism and now even in some Roman Catholic theological circles, that there can be no such thing as natural theology. Certainly this view has much to commend itself, and not least are Tillich's own considered observations about it. The question is, first, whether the dogma does not say too much and, second, whether what it says is not said in such a way that nature is inevitably devalued and frequently thrown out of theology's sphere of interest.

The latter can be briefly treated. It is only too clear that among leading modern Protestant theologians Tillich is exceptional in his regard for nature and in his attempt to deal with it systematically. For many if not most of the others, nature is ignored or else relegated to a remote corner of theological concern. The first part of the question is much more difficult to address. It needs, however, to be addressed a great deal more often than it is, even though no firm conclusions might be forthcoming. What follows is tentative and suggestive at best.

The first thing to be said is that manifestly there can be no *purely* natural theology. The critics of natural theology are right to assert this. Anyone engaged in the enterprise of theology would perforce take historically derived criteria to nature in the formation of "natural" theology. But does this obvious fact entirely obviate the possibility that nature, created and grounded in God and related to God actively and continuously through grace, has a kind of revelatory power in and of itself that may enter into revelation that is historically reached? Another way to ask the question is this: Is a *purely* historical theology, that is, a theology based exclusively on historically derived data, possible? It can be and frequently is argued that this is the *only* kind of theology possible—we are historical beings and thus all our thinking is necessarily historical. There is another factor, however, of which theology often does not take account sufficiently: we are not only historical beings, we are beings in and of nature. To move into the historical dimension is not to move out of the natural dimension. Since we carry nature with us into history, is it not likely that nature, within and without us, influences us and our thought a great deal more powerfully than we normally admit? That we are in and of nature needs to be taken with far more seriousness than theology normally accords it. When taken with the seriousness it deserves, the question may arise whether nature may not enter into our experience directly, immediately, and revealingly.

The affirmation that God is "the ground of being," to use one of Tillich's favorite phrases, is historically and culturally conditioned, arising out of a long tradition of philosophical and theological thought. But behind the affirmation is an experience of nature—the solid ground of the earth on which we stand. This experience is itself the condition for the theological metaphor. It is directly given in nature, it would seem, and is in a certain way revelatory in that it is the ground for the historically derived doctrine that God is the ground of being.

Something similar may be said of the *logos* structure of existence. *Logos* in us of course arises fully only in history, only in communal life and the power of speech, but behind this is the *logos* structure of our nature and the *logos* structure of all things, which can be grasped without historical factors as determinants. Our prehistoric ancestors experienced elements of the *logos* of being, or we would not be here today. That they did so is the very condition for our emergence into history.

Another primitive experience of great importance is that of the overarching transcendence of nature "out there" over human life. Its incalculable immensities and complexities, its richness and beauty, its beneficence and its terror, probably constitute the first inkling of human awareness of "that which none greater can be conceived." It is true that human self-transcendence occurred in relation to transcendence over nature, but the primal experience of the transcendence of nature has not been erased from memory, and in our time that memory is being greatly refreshed by advancements in scientific understanding and the menaces attending it.

What I am asking is: Whether the relation between nature and history is not more complex, more problematical than the line drawn between natural theology and historical theology (or cultural theology, as Tillich likes to put it) entails, and whether this is true even in the light of such an elaborate doctrine as the multidimensional unity of life?

In high Kantian fashion, Tillich says that "nature can only become an object for us through the medium of culture."[64] Now obviously this is true from one perspective. We have no experience of nature which is not historically and culturally *conditioned*, but this need not mean that direct experience of nature is an impossibility. We are not blind to light, impervious to cold or warmth. The solidity of an object strikes us immediately and directly. As R. H. Blyth puts it, "Earth is very real when you get a little bit in your eye." Categories of culture are not an issue at that point. Tillich says further that "for us nature derives its sole importance from the functions of the spirit."[65] A question arises at once in the face of this. Do we not eat? Do we not feed on nature? Are we not totally dependent on it for its sustaining forces? Eating can of course be a function of the spirit but it is always a natural necessity. The starving are not normally much concerned with the functions of the spirit; they are concerned with the quite objective issue of food. Tillich says also that "any religious import that may exist in nature lies in cultural functions in so far as these are related to nature."[66] If "religious import" as used here is meant in the sense of thematic deliberation, doctrinal formulation, or specific belief, then Tillich's claim is probably true. But behind "religious import" there is "religious impact," something that can derive immediately from the experience of external nature as that which immeasurably transcends culture and that without which no culture would be possible. "Religious impact" is prior to "religious import" as nature is prior to culture. Except by way of extreme abstraction, culture cannot become an "object" for us without the objective reality of nature as its ground.

These statements of Tillich's do not seem to accord easily with his idea of the infinite as present to the finite or of the possibility of our mystical participation in nature. The doctrine of the multidimensional unity of life would accord with them, one might suppose, since it is concluded there that the dimension of history includes all other dimensions of life. But even so, there are aspects of the doctrine that strongly suggest that nature does have a "religious import," and almost certainly, a "religious impact."

The issue here does not concern the possibility of natural theology as such. One need take no stock in the phrase or defend the validity of the enterprise. The term *theology of nature* is preferable on many counts. It is more accurate and descriptive of the process involved and should serve as a kind of meeting point for those who hold that natural theology is in fact possible, as well as for those who do not. What I do take stock in is that nature, both in its formal and material sense, be given its due in theology.

Nature encompasses our history. Our history, we are fast learning, does not encompass nature in anything but a most fragmentary sense. This implies no devaluation of history, of the historical development of freedom and cultural life, of the dimension of the spirit and the conscious, free possibility for the acceptance of the Spirit of grace. What it does imply is that we need to consider our history more contextually, more existentially, in the sense that human existence is a small part of the whole frame of existence and cannot be understood when divorced from that to which it belongs by nature *and* by grace.

Tillich's doctrine of the unity of life addresses this matter more fully than that found in any Protestant theology of the modern era. The criticisms raised above, although pertinent, are minor when compared with his achievements in working out the doctrine. Only Pierre Teilhard de Chardin has addressed the matter with comparable depth. Tillich himself notes the similarity between his doctrine and Teilhard's *The Phenomenon of Man.* Long after he had written his sections on the unity of life in the system, he came across Teilhard's book. He says that he was greatly encouraged to find that a scientist had developed ideas about the dimensions and process of life so much like his own, and that although he could not share Teilhard's optimistic view of the future, he was convinced by his description of the evolutionary processes of nature. He goes on to say rightly that theology cannot rest on scientific theory, but "it must relate its understanding of man to an understanding of universal nature, for man is a part of nature and statements about nature underlie every statement about him."[67]

It might be a good thing if this concluding remark of Tillich's were fashioned into a plaque and placed on the desks of theologians of historicist bent as a reminder of this crucial fact of human existence. Although it is probable that Tillich himself did not press his conviction quite far enough, he pressed it to the limits of his own historical conditioning, and with many happy results. As early as 1961 T. H. Greene remarked that Tillich's "interpretation of nature, animate and inanimate, as having a 'life' of its own" invites "our love, respect, and admiration rather than our contemptuous and callous exploitation."[68]

But while Tillich's doctrine became an important resource for a number of ecological theologians among others, it went largely unheeded by the main stream of Protestant thought because, one might guess, it looked too much like natural theology and was somewhat mystical in cast. Perhaps the time has come to give it a second hearing.

Tillich's doctrine of grace is of considerable scope but he does not offer us a full theology of grace. It lacks the starts and thrusts, the probing and rich detail, and finally the precision given to it by Karl Rahner, who in many instances reached conclusions similar to Tillich's. This is not surprising since they have a number of inspirants in common and since Tillich the Protestant aspires to include Catholicism in his theological standpoint and Rahner the Catholic is concerned not to exclude Protestantism from his. Each is successful to a remarkable extent. Tillich's doctrine of grace, however, requires supplementation. Rahner's doctrine not only goes beyond Tillich's by dealing more amply with the various categories of grace in tradition, it also delves into the issue in greater depth and with more "theological passion," to use a favorite phrase of Tillich's. The main difference between them is that Rahner has explicitly conceived the fundamental problem of theology as the relation of nature and grace whereas Tillich only implicitly and indirectly did so.

CHAPTER 4

Rahner on Nature and Grace
and Related Issues

THE THEMES THAT DOMINATE Karl Rahner's thought concern the necessary conditions for the human encounter with the mystery of divine love,
or how nature is related to grace. More commonly his question pertains
to what in being human makes it possible for us to receive a genuine
communication of God, but he goes beyond this to considerations of the
relation of nature as a created process to the divine grace. His writings on
theological anthropology, revelation and faith, Christianity and pluralism, epistemology and ontology, the incarnation, and indeed almost
every aspect of his thought, are either implicitly or directly expressions of
his understanding of the relation of nature and grace. Although he has not
reached complete clarity regarding the complex issues involved, he has
raised them in acute and systematic form and provided a basis for an
effective theoretical resolution of many of them. His thought has the
virtue of realizing that the problem of nature and grace, or something
quite comparable, cannot be obviated and that it lies at the basis of
theological reflection, whether on salvation or creation. While often
expressing his views in dense and sometimes tortuous ways, the effort to
grasp what he has to say is more than worth it.

Rahner uses the traditional distinction between the natural and the
supernatural, maintaining that such a distinction is necessitated by the
given realities of revelation and the implications of spiritual experience.
He uses it however not in the interest of any form of dualism that it might
suggest and that has suggested itself in the past, but in an effort to uphold
human freedom on the one hand and the absolute gratuity of divine grace
on the other. Though the distinction is less in evidence in his deliberations
on the relation of creation as a whole and the divine creative activity, it is
implied in his insistence on the independence and integrity God accords
to the world.

Since he has written more extensively on the nature of human beings in relation to redemptive grace, I will speak of this first and then turn to the underlying issue of grace and created reality. Fundamental to Rahner's position is the view that there is no such thing as a *merely* natural relationship of human beings to God. He rejects the Roman Church's teaching, following the Council of Trent, that grace is a supernatural structure above humanity's conscious, spiritual and moral life. This teaching, he rightly holds, is extrinsicalness at its worst and that, if followed, nature would have to be considered as what we experience of ourselves apart from revelation, or apart from grace; it would be nature and only nature. This sharply circumscribed understanding of human nature entails both too much and too little. It assumes that we know precisely what human nature is and that grace is in no real sense a constitutive element of it. While the tradition admits of a *potentia obedientialis,* a potential for responding to grace in the human constitution, it is understood negatively, as "a non-repugnance to grace."

Our actual nature, Rahner insists, is *never* pure nature. "It is a nature installed in a supernatural order which man can never leave."[1] So long as grace is understood as something lying beyond the range of experience, coming to us from without, as something imposed on nature, God's call to grace must remain only *ex additu,* only through verbal revelation. But grace as Rahner most frequently describes it is the actual self-communication of God and, as experienced, it is participation in the divine life itself.[2] As such it affects our conscious life, our existence and not just our being; it affects our very manner of life in the world and is thus not to be thought of as a "layer that is placed carefully on top of nature so that the two interpenetrate as little as possible." Indeed, for Rahner, nature is enveloped in grace and grace bears upon our inmost reality.[3]

His question is whether our present experience would be the same if there were no call to grace, no call to supernatural communion with God. If we are created for grace, ordinated toward fulfillment in grace by the divine intention in the act of creation, as Rahner believes, the very question one asks oneself is altered; namely, to what extent does my existence already contain, or may it contain, elements that transcend a purely natural conception of being human. Ontologically it is difficult to accept the view that a decree of God making us subjects of "an absolute finality" could remain external to the inmost reality of our subjective existence. The extrinsical view of grace, which regards it as merely a superstructure imposed from without upon a nature indifferent to grace, has to be deeply questioned. Concrete human existence is so ordinated toward grace that our existence cannot be conceived apart from it.[4]

Given this basic ordination, which admittedly depends on certain premises of Catholic tradition, the assumption that we know precisely what human nature is becomes highly questionable. Human nature is what it is, Rahner declares, only by virtue of the prior divine intent. Hence what we know about human nature is unavoidably *imprecise*. It is clear however that the ordination of the human being to God's grace, "even though an implicit and a priori transcendental, makes him what he experiences himself to be, precisely *capax infiniti*," that is, "he has as his constitution a desire, a longing for the supernatural, an openness for grace, and this determines his essential character. This desire, this longing, is inescapable. It makes human 'nature' a nature directed toward the 'supernatural' and so a nature determined in the end towards grace."[5]

Rahner believes that our intrinsic ordination toward grace radically excludes any dualism between nature and grace.[6] In my own view some residue of dualism remains, and it might have been more accurate to say that the interior ordination to grace excludes any form of radical dualism rather than radically excludes any dualism. This judgment seems to be warranted by Rahner's designation of nature as a "remainder" concept, that is, a reality which must be postulated in us which remains when the orientation toward grace is "subtracted" from us.[7] Presumably the matter of "subtracting" the divine ordination is theoretical only since Rahner holds that it is ingredient to human nature by the grace of creation. The point therefore is not worth pressing except to note how hard it is to exclude all traces of dualism. Rahner tries very hard to do so and succeeds better than most.

"The recipient of God's self-communication, presupposed by the same, is what is called nature." "In contradistinction to the supernatural then, nature is seen as a necessary element in a higher whole, experienced in grace and explicitly declared in revelation." "The difference between nature and grace must be understood on the basis of the radical unity of God's free self-communication in love."[8] It seems evident from these remarks that Rahner holds that nature does not and cannot indicate a state of reality that is intelligible in itself or that can be understood apart from the divine grace, and at the same time that grace is not something imposed on nature from without.

Certainly for him there is no neat horizon between nature and grace.

Grace presupposes nature and nature presupposes grace, since grace sustains nature and orientates it toward its proper end in God. But however true this is, nature, Rahner says, remains nature, and it does so "for the sake of grace." But although nature cannot exist apart from the grace that envelops it and is constitutive of it, grace in the sense of the personal self-communication of God is not of the same level as the "grace and favor" of creation. The divine self-communication is not inevitably instituted with creation; it occurs as free, incalculable gift.[9] There are essential gradations in the gratuitousness of grace itself. The permanence of free will in the sinner can be termed a grace *in* Christ because it is willed and preserved by the divine decree as the presupposition of the self-communication of God in Christ, but though it is a "grace of creation," it is not in itself a grace *of* Christ since the communication of the Holy Spirit is grace in "the strictest sense."[10] Echoing tradition, he asserts that the grace of creation is a "lower grace," and the divine self-communication in redemption is the "higher grace," an issue I will comment on toward the end of the chapter.

Still, Rahner goes on, it is not true to say that "everything is of grace" because everything has been freely given by God. Supernatural grace is something uncalled for with regard to our nature, even prior to sin. Nothing is due de facto to human nature, even prior to sin. We have no rights, no claims on an endowment of the divine life. No restraints are on God to impart grace outside of the divine will of love. The experience of grace is an experience "as the unexacted event."[11] Rahner calls this one of the "kerygmatic" facts to which theologians must attend. Grace is unexacted from the divine side and its reception is unexacted from the human side. Although we are ordered toward grace, created with the capacity for grace, and even empowered freely to receive grace by grace itself, we are not necessitated to accept it. Grace must be accepted in a "dialogue partnership" which is free.[12] God creates us in such a way that we can receive and accept grace in an unexacted way. "We can only know what unexacted means when we know what personal love is." We do not understand what love is by knowing the meaning of "unexacted."[13] These last few remarks soften the dictum that we have no rights, no claims on God's grace.

Freedom to accept or reject the divine self-giving is the essence of Rahner's understanding of human nature. Theologically speaking, nature is "man's grasp of his metaphysical being"; it is "spirit in transcendence and openness." The character of grace is grounded in its utter gratuitousness: there is no possibility of positively preparing ourselves for it, or of obtaining it by prayer or any other spiritual exercises,[14] he affirms as any good Lutheran might.

The link between the supernatural and the natural is our self-transcendence and openness to grace. The link between them cannot be called supernatural even though it is in itself an orientation toward supernatural grace. To describe it as supernatural instead of natural "could only lead to hopeless confusion and blur beyond recognition the objective distinction between nature and grace" which is demanded by our experience and the Christian conception of creation and redemption. "Nature cannot be entitatively supernatural grace; it is morally supernatural." It "is not simply and non-dialectically non-grace but is something which—in the actual order of things—rests on its own foundations and is sufficient 'for itself,' even without grace." Here again we run into a seeming contradiction with a number of Rahner's other expressions on this matter, but he straightway tries to balance this remark with the further assertion that human nature is the presupposition of "the higher grace" and depends on it. In this sense, "nature is in grace" and in "the actual order by no means involves autonomy and indifference . . . to grace and covenant, as Barth thought."[15]

The distinction between nature and grace is clarified, Rahner holds, by pointing to the distinction between philosophy and theology. Theology has philosophy as its fundamental presupposition, as the condition of its own possibility. This is understood not simply in terms of the traditional view that there are two sources of the knowledge of God, reason and revelation. Philosophy is itself "an inner moment of theology" because revelation is theology the moment it is heard, however rudimentary the theology. The reception of revelation involves the prior knowledge and self-understanding of the one receiving it. This previous knowledge, however changed through the impact of revelation, is a necessary aspect of the resulting interpretation of the revelatory event. This is an insight of the first order, in my view. It prevents theology from being considered a "second order" endeavor, an adjunct to faith, and draws theology into faith itself where it necessarily belongs.

Since the reception of revelation involves human thought from the beginning, it involves philosophy from the beginning in that it incorporates the previous understanding of self and the world in its articulation of the revelation. Hence although diverse, philosophy and theology constitute a fundamental unity, certainly something more than a mere conjunction. Revelation is in one sense dependent on philosophy, but in another philosophy finds its higher entelechy and norm in revelation,[16] a view, I take it, in general accord with Tillich's method of correlation.

Philosophy as human self-understanding, as human historicity, is "nature," the condition and possibility of grace, which possesses its own integrity and autonomy. Revelation, the cognitive factor in grace, although not owed to those who receive it, is freely bestowed as that which illuminates and fulfills our self-understanding and our longing and openness for God. The truth of philosophy is willed by God in order that revelation might be addressed to one from whom it might be withheld, to "the philosopher who, because he himself experienced God as the one who conceals himself, could accept revelation from him *as a grace*."[17]

The "saving receptivity" in our ordination toward the "saving object" of the grace of revelation is frequently termed the "supernatural existential." Again, this human existential is not grace itself; it is "from grace towards grace," that is, the person is open to the ordination toward grace through the prior operation of grace which provides the condition for the person to receive grace in its primary sense, the unexacted self-communication of God.[18]

Since in Rahner's view our experience as such is always the experience of nature and grace or the refusal of grace, salvation history for him coincides with the history of the world, although the two are not identical. If God's will to salvation is universal, this will is the supernatural order that constitutes the goal of humanity, and every human life is lived within the supernatural or graced horizon.[19] This graced horizon is at the same time a history of revelation. What theologians normally refer to as the history of revelation—the specific revelation in the biblical witness—is the conceptualization through particular witnesses of a "primordial revelation" given to humanity as a whole. Strictly speaking, Rahner asserts, it is *Christian* grace and truth operative before and outside the Christ event itself. Owing to God's original intention in Christ, the Christian revelation finds inadequate but real expression in the history of religions and in the development of philosophy as well.[20]

Just as there is no such thing in Rahner's view as "pure nature," no more is there such a thing as "pure philosophy." This is so because the unthematic self-understanding out of which philosophy arises occurs within the universally present supernatural ordination and thus incorporates more than merely natural elements. The human spirit is already open to the divine life and because of this philosophy is unable to distinguish between nature and grace in its own performance. All philosophy is necessarily influenced by Christianity if the supernatural existential is accepted, whether in its Christian sense or not. Those philosophers outside the realm of the church are unknowingly touched by the divine grace, which as noted above, is a *Christian* fact and cannot be otherwise. "In every philosophy men already engage inevitably and unthematically in theology since no one has a choice in the matter—even when he does not know it consciously—whether he wants to be pursued by God's revealing grace or not."[21]

When however the pursuit by grace is recognized and accepted as free gift, when, that is, the objective revelation of God in the Christ event in its full and constitutive historical reality is received, the unthematic revelation in universal salvation history is made reflexively conscious.[22]

The doctrine of universal salvation history has led Rahner to develop a concept which he calls, for want of a better term, "anonymous Christianity," but which lies close to the core of his understanding of nature and grace. Its implications are very wide, gathering into concrete focus many aspects of his thought. I can perforce deal with it here only briefly. Its major premise is that Christianity presupposes a knowledge of God among the pagans; the gospel does not introduce it.[23] The express revelation of God in Christ is thus not something that comes to us from without as entirely strange, but as the explication of what we already are by grace and what we experience at least incoherently in our experience of transcendence.[24] The practical application of this is that the missionary can and ought to appeal to pagans as "anonymous Christians" and not seek to indoctrinate them *ab externa*.[25]

A criticism of his terminology by Henri de Lubac has led Rahner to say that the term *anonymous Christian* may be more readily admitted than *anonymous Christianity.* He goes on to say however that "Christianity" itself has to be seen in two aspects: (1) Christendom and the church and (2) "being a Christian" in the case of the individual person. In the case of the latter we can speak of anonymous Christianity as long as we can speak of anonymous Christians. There are after all degrees of membership in the church, not only in ascending order from being baptized to holiness, but in descending order from the explicitness of being baptized on down to nonofficial and anonymous Christianity, even though it would not describe itself this way.[26] On a basis such as this, Rahner avers, some people outside the church or who have not embraced explicit Christianity through no failure of their own, stand in a positive and salvific relationship to God; they are, in other words, "justified" and in a state of grace, and even atheists may be among them.[27]

Anonymous Christianity strives toward explicit expression; its relation to the historical Christian revelation is found in this very striving. The expressly Christian revelation becomes "the explicit statement of the revelation of grace which man always experiences implicitly in the depths of his being."[28] Explicit preaching of faith is therefore in no way superfluous, because the grace which is preached is prior to the preaching as its condition and as the content of the preaching. Indeed, "precisely because it is prior to the preaching, the grace itself demands to be preached."[29]

The concept of anonymous Christianity is one of the chief means Rahner uses to deal with the problem of pluralism, particularly religious pluralism. It is therefore an important aspect of his theology of non-Christian religions.[30] Although Christianity cannot relinquish its absolute claim without ceasing to be itself, he declares, and must comprehend pluralism by understanding itself as "the higher unity of pluralism," it must become much more generously open to different world views, recognizing that the grace of God extends itself into all the dimensions of historical and social life.[31] Non-Christian religions are to be seen as legitimate religions which contain not only real elements of a natural knowledge of God "but supernatural moments of grace." Going further, Rahner says that he believes that Christians ought not to expect those who live outside of the sphere of the Christian religion to forsake the religion that their society provides. Such an expectation would be based on a definition of religion as something completely interior rather than radically social in nature. The human being "can live his proffered relationship to God only in society and must have the right and indeed the duty to live his relationship to God within the religious and social realities offered him in his particular historical situation."[32] If this point were heeded, it would transform the theology of mission and so of grace.

Under these terms, a member of a non-Christian religion would be regarded not just as a non-Christian but as Christian. If such a person later confesses Christianity, that person's previous anonymous Christianity becomes part of his or her Christian development. Acceptance of the reality for which anonymous Christianity stands, whether the term is accepted or not, would broaden the church's understanding of itself greatly, Rahner holds. It would no longer see itself as the exclusive community of salvation or even the guardian of salvation, but rather as the historical expression of what exists outside of itself, "as a representative people who symbolize the whole of mankind as the covenant of universal salvation." Even when the church confronts growing opposition in the world, Rahner goes on to say, part of its hope is that God's grace will triumph whether the church is seen to triumph or not. The church is not the communion of those who have grace against those who do not have it; the church "is the communion of those who can explicitly confess what they and others hope to be."[33]

The supreme expression of the relation of nature and grace is in Rahner's view the supreme sacramental reality of redemption, the incarnation of God in Christ. Since grace is "the essence of God's self-communication in love,"[34] is "God himself," a work which "is really *himself*,"[35] the incarnation must be interpreted in terms of it. The hypostatic union in Christ "is not a mystery *beside* the mystery of the absolute proximity of God as holy mystery in human experience; it is this mystery itself in an unsurpassable form."[36] Although a "unique event," and when seen in itself, "the highest conceivable event," it is yet an intrinsic factor of the whole process of the bestowal of grace in general.[37]

I will make no attempt to develop a full account of Rahner's Christology here but reference must be made to it if justice is to be done to his understanding of the nature and grace schema. While not always directly employed in his christological reflections, given the principles set forth just above, it seems clear to me that the schema is a major key for their interpretation.[38]

In a probing but rather typically convoluted essay, "On the Theology of the Incarnation,"[39] Rahner begins as is usual with a number of anthropological observations: "man is a mystery in his essence, his nature; he is not in himself the infinite fullness which concerns him," but is a being who is referred to this fullness. Human existence, the whole of it, is the acceptance or rejection of the mystery to which it is referred. In Christ human nature is assumed by God as God's own reality and thus arrives at the point to which, by virtue of its essence, it always strives. The incarnation is therefore the supreme actualization of human reality, "which consists of the fact that man *is* insofar as he gives himself up" to the divine outreach. We are called in our action to confront our nature, to come to ourselves. Our nature is "substance in action," and the substantial acceptance of the Word of God "is substantial self-dedication." This acceptance "in self-surrender belongs so little to human nature itself that it becomes the nature of God." Still, the possibility of acceptance is present in our nature, "the possibility of being assumed, and becoming the material for a possible history of God." In Christ our nature reaches total openness to the mystery of God's love; in him the Word *becomes* flesh. In the act of incarnation, God remains infinite, but gives the finite "an infinite depth."[40]

Although all of us have the capacity by nature as created in grace to receive the Word and may in fact do so when opened to the divine self-giving in fulfilling grace, it is in Christ alone that the hypostatic union between God and human nature occurs. "In him the question which is human nature has become unquestioning." The incarnation is not a priori. "It is not independent of the revelation in its *de facto* existence." While willed by God from the beginning, it took place in history at a particular moment in a particular person. What happened in Jesus was precisely the history of the Word of God, a process which the Word underwent.[41]

Rahner is intent on affirming the link between creation and redemption. "That God himself is man is both the unique summit and ultimate basis of God's relationship to creation." The positive nature of creation "reaches its qualitatively unique climax, therefore, in Christ."[42] The doctrine of creation, however, is *not* the basis of the fundamentally Christian concept of the world. As in Irenaeus, creation is for Christ. The ground of the Christian understanding of the world is the history of salvation, the central theme of which is "God's will to communicate himself *ad extra* to what is not divine." Thus "Jesus Christ as the incarnate Logos and God's supreme self-communication to the world is the reason for bringing the world into existence."[43]

Another important aspect of Rahner's Christology concerns its relation to evolution, as I have suggested above, and his doctrine of the unity of spirit and matter. With regard to the latter, he says in a luminous phrase that since "grace is the secret essence of all eligible reality," natural history and human history form a unity, though there is a manifest diversity within the unity.[44] Human beings are distinguished from material beings but without injury to their biological evolution.[45] As in Tillich, matter and spirit do not exist side by side in alien departments; they are "everywhere correlative constituent moments of the one reality."[46] Our relationship with God is always in terms of the material constitution of our existence. The unity (not uniformity) of spirit and matter is grounded in the single goal of each, which is participation in and by the divine will of love. Materiality is therefore *not* provisional; it is a factor in the process of perfection itself, for it is the world we concretely experience that is to be fulfilled and transformed.[47]

Rahner is at pains to stress that spirit and matter are not static entities; they have a history, they develop. Although spirit is inextricably rooted in matter and has no existence apart from matter, it is not reducible to matter in and of itself. This transcendence does not emerge by a merely intra-mundane process of becoming. There is no independent leap of material into the "noosphere" by an inherent means or power. Anything of this kind would unlimit the essentially limited reality of matter.[48] Behind the process is the divine will to communicate itself. The action of grace is *for* self-communication and *toward* the consummation of the entire material realm. A finite causality must of course be assigned to finite being, or as Rahner often puts it, "matter develops out of its inner being in the direction of the spirit."[49] It does not do so however apart from grace. "Finite causality works in virtue of the absolute being within the finite,"[50] or, put another way, the world emerges within the process of God's self-bestowal.[51]

In the incarnation, the evolutionary process, "the becoming of the world in its history," reaches the point to which from the outset it was ever striving to attain. Indeed, the incarnation is the explicit objectification of a process occurring all the time and everywhere, for in it "man attains to God in an ultimate act of self-transcendence" and "God's self-bestowal on man finds its most radical form."[52]

We need to note with emphasis that by "man" Rahner means nature or the world as such, not only humanity in its historicity, but all the factors which both underlie and are included in human historicity.[53] Jesus "is absolutely everything which belongs to the nature of man"; he is "truly a part of the earth," "truly a moment in biological evolution," and in him the Logos of God becomes "world," becomes "irrevocably present in matter."[54]

Since grace may be regarded "as the highest, freely given and unsurpassable step and phase" in evolution,[55] the hypostatic union in Christ is "absolute grace," God's "absolute self-communication," present in both declaration and acceptance. In one sense, the "end" of creation, the end term of the evolutionary process, has arrived; in another, it has reached a new phase of becoming. The first advent of Christ and his second constitute a unity, "a single event still in process of achieving its fullness."[56]

The incarnation, as Rahner frequently puts it, is the "asymptotic" goal of the world reaching out to God.[57] This word, a favorite of his, is defined as a line which continually approaches nearer to some curve but even though it were infinitely extended, it would never meet the curve. In this connection, it means that the fullness of creation, its consummation, is not an inherent emergent but awaits the grace and glory of God's final gift to it.

When the world as a whole is illumined by and brought face to face with the immediacy of God, "in this sense Jesus himself will have 'come again.'[58] Only in him will the divine immediacy be present to us.[59] Christ can only be rightly understood, Rahner says, "if in him the 'head and body' which is the church, and ultimately the world itself, are apprehended in their unity as constituting the one and whole Christ." Through the grace of the incarnation, the world is given a true direction and hope, and the freedom to cling to it, precisely because "it achieves its fullness in the dimension of God's uttering of himself . . . as the absolute future."[60]

No more need be said, I think, to indicate Rahner's general position on the relation of nature and grace. Even though I have not entered into many of its intricacies and complexities, his grasp of the magnitude of the problem and bold engagement with it have been indicated.

To a very considerable extent Rahner has overcome the dichotomizing tendencies evident in much modern theology by affirming and attempting to demonstrate the fundamental unity of creation and redemption in the divine self-bestowal, and by taking nature with a theological seriousness second only to that which he accords to the history of salvation. It is clear too that he has gone a long way toward transcending the post-Cartesian disdain for the material world so prominent in many strands of Roman Catholic and Protestant theology, and that he is less prone to bifurcate historical reality and natural reality than many other modern theologians. While we can only stand in appreciative awe of the subtlety and force of his deliberations, a number of questions emerge in the face of them.

Foremost of these questions concerns his refusal to admit creation per se as one of the cardinal mysteries of faith. The great mysteries of faith in his view are grace as divine self-communication to human beings, the hypostatic union of grace and humanity in the incarnation, and the divine Trinity.[61] He speaks also of the beatific vision, of grace and glory, as a great mystery of faith and thus includes consummation; he does not however speak similarly of creation. I find this curious. That there is anything at all, that the world is ordered to life, that reality exists in untold immensities, that the least feature of its constitution is complex beyond all present calculation, and that conscious beings arise within its orb—is this not a mystery? That the whole is created by divine love compounds the mystery a thousandfold, I should think, rendering it an unsurpassable mystery of faith.

The tendency to assign creation a subordinate status in theology is of course too marked and tenacious in tradition to be accidental. It is possible and necessary however to call it into question today. The tendency emerged and gathered force in a time when comprehension of the world was very limited. The world was "there," it was "ours" in a way it has not been for some time now and will never be again. In company with this tendency was the deeply entrenched Neo-Platonic devaluation of the material order, one that lurks about still in many pockets of Christian consciousness. Demeaning creation became a theological habit early in the tradition, and in modern times it was powerfully reenforced through the influence of the Enlightenment. But when creation is demeaned, the creator is demeaned and so too the redeemer of creation.

Rahner rightly points to the existential centrality of the *whither*, the sense of the limitless horizon of human life, its openness toward an absolute future,[62] in the process of human self-understanding and in commending faith in our time. In a more settled age than ours, however, Schleiermacher used to talk about the *whence* of existence and "the sense of absolute dependence" it evoked in human consciousness.[63] I suspect that the existential centrality of the *whither* of existence has not altogether supplanted the sense of the *whence*. It is not likely that the former could arise except on the basis of the latter. The two are at least fraternal twins. But however this may be, creation should be given its just due in Christian theology. Perhaps it would be best to regard creation, incarnation, and consummation as aspects of the divine self-communication, as Rahner himself at one point suggests, with the Trinity as disclosed in the incarnation and as operative in all three movements of the divine grace. At all events, if we fail to witness to creation as a cardinal mystery of faith, theoretical physicists and anybody else for whom nature provokes awe and wonder will probably find our theology existentially entrapped and unrealistic.

I am made a little uneasy with regard to the notion that the world, given a relative independence by God, is *in* grace only. If creation is a continuous process, something that happens and not something that simply has happened, as Rahner everywhere affirms, then the independence given the world is continuously dependent on the gracious will of God, on an always operative grace. It is *in* grace, we may believe, but beyond this it has its existence and independence *of* grace. The *"in* grace" phrase may point to a quasi-deistical view, one that does not have due regard for the intimacy of God's relation to creation and is thus insufficiently theistic. Although the integrity and relative independence of nature need always to be upheld, it is within the constant creativity of the divine will, within the continuum *of* grace itself, that it can be so.

A question arises too in connection with Rahner's idea that there is something in nature which has meaning and the possibility of existence without grace. If this were not so, he holds, there would be nothing for grace to address itself to freely. Although this must be affirmed in the religious and moral sense, it may be logically more "imprecise" than Rahner implies and may accord to us more freedom than we actually have. At one juncture he himself seems to acknowledge this. In discussing the relation of philosophy and theology, he observes that those philosophers outside the sphere of specific Christian faith are unknowingly influenced by the divine grace, which, as we have seen, is a specifically Christian fact. In every philosophy philosophers already and inevitably engage in theology since *"no one has any choice in the matter."*[64] To speak of a possibility of nature existing without grace does not easily accord with this emphatic affirmation.

Rahner also asserts, following tradition, that our choices in this life determine forever the state of our souls, whether to eternal life or to eternal loss.[65] The question has to be asked whether this view sufficiently recognizes, here again, the relative character of our freedom. If it is true that we are only relatively free in this life, not absolutely free since absolute freedom belongs to God alone, our status in "the world to come" may be rather more open than Rahner supposes and than tradition affirms. If our freedom is freedom *of* grace, and not simply *in* grace, as I believe it to be, comparable with the relative independence of the world, then our possibilities for response to grace may be immeasurably extended beyond this life. Understood in this way, grace would be the term of God's never-ending relationship with all of us and not only some of us.

A further feature of Rahner's thought, a feature central to it and to tradition as well, is the affirmation of the *absolute* character of the divine self-communication in Christ. To give up this absolute claim, Rahner holds, would mean that Christianity had ceased to be itself. While devotionally and emotionally some such claim must inevitably arise, I am not

sure that it is absolutely essential for Christianity to affirm it dog-
matically. Perhaps Christianity, following Jesus, should not seek to establish itself as anything except servant, should not seek its own but should
give itself for the life of the world, witnessing always to the one absolute
to which he witnessed, the absolute love of God. If it be argued that Jesus
was absolutely open to the love of God and so the absolute embodiment
of it, two things must be said. First, a glad and grateful acknowledgment
of the bestowal of the divine love in his life and death and as sealed in his
resurrection must be put forth. Second, it has to be said that since that
bestowal was in a particular humanity and historicity, the absolute was in
some sense relativized in Christ, made *relative* to us and our fulfillment in
God. Can there be an embodiment of the absolute absolutely without the
absolute ceasing to be absolute?[66] The absolute can however embody
itself relatively, that is to say, in humanity, which is by definition relative,
limited and finite. It is necessary and legitimate to affirm that the absolute
was humanly, finitely present in Jesus as the Christ, that is, as fully and as
absolutely as the conditions and limitations of human nature afford. To go
beyond this may be to move away from incarnational theology to something like docetism. God as incarnate is precisely God related to the
world and human beings.

The Pauline statement that in Christ "dwells all the fullness of the
Godhead bodily" (Col. 2:9) is frequently applied to the life of Jesus, or to
the incarnate Christ. In the text it is not clear whether Paul is referring to
Christ in glory, on earth, or a combination of the two. But whatever his
own usage, the statement is misapplied when taken as dogmatic dictum
concerning the incarnate life. Paul is rhapsodizing at this point anyway
and, as a good Jew and as a rational human being, he could not have
meant that the fullness of "the consuming fire" of God was present in
Jesus. The consuming fire image in Scripture points to the inex-
haustibility of the divine, the fire that is never exhausted—the bush that
burns but never burns up. God's inner being is inexhaustible and cannot
be exhaustively revealed. God can however exhaustively reveal himself in
relation to the character of those to whom the revelation is given. This
means here again that the revelation in the Christ is as full and complete as
the body, mind, and spirit of Jesus allow. It is relative to him and relative
to those who confess the grace embodied in him. Revelation in him as
divine self-communication is sufficient for human needs but not exhaustive of the Godhead.

If this is the case, provision might be made for the view that along with the relatively absolute or the absolutely relative revelation in Jesus as the Christ there are other quite significant and valid revelations in the non-Christian religions of the world. The grace revealed and operative within them, which has been systematically demeaned in Christian tradition, might be accorded a much enlarged validity, larger than Rahner himself accords it. This would help to make dialogue with them really possible. So long as the Christian claim is absolutist, dialogue will not be a genuine possibility and Christian imperialism, so marked in our history, will be suspected and feared. Similarly other religious groups would have to temper their claims for absoluteness, but Christianity might well have to exercise leadership in this direction.

The establishment of an absolute claim in contradistinction to an assertion of it would rest on the universality of the basis of the claim. All the higher religions, including Judaism, have within themselves a thrust toward universality developed out of their own peculiar historical circumstances and view of the world. They raise questions that are sometimes quite beyond Christianity's sphere of concern. For example, there is the question addressed by *karma* in Hinduism, to cite an obvious one. Why are people born in such extremely differing situations—some with every possibility stretching out before them and others with virtually every possibility closed to them? Some Christian theologians are prepared simply to dismiss this question, opining that what Christianity has to offer is not a theodicy but an eschatology. But can it or should it be so easily dismissed? The karmic myth is deeply engrained in a huge segment of human consciousness. Can it be summarily ignored by any religion claiming universality?

That there is an enormous drive toward universality in Christianity all would admit. The incarnation doctrine is pivotal to this, and also and equally the eschatological dimension of faith. It may be that in some distant and undesignated future Christianity will establish its universality. Meanwhile however its universality remains an assertion. Perhaps Christianity will have to surrender its claim for itself in order that the claim might be established. Perhaps only through an openness to the love of God, which exclusivistic claims may impede, will it be able to become itself. We may well hope, as Tillich puts it, that Christianity will prove to be the most inclusive and universal of religions,[67] but the way to realize it is likely to be found through self-giving service, not through assertive claims.

Rahner's idea of "anonymous Christianity" is an updating of a strand of

Logos Christology of the ancient church, and in some ways is very attractive in terms of Christian self-understanding in confrontation with the plurality of religions. It may well be true that the grace resident and operative within the other religions is of Christ, that it is "specifically a Christian event." For those of other religions, however, this claim can only sound like another Western form of exploitation, of imperialistic aggression. And perhaps in reality it has a tinge of this about it and is *not* itself of pure grace. Since the covenant of grace extends to all other religions, they have something to teach us that is distinctively *theirs.* The Christ is and should remain central to us as Christians, but if those without are to come to confess his centrality, they will be led by love and not by anything like talk of "anonymous Christianity" or "anonymous Christians."

It is possible, even probable, that the plurality of religions will never be resolved. We may hope that it will be eschatologically resolved, but the eschaton may be full of surprises for Christians no less than for members of other religions. In the grace and glory that awaits us all, all manifestations of the divine will of love will be gathered up and crowned, we may suppose, and God will assign to all their proper places. For the time being, we should try to be much less anxious about making absolute assignments following upon absolute claims.

The last problem I will mention here has to do with the view that we have no claim on, no right to God's self-endowment, that God in effect owes us nothing, which Rahner affirms along with a very strong strand in tradition. This tradition, I suspect, was developed largely through the interest of Greek speculative theology. While it has much to say for itself and has the support of a long line of prominent theologians, I find that I am increasingly critical of the notion, so much so that I am prepared to raise a question or two in the face of it. The first is this: If God as Creator is in some sense "parent" to us, might we not, analogously with the parent and child relationship as we experience it, have some sort of "claim" on God? Children cannot *exact* nurture from their parents but they can and must claim it, and have, we can only suppose, a "right" to do so. I am not referring merely to food and shelter but to the nurture of mind and spirit, the self-giving grace of genuine parenthood that leads the child into freedom and responsible adulthood. It is true that parents do not *have* to nurture their progeny, yet they "owe" it to them and are constrained, we may believe, by nature and grace to provide it for them, however imperfectly or sporadic. Since we owe something to the children we bring into the world through our own will and pleasure, does not the God of love who creates us out of love, who brings us into an existence we did not ask for, "owe" us something? If God owes us absolutely nothing, if we have no claim whatever on the divine grace, then by analogy at least there may be something deficient in the divine "parenting." These questions raise a lot of difficulties, I know, but they may accord better with the biblical saying that if we know how to give good gifts to our children, God knows immeasurably more how to do so.

Despite the criticisms I felt it necessary to make of Rahner's viewpoint, and there are others I could have made, his teaching on nature and grace has a fullness and an inner consistency about it which should commend it to anyone concerned with the issue today. His position has the great merit of realizing the indistinctiveness of the distinctions that have been so sharply drawn in traditional theology between nature and grace. He is glad to affirm that nature is in grace and that grace is operative within the process of nature as such, even though his principal concern is with nature as found in human beings. As indicated above, I am not at all sure that he has gone far enough in allowing for the operation of grace within nature, but he has made significant movements toward it by reducing the bifurcating tendencies of tradition to what often seems a shadow of themselves. He does however tend to bifurcate nature and history, despite his emphasis on the unity of spirit and matter. This is not nearly as blatantly so with him as with other contemporary theologians, yet it is apparent that he ascribes to history complete centrality by subsuming nature under the rubric of salvation history.

It is quite possible that Rahner derives his anthropocentric orientation from Thomas Aquinas, as he himself believes, but his indebtedness to Heidegger and other strands of existential philosophy were doubtless contributory. Existentialism, as we have seen, does not generally concern itself with nature in a positive sense. Rahner clearly breaks out of existentialism at this point and shows himself much concerned with evolution and material reality. But even so, he is so preoccupied with history that his concern with nature suffers. This has decisive consequences for his theology of creation and nature generally.

In the next two chapters I shall examine the thought of two theologians who exalt history more single-mindedly than Rahner and to indicate the bearing of this exaltation on their views of nature and grace. Some of the criticisms made of them will apply to Rahner, though less obviously. While Rahner is more generously disposed toward nature than the others, in the final result his theology is closer to theirs than its differences might at first sight suggest.

CHAPTER 5

Metz and the Social Dimension of Grace

JOHANN BAPTIST METZ, a student of Rahner who learned much from the master but found it necessary to differ from him at crucial points, is highly negative toward the doctrine of nature and grace. He holds that much of nature and grace theology tends to become privatistic and individualistic, failing to bring into consideration the social and political dimensions of a properly Christian view. It overemphasizes the actual moment of a believer's personal decision for grace and ignores the future element of faith. By making the world merely the scene of individual salvation, most theories of grace denude temporal history of significance; that is, the temporal history of the world itself does not enter into the scheme of salvation. It is "historical" only in the sense of taking into account the personal, individual histories of those who decide for or against grace.[1]

Since this is so, Metz holds, history has no real pertinence to God's saving purpose in many, if not most, of the nature and grace schemes; history's futurity is notably absent from them and, when the future aspect of history is not allowed a place in salvation history, there is no real history of salvation.[2]

Metz attempts to supply a corrective to the privatizing tendencies of anthropological and existential forms of modern theology. He begins by calling for a recognition that biblical faith is rooted in the promises of God, which initiate the future and direct history and faith toward that which is to come or to be realized, toward, as he often puts it, "the not yet." The biblical revelation shows a God who is not above us, but before us; a God whose transcendence is our absolute future.[3] This future calls forth unrealized human potentialities and exerts a liberating power over the human present. The absolute future of humanity finds its eschatological realization in the self-communication of God in Christ. Faith finds in Christ the abrogation of "what is" and the invitation to realize in history "the not yet" of God's promises. Faith therefore is essentially directed toward the future, the promised kingdom of God. Hence a biblically oriented theology cannot be a mere theology of the cosmos, of the world as the space in which history occurs; no more can it be a mere theology of the human person and human existence. It is rather a theology of the emerging and political order informed and empowered throughout by promissory faith. Such a theology places itself in direct communication with the prevailing political, social, and technical realities of the times, and also aligns itself with contemporary promises for justice and peace.[4]

This platform for a political theology has important implications for the doctrine of grace. They are not frequently designated as such in Metz's writings, even though they are everywhere suggested.[5]

Salvation for Metz, we have seen, is something that is mediated through history and that has an essential relationship to history, not just to the inner core of personal life or existential decision for faith. Grace therefore transcends the exclusively private and individual realm and becomes a social reality. It can no longer be couched simply in categories of the intimate, the I-Thou realm of human subjectivity, or in that of the apolitical. It must be at least equally operative and effective within the public and political world.[6] Grace is the horizon of the soul as a part of a larger whole, and it is on the larger whole that Metz places his emphasis. In his thought grace is primarily, though not solely, the dynamic summons to the world to realize its potentiality; grace gives history its forward thrust. World history is not separate from salvation history but is itself salvation history. The summons of grace is universal since every human being shares in the responsibility for fulfilling the potentialities of the world. The call and responsibility for creating a better, more humane world are what unite or can unite all people into a global society.[7] God's summons and the response to it in history constitute, we might say, the social dimension of grace.

The social reality of grace can never be identified with conditions in existing society, for society, Metz says, exists in "an eschatological meanwhile." Its standards and norms are provisional only, and are only provisionally valid insofar as they move toward the eschatological promises of God, toward liberty, peace, justice, reconciliation. But since these are aspects of the message of the promised kingdom and are bound up with the actual social and historical process, they are of grace. The promises of God have a definite "now" quality and demand of faith that it be a critical, liberating force in society, working toward the realization of the "not yet" of the kingdom.[8] When and wherever the promises of God are realized in social structures and movements, and to whatever extent, so too grace is manifested in its effects.

The full meaning of "social grace" or the social dimension of grace cannot be known, Metz would own, apart from the specifically Christian covenant of grace. He clearly sees however that it is necessary for Christian thought to push beyond the borders of that covenant to the whole of human society in its effort to be true to biblical religion and to understand and articulate the doctrine of grace. His emphasis upon the public realm as the place where God's grace can be consciously acknowledged and adhered to points to an essential ingredient in the doctrine of grace and helps to make it intelligible. This is true also of his endeavor to show that grace is operative whether or not it is consciously received. Grace operates beyond individual conscious awareness; God's gracious design has direct bearing on the societal, the political arena; it must do so if it is to have any bearing on the personal realm since the person is nothing if not social and political.[9]

The mediation of grace in the public and political realm finds its supreme though not sole sacramental focus in the church's witness to hope. As a historical and social reality, the church is always active as a political factor; it is "political and acts politically before taking up any political position."[10] On this basis, Metz insists that it is essential to evolve a critical and political form of hermeneutics of the church in order to prevent it from being uncritically identified with specific political ideologies and to prevent Christianity from becoming a purely political religion. Political theology is thus not "a regional task" of contemporary theology but "a fundamental task." It is so because such a theology, based on eschatological hope for the future, helps to define the relation of the church to the world and to make it clear, or clearer than is all too often the case, that the church is not the goal of its own strivings, but that this goal is the kingdom of God. "The Church has a hope and witnesses to a hope, but its hope is not in itself. It is rather a hope in the Kingdom of God as the future of the world. *Ecclesia est universale sacramentum spei pro totius mundi salute.*"[11]

As the sacrament of hope for the salvation of the world, the church is related to the world temporally and not spatially. It is the eschatological and exodus community. Its institutional and sacramental life is grounded upon this eschatological character. "The Eucharist is the sacrament of the Exodus; it is the commemoration of the death of Christ *as promise.*"[12]

Metz's view of grace operating within the church's life as the grace of hope, based on the promise of the kingdom, does indeed provide an effective theological corrective to prevalent individualistic doctrines in both Roman and non-Roman churches. Although his political theology has been criticized from almost every angle by conservative and leftist thinkers, Christian and Marxist alike,[13] it nonetheless marks a very significant movement in Roman Catholic thought toward a more critical theology and a broadened, more inclusive doctrine of grace. With the attacks on his thinking, and some have been quite virulent, I am not here concerned. The chief difficulty I have with his theology is the understanding of the relation of nature and grace it gives rise to, not really at any other point. Although the difficulty I find with it constitutes the very basis of his contributions to contemporary theology, it is the precise locus of its most notable inadequacy. Apart from this inadequacy, it is not at all likely that he would or could have concerned himself so singly and rigorously with the social and political dimensions of the Christian life.

However this may be, the difficulty to which I point has to do with the fundamental presupposition of his thought. This presupposition arises from his evaluation of history and his all but exclusive preoccupation with it. It is apparent almost from the outset of his *Theology of the World* and *Faith in History and Society* that Metz shares and in a real sense celebrates the modern world's loss of a positive feeling for nature. In fact Christianity is itself responsible for this loss. It has dedivinized nature and rendered it material for human self-completion in history. "We encounter the world as the world of man," Metz says. "What primarily meets our eye is not the *vestigia Dei,* but the *vestigia hominis.* The 'creation' of God is everywhere mediated through the 'work' of man. It has a distinct 'anthropocentric' orientation. This is all fundamentally a Christian event."[14] The historical power of the Christian faith has secularized the world, and although this secularization is not to be identified with modern secularity, the basic tendency of the modern process of secularization is to be understood in a positive Christian way as that which frees humanity for history and from the divinized view of the world that pertained in earlier ages.[15]

Along with Rahner and many other contemporary theologians, Metz rejoices in "the epochal shift" from the cosmocentricity of Greek thought to the anthropocentricity that marks modern thought. He attributes the impetus for this shift to Aquinas, though it might more properly be traced back to Augustine. In a more immediate way, however, it derives from Kant and the Neo-Kantians. It is to them that we owe most directly our subjective, anthropological, and ontological understanding of humanity and the world. Metz is as opposed to metaphysics as any Ritschlian theologian. Metaphysics concerns the world as world, that is, as cosmos, as that which immeasurably transcends the human continuum. As he sees it, conceptualization within the horizon of nature, of the cosmos, belongs to a past age, one never to be recalled. The shift from nature to history, from *Umwelt* to *Mitwelt*, in Christian thought is complete. Though it was a long time coming, it was necessitated by biblical religion itself. All teleological interpretation of revelation and transcendence must be entirely eschewed in favor of concentration on "the world of man," the shared intersubjectivity that constitutes history. So great is the distance from nature and history that Metz can say that in relation to the world as nature, something like a "cosmological atheism" is justified.[16]

This split between nature and history, everywhere evident in Metz's thought, receives especially luminous articulation at certain crucial points. As with Marx and modern Western thought generally, Metz tends to see nature simply as that which affords the raw matter for human history, even while he deplores human exploitation of nature.[17] He cites Bacon's dictum *Scientia et potentia in idem coincident* ("knowledge and power are one and the same") as that which characterizes the modern conception of science as control over nature, but nowhere balances it with Bacon's further stricture that nature must be obeyed if it is to be made to serve human ends. As a matter of fact, he counters Bacon's dictum with an appeal to the uses of a kind of antiknowledge *ex memoria passionis*, a recollection forming in modern society of the suffering in history which profoundly moderates our tendency to define history only in terms of the successful and the established.[18] This very suffering is developed in this context as the precise reason why there can be no theory of reconciliation between humanity and nature, "no 'objective' reconciliation and no visible and manageable unity between them."[19] The slightest trace of senseless suffering gives the lie to all affirmative theories of nature and all teleology. Not only so, for "the anthropocentricity of power over and control of nature asserts itself to the same end, over all cosmocentricity."[20]

Metz's use of the *memoria passionis* makes a fundamental appeal to us.

It is certainly true that the conquered and defeated, the forgotten and suppressed hopes of historical existence need to be given a place in history (as antihistory if nothing else), especially for Christians. The midpoint of Christian faith is after all, as Metz finely says, "a specific *memoria passionis,* on which is grounded the promise of the future freedom for us all."[21] Still, does human suffering justify the line that Metz has so decisively drawn between nature and history? There is much that can be said to make the line a good deal less decisive.

The lack of reconciliation between human beings and nature is today a source of suffering; it is itself one of the deepest roots of human pain, of a searing sorrow at the core of modern Western civilization. That pain cannot be removed by asserting that no reconciliation is possible and by locking ourselves into history, into "anthropocentricity." To turn our backs on the problem is simply to drive the anguish of being separated from our ground—most literally, our ground—into more and more hidden recesses of our spirit, only to find it erupting in social strife and warfare. The claim that modern Western people are rootless points to something more than their being without familial and social ties. Rootlessness has deeper dimensions than this. Among other things, rootlessness indicates that our affinity with nature, our very rootage in the soil, has been and is being increasingly lost sight of. This is the most fundamental of all losses.

The way to deal effectively with this problem does not lie in the celebration of secularization that is so frequently found in theology today. This deepens and exacerbates the problem. It pulls people more and more into the narrow tunnel of history that they have dug through nature, the darkness of which prevents them from seeing that the tunnel is surrounded by nature and could have no reality whatever apart from it. I cannot see how any useful purpose can be served in our time by continuing to relegate nature to the realm of utterly secondary concern and by exalting history to a level of significance that, stripped of its ground in nature, is a first-order abstraction. It may be true that history cannot be supported by a theory of nature, as Metz holds, but it is certainly no less true that no theory of history could arise apart from the facticity of nature. Yet there is more to be said, for nature is not only the prior condition of history, it enters into the very substance of history itself in our own corporeality, in that of which we take knowledge, in what we value and fight over, feed upon and return to at our demise. Certainly the discovery of the structure of nuclear energy has enormously deepened, or should have deepened, our understanding of history as something we have with nature or not at all.

At all events, due weight must be given to nature if there is to be any balance in our self-understanding, if our history, our "anthropo-centricity" is to find a somewhat more realistic place in the scheme of things. So far as I can see, the task of devising a theory or vision of nature is a crucial call upon theology and human thought as a whole. And the theory can be positive, at least far more positive than Metz allows.

Philosophy and religion in much of the West, the Near East, and in China at least are rooted in the belief, the faith *and* feeling that life is good, despite the suffering it entails. If this affirmation fades away, the prognosis of history will be very grim indeed. That there are signs in Western culture which point to a growing dissolution of this affirmation few social critics would doubt. Is this not closely related to the separation modern people feel from the world as nature, to their sense of isolation in their ego-centrism? The anthropocentricity that Metz celebrates and that derives from the dogma, long dominant in the West, that history is the horizon of humanity with nature as merely material for historical action,[22] cannot but be ingredient to this dissolution. "The sense and taste for life" are inseparably bound to an affirmative feeling about the processes of life as a whole, a feeling that lies deeply submerged in biologic urges that human beings share with the realm of the nonhuman or, perhaps better ex-pressed, the prehuman realm of nature.

Metz is rightly opposed to the Heideggerian view that human beings are "thrown" into existence. Rather than a sense of "throwness," he says, they enter into existence with a sense of "sharedness." That sharedness is however, as he would have it, strictly limited to history. The world of experience is a shared world insofar as it is history, that is, human intersubjectivity. Although one appreciates Metz's stress upon the essen-tially social character of being human, the limitations of his notion of what constitutes human beings are perhaps too obvious to be mentioned. All that stands as the very precondition of history is surely a shared inheritance. Nature is shared in our very constitution. Others are "bone of our bone, flesh of our flesh." We share with them "intersubjectivity" only because we first share with them "interphysicality," our composition and structured reality as human beings, along with all those factors and forces in nature which provided for our emergence. It was necessary for nature to be "hospitably disposed" toward the rise and development of our species, else we should not be here on the surface of the world, proudly boastful of our history or anything else. An excessive preoccupation with ourselves, our shared history, can make us all but oblivious to aspects of being human that are given in and with nature, to the ineluctable consanguinity—affinity is too weak a word—we have with "the great appearances of nature" (Coleridge), of which we are one and in the most fundamental sense with which we are one. Nature's "hospitable disposition" toward us, despite the struggle and strife against its forces that we have had and have to bear in order to survive, is certainly among the factors that induce the feeling that life is good and that sustains humanity. We share historical life because we share that which underlies and conditions historical life in all its parts. Negativity toward natural reality not only distorts sight and understanding, it makes us ingrates, spurners of the wonderfully fecund world from and in which we have our being.

One of the troubles with positions such as Metz's is that it tends to divide consciousness and truncate our grasp of the human situation. Before we are situated in history, we are situated in nature. This is true for the race and for the individual. Situationally, we are and remain in both realms. We cannot be "thrown" into one and "share" in the other. The very notion that it could be otherwise produces a profound disturbance of the spirit. The sharp bifurcation between nature and history, so marked in our culture and so well exemplified in Metz's thought, is the precise issue we need to address and, if humanity is to have a good prognosis, to overcome.

I do not think moreover that it will do to hold up suffering as the only effective counter in history to scientific and technological dominance. Metz is right to point to suffering as something which characterizes human life on a scale so massive that it stuns the mind and defies all descriptive powers. Certainly history is scarred by suffering in its every dimension, but however deeply etched suffering is within it, history is also marked by many other things: creativity, pleasure, joy in discovery, delight in one's progeny, the ecstasy of sexual fulfillment, and the ecstasy of mystical experience, whether in the sense of union with nature only or with the divine transcendent power. All of the "unities" we experience, fleeting though they may be, with elements of the world, with people in a common cause, in the battle against injustice, in the crusade for freedom, and above all in love of and by others, are deeply etched in history too. It is true that these things are ambiguous and may and often do occasion suffering. But they provide grounds for the affirmation of life which no form of Christian theology should be allowed to obscure. And of course suffering itself is ambiguous. Poverty and tyranny occasion suffering on untold counts, privately and publicly, but this suffering often harbors the seeds of new hopes, no doubt limited but promising to some degree for whole segments of the race. The things that make life endurable and even sometimes enjoyable have a legitimate place in responsible theology. They help to give substance to the affirmation that creation is good and that not everything devolves on the "futurity of faith," on the eschatological consummation. In fact they are ingredient to the hope for that consummation just as surely as suffering.

A question about Metz's eschatological claims presents itself at this point, but since I want to discuss the eschatological stance of modern theology in connection with Moltmann's position, I shall say only a few words about it here. It is not clear to me that the eschatological hope for the future freedom of man, as Metz develops it, is any more essentially Christian than the idea of the divine moving within nature toward human fulfillment. What is even less clear is whether, as Metz avows, these two views are mutually exclusive. May it not be that God is working toward the realization of the kingdom in ways other than those designated as historical? I suspect that we ought to be prepared to credit God with more avenues of operation than one, natural and historical, teleological as well as eschatological. History cannot be divorced from nature if the creative grace of God is the ground of both.

CHAPTER 6

Moltmann and the Ultimate Future

ANYTHING THAT JÜRGEN MOLTMANN writes is of immediate interest and importance. His massive and constructive trilogy,[1] dealing with eschatological hope, Christology, and the Spirit and the church, has established him as a frontrunner in theological scholarship and skill. A collection of his essays entitled *The Future of Creation*,[2] which includes writings integral to the development of his major works, is of special significance for the purposes of this study. The title itself is arresting, particularly since to my knowledge he had not been wont to say a great deal about creation before.[3] It had been my hope to find something fundamentally new in this volume. I was not disappointed. Although Moltmann not surprisingly declares here that the scheme of nature and grace has to be dropped, he proposes a highly schematic replacement for it based on "the Christian hope for the ultimate future," as he puts the matter.

At certain strategic points, he insists that this hope must not be allowed to obviate the hopes for what is developing in the here and now. The knowledge "of the future of God" which began in the crucified Christ and which brings Christians into critical conflict with technocratic notions of development, is a conflict waged not "in the name of the ultimate supernatural hope against the penultimate earthly hopes," but in the name of the people who now and in the future "are excluded from the development process: the neglected, the oppressed and the outcasts."[4]

In an essay entitled "Creation as an Open System," the most searching and systematic in the volume and where Moltmann specifically outlines his proposal for replacing the nature and grace scheme, he begins his deliberations by calling for a convergence of science and the theological understanding of creation. If there is to be any such convergence, he says, there has to be a revision of both theology's concept of creation and of classical science's concept of nature. In the past, theology has sought to adjust itself to the progress of science either by deistically limiting belief in creation to the origination of the universe or by existentially limiting it to the personal realm of human life. If it has not taken one or the other of these apologetic paths, it has cut itself off from the sciences. The progressive destruction of nature we call the ecological crisis was brought about by Christianity and science together. If the race and nature are to survive, "then Christianity and science must together revise both the picture of man found in the traditional belief in creation ('subdue the earth,' Gen. 1:28) and the picture of man reflected in Cartesian science ('*Maitre et possesseur de la nature*')."[5]

The traditional view of redemption in the light of and for the sake of creation, he goes on to say, can no longer serve. It is a *protological* understanding of faith that makes the history between creation and redemption primarily the history of the fall. It is therefore a closed system; it cannot bring anything new. The revision proposed is an *eschatological* understanding of creation. Modern exegesis, it is here claimed, shows that faith in salvation as a historical process determines belief in creation, and insofar as faith in salvation is eschatological, eschatology determines the experience of history and belief.[6] In the J and P documents creation in the beginning does not mean an "unscathed primal condition" but the history that precedes creation, as that which opens up the historical prospect and aligns creation toward the future. And since time is established with creation, it cannot be a closed system; it is an open system, "open for a future which does not have to be the return of what was at the beginning, in the form of *restitutio in integrum*."[7]

On such a basis as this, Moltmann says, theology has to concern itself with creation not only at the beginning but also in history and at the end. It has to have in view the total process of divine creative activity, maintaining the continuity and unity of the divine creativity itself. In traditional terms this means the unity of the *regnum naturae*, the *regnum gratiae*, and *regnum gloriae*, each considered eschatologically. The inner ground of creation in the beginning is not the covenant of grace, for that covenant is only given with the promise of the kingdom of glory. The kingdom, Moltmann concludes, "is the inner motivation of the divine history of the covenant," and the process of creation "is totally aligned towards glory."[8]

Following these observations, Moltmann goes on to develop his doctrine of the consummation. It is a splendid and imaginative achievement into whose details we need not enter here. I want rather to point to some of the implications of his doctrine of creation. In regard to the crucial matter of maintaining that creation is not a closed system but an open one, Moltmann has much to teach us. His judgment that the traditional doctrine has led to a view of history between creation and redemption as primarily that of the fall, and the history between redemption and the consummation as the restoration of creation as it was originally, cannot be gainsaid. Such widely differing theologians as Thomas Aquinas and Rudolf Bultmann are cited in support of the judgment. Aquinas holds that the end will be like the beginning,[9] and Bultmann does so unequivocally, as in his often quoted remarks that "[n]o light shone in Jesus other than the light that always shone in creation" and that the meaning of redemption "is that the original relationship of creation will be restored."[10] Such a picture of creation clearly does not allow anything fundamentally new. Moltmann justly complains that it does not take into account the death and resurrection of Christ as "the new creation," as the introduction of "the absolutely new reality of life through death" and the consequent consummation of God's indwelling of the new creation of heaven and earth. In the kingdom of glory humanity is not merely restored to the image of God; it is glorified, it participates in the life and glory of God. And along with humanity, the whole creation is to share in the all-permeating glory of God,[11] Moltmann says, clearly echoing the Irenaean tradition.

This is finely conceived and said far better than the mere paraphrase I have given. It presents, however, a real difficulty. Its essential thrust is toward the eschaton as promised in Christ and as it is to be manifested in the new heaven and earth. Universal history prior to Christ does not significantly enter the scheme and creation in the beginning and in the present is devalued.[12] There is scarcely an appreciative word about the manifestations of glory in the religious history of mankind, scant recognition of the emergence of the "new" in the created order, from the primal elements to conscious life. It frequently appears, under this view, that humanity existed in a closed and isolated world between original creation and the coming of Christ, that God's openness for the world awaited the Lord's death and resurrection. Prior to that, it is almost as though the divine eyes were closed to it, once created.[13]

If the entire creative activity of God were to be viewed eschatologically, as Moltmann affirms it must be, there would, one might suppose, be numberless eschatological manifestations of his glory, at least "proleptically" so. Would not the first fires of revelation, wherever and in whatever circumstances they appeared, be such; would not every step toward civil order from the beginning of history until now be another; would not the development of technology, however ambiguous in expression and use, be a possible candidate; would not divine judgment and wrath against injustice and the misuse of the goods of the earth and of human artifacts be yet another, and behind all this, would not the first flickers of life be a moment of eschatological glory, especially and wonderfully so when creatures emerged with sufficient awareness to realize that they were creatures and who found it possible "to orient themselves toward the future," and to "fall" in freedom and at times at least, to rise in love?

If eschatology is the central focus of theology, the eschaton, reaching a climax in the Christ, has to be seen as always and everywhere fragmentarily manifested, at the least adumbrated in all that preceded his coming. In Moltmann's view the eschatological dimension manifested in the Christ has no fundamental bearing upon the past. It is limited to the future.

That God's openness in the world becomes manifest in Christ is basic to the church's faith, but that openness should not be considered as openness solely toward the future; it should be seen as the disclosure of what in some basic sense has ever been so, even if considered more fully so after Christ's advent in history. Some such view would give us theological grounds for appreciating the manifestations of the divine glory in the minute structures of a single cell, the unfathomable complexities of the human brain, the relation between the two and the long reaches of evolution behind them. These things are not of nature only; they are of grace. They are anticipatory promises of the fulfillment of nature and history, universal in both their past and present scope, and as such are eschatological signs, "moments" in which the eschatological glory of God is revealed and recognized, presaging greater things to come.

The "mystery of inequity" which so deeply dyes past and present history and upon which Moltmann focuses so much of his attention here should not be suffered to obscure another mystery equally as great, the mystery of the drive within us toward the good, toward order, justice, righteousness, even love. This mystery needs to be attended to theologically and systematically, equally with the dark mystery of sin. When it is allowed a significant place in theological reflection, the scope of theology is broadened very considerably, including, 1 believe, the eschatological dimension.

It is doubtful whether faith can long be maintained when it is entirely or even almost entirely directed toward the future, if hope supercedes rather than conditions all of its other dimensions. Such a supercession not only threatens the continuity of faith, it diminishes severely that which succors and sustains faith now. In its light, all active and loving signs of the divine in the forms and forces of nature and historical life become peripheral, if not inconsequential.

God does not merely confront creation, as Moltmann implies, but indwells it, permeating it with glory even now. We may hope that God will do so fully in the end, but when such a hope dulls our sense of God's power and presence in the immediacies of existence, a division of soul is the direct result, one in which faith finds itself torn and tortured. In the kingdom of glory, we may conjecture with Moltmann, all finite life systems will be open for infinity,[14] yet must we not insist that a fundamental ground for the hope lies in the belief that all systems of life already to some extent lie open to it and have been from the beginning?

In "Creation as an Open System" Moltmann gives evidence of a more positive view of nature than found in the other essays in *The Future of Creation*. Account of this must be taken if we are to be fair to his perspective. It appears in connection with his criticism of the scientific understanding of nature during the past few centuries, which dates from the time when Bacon and Descartes described the relation between human beings and the world as subject and object. Such a division brought about a pattern of domination and exploitation, which quantum physics, Moltmann notes, has realized. "The old division . . . is no longer a suitable starting point for our understanding of modern science. Science, we find, is now focused on the network of relationships between man and nature" and "sees itself as an actor in this interplay between man and nature."[15] From this standpoint, Moltmann speaks of nature as a cohesion of open systems of life with its own "subjectivity" and to the "symbiosis" between human and nonhuman systems. He says moreover that rather than domination over nature, a model based on communication with it is required. "In the light of Christ's mission, Gen. 1.28 will have to be interpreted in an entirely new way: not 'subdue the earth' but free the earth through fellowship with it."[16] No social justice, the most important element in the further development of civilization, is possible without justice to the natural environment, just as justice for nature cannot be achieved without social justice. "Justice is the form of authentic interdependence between people, and between society and the environment."[17]

These and other such remarks point to a nascent theory of nature, affirming its relative independence of history. This is a welcome perspective. It is not permitted however to lessen the force of Moltmann's eschatological priorities. The whole creation is "enslaved" and simply waits for "the glorious liberty of the children of God" in order for itself to be free.[18] The totality of nature, that is, is subsumed under the eschatological fulfillment of humankind.

Although emotionally compelling and scripturally warrantable, it seems to me that the eschatological schema places a weight on human history which it cannot bear. Such a scheme may have been viable prior to the development of astrophysics, but to make the whole of reality as now conceived adjunctive to salvation history strains credence. It appears to be another enthronement of anthropocentricity, a conception fitted to a view of reality depicted in such phrases as "man and his world" but hardly one that fits "planet earth in the midst of a system of unimaginable vastness."

The "end" in store for our history may have little, perhaps nothing much at all, to do with the vast beyond, which quite possibly is independent of our history and wholly impervious to its fate.

A perspective of this kind has the virtue of putting a limit on the aggrandizement of human history, whether by the theological or the scientific community, and inducing a humility that *Heilsgeschichte* schools of thought do not normally accommodate. This sort of humility may point with more accuracy to our position within reality than contemporary eschatological theories that bulge with anthropocentricity. It may also bear significantly on our theology of nature and our theology of grace. The humanly centered views that have so long informed our theological thought need to be subjected to deeper and deeper criticism. The fact that we now find ourselves in an overwhelming immensity of interstellar space may be itself revelatory, a "word" of God to us about ourselves and our place within "nature," a nature from whose stardust, billions of years old, we perhaps got our start, and from that we only recently—very recently indeed—emerged into history.

Theologically, such a "revelatory" word could be of great importance. If accepted and acted upon, it would *declare* (as the heavens are said to declare) the glory of God in "the very heights," that is, that the divine glory exceeds anything that can be remotely imagined from the vantage point of the earth and its people; it would declare too that our historical life is perhaps but a moment in nature's life and that in a far larger sense than ever realized before, we are formed from the dust and have our life in total dependence on the dust from which we derived. We might really grasp the fact that nature is not ours but is independent of us and has an integrity and life of its own.

Ecologically, this enlarged vision of reality might bring with it a much deepened awareness that our survival depends on recognizing and honoring that independence. So long as nature is considered an adjunct to our history or dependent on our history for its consummation, we shall continue to regard it as that which belongs to us, as material for historical activity, and so for our domination, whatever shifts may transpire in this through efforts to achieve "justice to the environment." This very phrase implies that nature is less than an equal partner in the enterprise of life, that we have the upper hand in regard to it. It may just be however that justice to nature is not to be accomplished without our recognizing its overarching independence of historical ends.

The doctrine of the eschaton, despite all disclaimers, is a mythological construct. Modern eschatologists, however, persistently speak of it as though it were the final biblical instrument for the demythologization of religion. Thus Moltmann understands the view that the original relationship of creation will be restored at the eschaton as an age-old mythological scheme, "the myth of eternal return."[19] This myth, he says later on, is not demythologized by talking about "authentic existence" instead of heaven and "alienation" instead of hell, as in Bultmann.[20] But does talk about "the new beginning of man's becoming man at his end," about "the absolute future of God," the "eschatological glorification of man and through him all creation," perform the task of demythologizing the Christian hope? Not at all, for it merely introduces other mythological categories. The resort to myth is essential and inevitable if voice is to be given to that which transcends human experience and powers of description.

We can appreciate Moltmann's motive in denying the doctrine of restoration in the interests of "the new" in creation, as that which is eschatologically directed toward the transformation of the unjust world, and as that which prevents the gospel from becoming "the uncritical compensation for existing evil."[21] But the trouble is that the new creation as he conceives it is "the absolutely new." The resurrection of the crucified Lord is, he says, *nova creatio per annihilationem nihilii:* "out of the annihilation of nothingness the Being emerges that has overcome death—this 'absolute death'—and is hence life and eternal bliss." The new creation, Moltmann says, "does not emerge out of the restoration of the old creation: it follows from creation's end. Out of 'the negation of the negative' a Being arises that has overcome the conflict between being and non-being and is hence absolutely new.'"[22]

This is said with such urgent insistence that is implications may be obscured. It needs to be noted first that the assertion's Hegelian phrasing does not make it philosophically immune to challenge. More to the point is the split it implies between creation before and after Christ's death and resurrection. To posit "the absolutely new" in Christ and mean it, as Moltmann evidently does at least here, is to take him out of the context of life, to see him as having no part in human emergence, a nonparticipant in the created processes of existence. It is to divorce him from prior history and to separate him from all those in other religions who have had a little something to say about hope.

We have heard a great deal about "the absolutely new" reality in Jesus as the Christ since so much of contemporary theology is apparently enthralled with the phrase. It is motivated by a desire to exalt the Lord, and in some sense perhaps dictated by devotion. But however this may be, it should be understood as an exaggeration that is theologically dubious, if not inadmissible. Docetic in fundamental tendency and implication, it removes the Christ from nature and ordinary history. If his death and resurrection constitute "the absolutely new," then it is *too* new, too new to be appropriated in experience and made the basis of hope, at least for those to whom its Docetic and Gnostic tendencies are unacceptable.

Is it not enough and more accurate to speak of the Christ event—in its entirety and not simply of the death and resurrection—as "the radically" rather than "the absolutely new"? The latter phrase implies an insertion into history, totally from without, while the former makes provision for that which is new in a radical way from all that came before it but is yet sufficiently rooted in common life and history to bear upon their very basis. Emergence is a bad word among dialectical theologians but it is not altogether without use. In some sense, the Christ must be seen as an emergence *in* history and the nature which provides its basis, not however as something simply originating in history and nature but in the divine grace. Grace gives the Christ event the radically new character of a gift, yet a gift made in accordance with the life and experience of those to whom it is made.

On terms such as these, it would not be necessary or even possible to resort to the category of restoration, and certainly creation could not be considered a closed system. On the contrary, the creative process under these terms is understood as continuously open to the new and especially to the radically new reality in Christ as that which works toward the transformation of history into the nearer likeness of God. Such a view allows for more than a verbal continuity between creation, incarnation, and consummation (in Moltmann's usage, the *regnum naturae,* the *regnum gratiae,* and *regnum gloriae*) and between history before and after Christ.

A strict interpretation of Christ's death and resurrection is central for understanding Christian faith, to be sure, yet his death and resurrection take place within a context of human experience and hope without which their centrality for faith could not be real. Contextually they are absolutely central, but their very context prevents them from being "absolutely new," even while being "radically new."

No one has written more searchingly on Judaism and its place in the covenant than Moltmann,[23] but if Christ is "the absolutely new," he is absolutely cut off from all that came before him, including the people of the promises, not to mention the immemorial hopes and sighings of humanity, its worldwide religious visions, teachings, and worship.

In the preface to *The Future of Creation* Moltmann says that the essays are offered in the hope that they "will serve to deepen and crystallize eschatological thinking, and to show how open-minded and how ready to learn that way of thinking is."[24] In some instances open-mindedness and willingness to learn are very marked, and in other instances one-sidedness is equally marked; in all practically everything learned is made to fit into the eschatological mold as Moltmann interprets it. Although variously dated, the essays do not merely represent stages in his progress but are ingredient to the methodological and factual basis of his thought. No suggestion of amendment is made, though of course shifts in perspective are evident in his other works, most notably perhaps in *The Church in the Power of the Spirit.* In the essays, however, Moltmann tends to tow a single line, frequently making statements and proffering arguments that indicate a curious imbalance in his thought, more so perhaps than those already mentioned. Some of these statements and arguments are pertinent to our discussion and will be briefly described below.

Anticipation of the future, Moltmann remarks truly, makes Christian faith aware of its provisional nature in all its manifestations.[25] But having delivered himself of this cautionary word, he proceeds to make statements that seem anything but provisional, sometimes countering others of a similarly "provisional" nature. At one point he says that "the coming kingdom of God is not to be found anywhere on earth, except in the Cross of Golgotha. The divine future confronts us not in dreams of the future but in the face of the crucified Jesus."[26] Taken at face value, this deliverance poses a few questions. Is there no hint of the coming kingdom in the Exodus, in the covenant with Israel, in prophecy? Are there absolutely no anticipatory signs of it in religious and social history the world over? And what happens to the earthly hopes and aspirations Moltmann shows himself so anxious to protect, especially those of the poor and the oppressed? Does it not sweep all history prior to the cross into the dust, and rule out any possibility of a relation between human aspirations and Golgotha? One can certainly hold that the coming kingdom is to be found in the cross with a power and effect found nowhere else, but taken discretely Moltmann's statement makes the cross utterly disparate from everything else.

Another declaration to be noted is this: "The cross of Christ reveals the godlessness and God-forsakenness of the world."[27] From one standpoint this is true, from another it will not hold. The cross discloses human sinfulness in its depth but at the same time it discloses the human potentiality to respond through grace to the divine action in the cross. Apart from this potentiality, the resurrection would not have been perceived, not at least specifically as the resurrection of the crucified one, unless indeed one supposes that belief in it came about through a sheer miracle of grace, having nothing whatever to do with the human component, with the minds and hearts to whom it was revealed. The cross unfolds the world's godlessness, to be sure, yet at one and the same time it unfolds its godliness, in the sense at least of indicating the capacity of human beings to acknowledge God in self-communication in the cross. If we were totally godless, we would not be able to recognize God in any self-manifestation, not even in the cross.

Moltmann deals with the principle of revelation of the opposite and of knowledge of the unlike in some little detail. Using Hippocrates' principle *contraria contrariis curantur,* he reasons as follows: insofar as God is revealed to people in the contradiction of the God-forsaken, this knowledge brings them into correspondence with God and even makes them like God. Contradiction and correspondence are opposites, but they belong together and compliment one another. "Knowing begins within contradiction and ends within correspondence. It begins with pain and ends with joy."[28] This sounds good homiletically, perhaps, but does it possess logical rigor? Could those completely locked in godlessness be thrown into pain when confronted by a holiness of which they had no inkling whatever? They might be thrown into confusion and possibly awe, but hardly pain.

Moltmann's use of Schelling's dictum "Every nature can be revealed only in its opposite—love in hatred, unity in strife" to support his thesis helps little, even when, as he suggests, Schelling's "can only" is changed into "is in actual fact."[29] There is of course a measure of truth in this line of thought: we value love the more we see of hatred and are more urgently mindful of the necessity for unity the more we see of strife, but Moltmann's reasoning begs a question a good deal more fundamental than is admitted as a term of his argument, at least at this point. If we had no prior idea at all of love, if we lived in a completely loveless world, no amount of hatred, however intense, could produce a knowledge of love. Hatred would be simply the determinative factor of life, and similarly so with strife in respect to unity: no one would remark on strife if that were all we knew. Its recognition depends on an awareness, however elemental, of its opposite, of the desirability and indeed necessity for unity. In another context, Moltmann himself says as much. "The negation of the negative must itself be founded on an anticipation of the positive, latent though this anticipation may be. If this were not the case, the negative could not be experienced as negative and judged accordingly."[30]

These critical remarks are not captious entries. They bear directly on Moltmann's distrust and disavowal of the principle of analogy, a pivotal matter in the theology of nature and grace. He will allow no similarity in the revealer and those who receive the revelation. That given in revelation "contradicts" its recipients, and it is only in the contradiction that godliness or grace can be known. This raises epistemological questions of a searching sort, questions that may send one back to Rahner's theological anthropology with both relief and gratitude. But it is of a piece with Moltmann's refusal to place a positive evaluation upon human capacities in his theology. It is also of a piece with his tendency to make distinctions absolute when they are much less so in fact and experience. His dismissal of the *analogia entis* illustrates this tendency well. Aristotle's principle that "the knowledge of like comes into being through like," on which the analogy of being doctrine is based, is rejected on what seem to be highly questionable grounds. Theologically, Moltmann says, if the principle of likeness is understood in the strict sense, God is known only by God.[31] But likeness has never been so conceived by responsible theologians. All that has been claimed is that human beings are sufficiently akin to God that they may respond to God's self-communication. If this were not so, then God's self-revelation would be to naught, pointless and without issue. Even if the revelation be conceived as contradiction, some little element of correspondence with God would be necessary to grasp what the contradiction was all about.

Moltmann's contention that the principle of analogy supports *apatheia* and prevents sympathy with the stranger and people who are different is far from a conclusive argument against it. The contention may well have point, doubtless does, in the moral sense. It is true that "[l]oving people like ourselves is a matter of course," is self-affirmation and may, as is alleged, eventually make us apathetic. And it is here that love "for the person who is different, for the stranger and the enemy" is what socially and ethically justifies the other.[32] But these judgments do not logically validate the principle of correspondence in contradiction—the stranger, the enemy is after all a *person*. These judgments logically support the *analogia* doctrine even while pointing to some of the moral difficulties it might give rise to.

There is the further matter of the cross as the revelation of godlessness in history. Can one thing bear so great a weight, however central in Christian thought and devotion? Are there not other revelations of god-lessness in history? The Holocaust comes to mind as a possible candidate. There millions and millions of people were systematically, coldly put to death with sophisticated scientific methods. Surely this can only be considered one of the greatest perfidies in history, one pointing to god-lessness and godforsakenness on a vast scale, to something unimaginable in its horror and its demonic depth. It is necessary to claim that the cross reveals godlessness in a vast number of its dimensions and depths, and that that revelation can provide the symbolic and systematic focus for other such revelations, but need more be claimed?

That Moltmann pursues his eschatological vision with such intensity and fervor and sometimes make statements that are quite extreme is the very feature of his thought that accounts in large measure for the impact he has made on contemporary theology. But there are other more significant features of his thought that lend a compelling attractiveness to it. One of them is sheer depth, the power of taking an issue to its very basis. Another is the seriousness with which he regards biblical faith as the foundation of all theological thought, and his refusal to look either to the right or the left of it. Still another is the passion and precision with which he states his views. In short, he is very persuasive. Fortunately for those whom he serves as theological mentor, he is quite frequently right in his judgments. What he has to say commends itself not only to those who share his premises and cast of mind, but to many who are floundering and in search of a satisfying theological perspective.

It is often said that people in this age are looking for a new mythology, one that can command our allegiance and to which we can give ourselves in life and thought. Eschatology for a good many people within the church today is that new mythology, something that makes sense of faith and hope. Moltmann and those of similar mind have met a real need, providing the new mythology with theological depth and intellectual power. Still, a few questions arise in the face of it.

Is the new mythology adequate to life as it is lived today and will be lived tomorrow? Is the pluralism that constitutes one of the great problems of the age met at all effectively, or is our increasing knowledge of the immensity of natural reality addressed, and how far are our minds, feelings, sympathies drawn toward unity by it? Is it not possible that what we need is not so much a replacement for the doctrine of nature and grace as a revision, inclusive of eschatology and "the future of God" but extending beyond it to the whole order of existence in whatever minute earthly occurrence or whatever distant realm? A revised scheme of nature and grace might afford some important leads toward a view that would address these issues.

Both Moltmann and Metz have made lasting contributions to the theology of grace. In the case of Metz, the emphasis is on the social dimension of grace, specifically grace in the political arena as hope for the eschatological future of the kingdom of God. Moltmann's thought reaches similar results. In his view grace becomes effectively eschatological grace, that which finds its basis in the death and resurrection of Jesus as the Christ and the eschatological future of the kingdom. With him as with Metz, the life of the Christian community is one of hope and action in the world springing from hope for the future. Moltmann's grasp of the centrality of hope in the Christian life, his powerful exposition of the promissory character of the Scriptures and his single-mindedness in doing so have given the eschatological dimension of grace a prominence it had scarcely had since the early ages of the church. He has had of course coworkers in this development, but few have had quite the same impact.

Grace in its eschatological dimension will be critically tempered, to be sure, just as "realized" eschatological thinking before it. It will also be seen that grace is operative in nature, not merely as an exterior power but as its imminent ground. Modern eschatologists have gone too far in their views that biblical religion has "dedivinized" and "desacralized" nature, tending to interpret this to mean that nature had been denuded of grace and thus confining grace to history. Some kind of *modus vivendi* is not only possible but necessary.[33]

CHAPTER 7

Whitehead on Nature and the Nature of the Divine Life

IN SHARP CONTRAST TO THE POSITIONS of Metz and Moltmann, and to a lesser degree of Tillich and Rahner, Alfred North Whitehead presents a metaphysic of nature which includes human history as, in his terms, "an extreme event in nature." Although human experience is taken to be the key to the understanding of nature, it is seen as one element in a single, unified process or "organism." Whitehead tries to present an inclusive metaphysic, "a system of ideas which bring aesthetic, moral and religious interests into relation with those concepts of the world which have their origin in natural science."[1] His categories of interpretation are metaphors drawn from immediate experience that are reckoned to be universal, that is, to be exemplified by all the entities of the world and to be applicable to all elements of experience. Reality is seen as a process of becoming and its basic components are seen as interrelated dynamic events. Everything is interdependent and participates in everything else, from atomic particles to the highest reaches of human community. Even God is a participant in the process. While occupying a singular position within the process, God is yet subject to its metaphysical principle, or as he puts it, "in its grip."

A scheme so imaginative and inclusive as this could not but attract the attention of theologians who are concerned with a unified vision of reality and who want to affirm nature in a theologically significant way. The number of Whitehead's disciples among theologians, far from diminishing through the years, has continued to increase and is likely to grow a great deal more owing to the influence of the astute group of theological thinkers who acknowledge him as a chief inspirant. Indeed, the Whiteheadians of today might be likened to the Hegelians of the last century, for it is possible that Whitehead might in time exercise an influence in theology comparable to Hegel's and perhaps with better results. If this should prove to be the case, it will be because of the commodiousness of his system, one able to support a wide spectrum of theological viewpoints. Even theologians who are not directly indebted to him are already subject to his influence through the thought of those who are under his spell.

Whitehead's doctrine of God is the principal stumbling block for the many who find his system unacceptable. There are many attractive features about it but there are others that are less so. It is not necessary, however, to adopt all the implications of his theism in order to appropriate much else in his thought, chief among them, his general understanding of nature. This aspect of his system affords an important means for structuring a theology of nature and of grace as well, along with the relation between the two.

In what follows the principal concern will be with these issues. No attempt will be made to give a full account of Whitehead's thought.[2] My aim is rather to sketch his overall view of reality and its bearing on nature and grace. I had hoped to be able to do so without resorting to his technical distinctions and often opaque language, but found that distortion would likely result from such an effort. Hence I have kept largely to his own manner of expression, simplifying where it seemed feasible.

The doctrine of God in Whitehead's thought is not the beginning point of his deliberations on the world process; it is a consequence of them. This should not be taken to imply that he stumbled on the idea of God through his analysis of experience or derived it purely from the requirements of his system. The idea of God was no doubt prior to the analysis since Whitehead was a Christian, at least in the sense of cultural inheritance, but the idea was given specific shape and focus through his interpretation of immediate experience. Owing to this, I shall consider in this chapter the epistemological basis of his philosophy and his analysis of the flux of events in the world, dealing with his critique of Christian theism and contributions to theology in the following chapter.

The mystery of personal identity, "the mystery of the immanence of the past in the present, the mystery of transience,"[3] is the epistemological basis of Whitehead's metaphysics. Penetration into this mystery involves analysis of the exceedingly complex character of our experience, though in the recognition that there is no definite area of our experience where complete clarity can be reached. Systematic analysis can take us only so far, beyond which "all is dark." Nor is it true that the elements of experience are important by virtue of the clarity they may reach in consciousness itself. Indeed, the simplicity of clear consciousness is no measure of the complexity of complete experience.[4] Consciousness flickers amidst "a large penumbral region of experience which tells of intense experience in dim apprehension," and suggests that consciousness is "the crown of experience, not its necessary base."[5]

The first principle of epistemology for Whitehead is change: the "changeable, shifting aspects of our relations to nature are the primary topics for conscious observation."[6] A second principle is to be found through the recognition that sense perception is *superficial.* The sense of reality cannot be adequately sustained amidst mere sense, whether of sound or sight. Whitehead's main quarrel with modern epistemology has to do with its exclusive stress on sense perception for the provision of data about nature.[7]

Sense perception does not, he insists, provide this data. The narrow formation of such perception excludes all of the really fundamental factors that constitute our experience.[8] The direct feeling of the derivation of emotion from the *body* is among our most fundamental experiences.[9] The whole complexity of experience is either derived from or modified by it. Hence the basis of experience is *emotional;* experience arises out "of an affective tone" originating from things in nature whose relevance is *given,* not merely perceived. But although the primitive experience is emotional, it is important to note that in the case of human beings or even in the case of higher animals, emotion is never bare emotion; it is emotion interpreted, integrated, and transformed into higher categories of feeling. Yet while this is so, "the emotional appetitive elements in our conscious experience are those which most closely resemble the basic elements of all physical experience."[10] This pivotal fact points to our essential affinity with nature. For all that, there is no definite boundary to determine where our bodily nature begins and external nature ends. The human body is a complex of occasions which are part of spatial nature. Psychologists and physicists agree, Whitehead says, that the body inherits physical conditions from the physical environment according to physical laws. There is thus a general *continuity* between our experience and physical occurrences, and the elaboration of this continuity is one of the more obvious yet more important tasks of philosophy,[11] and one of the tasks where Whitehead is at his best.

Given the radical character of this continuity, the whole conception of the relation of the subject and object as entertained by modern philosophy requires radical revision. Whitehead agrees of course with this conception but not in the sense in which subject and object are identified with knower and known.[12] Subject and object are relative terms. Any given entity in nature is a subject regarding its special activity in relation to another entity, and every entity is an object in regard to its provocation of some special activity within a subject. Analogously so with us, all things are imbued with "emotional tone." All things have what is to be likened to "subjective aim" in human beings and all things strive for "satisfaction," again in some sense like human beings. *Universal reality, this is to say, consists of elements disclosed in the analysis of experiences of subjects.*

Following Hume, Whitehead was able to say that "nothing is to be received into the philosophical scheme which is not discoverable as an element of subjective experience."[13] This is the ontological principle that determines epistemology.[14] But quite unlike Hume, his view entails the ascription of subjectivity (and objectivity) to *everything*.

The reformation of the subjectivist principle in Whitehead's thought is based on the refusal to place human experience outside of nature and the consequent effort to find in descriptions of human experience factors which also enter into the descriptions of "less specialized natural occurrences" than we are ourselves. An occasion of experience which includes human mentality is *"an extreme instance, at one end of the scale, of those happenings which constitute nature"* (italics mine).[15] What we have otherwise is, Whitehead says, perhaps stretching the matter, a form of strict dualism. This can be avoided only if we point to identical elements that connect our experience with events in nature. Our self-identity is knowledge of a special strand of *unity* within the general unity of nature, a locus within the whole, exhibiting the general constitution of the whole. Thus an analogy between the transference of energy from particular occurrence to particular occurrence in physical nature, and transference of affective tone with its emotional energy from one occasion to another in the human sphere, is—if the subject-object principle is to be adequately grasped—philosophically necessary.[16] If it is too much to claim that the subject-object relationship is reproduced in physical nature, Whitehead tells us, the phrase *vector relation* of one particular to another may be proposed as a way of putting the matter.[17]

Now Whitehead is aware of the limited nature of his analogy. The multidimensional character of the seriality of physical events places severe limits on such a scheme. But it has point, he holds, by the fact that our experience is not a one-dimensional thing at all; it is not simply *personal*. The one dominant inheritance we have—the personal dimension—is broken into by many others, sensitive nerves, viscera functions, disease, emotions, hopes, fears, inhibitions, and deep frustrations among them. The personal and the physical therefore are fused inseparably together in us.[18]

However true this is, and however necessary it is to take account of our experience as a genetic relation between occasions in nature, no attenuation of human personality as such is intended. It is important to take due note of this intention if we are to understand Whitehead's point of view. Personal unity is an inescapable fact; it is that by which we receive all occasions of our experience. Although it differs in character at different times, it is yet a unity. Without it we would have no personal identity. The unity of the soul (personality) "is the natural matrix for all transactions of life and is changed and influenced by all that enters it," remaining all the while itself.[19] Still, there can be no excision of personal unity from its matrix in nature.[20] Even our most compelling experience of nonsensuous perception, our experience of the past, which is constituted by a group of focused occasions having no perceptible immediate fact, is nevertheless rooted in activities that are primarily in the past of our bodies and, more remotely, in the past of the environment in which our bodies function. *Fatigue* is a form of bodily memory; it enters into our perception and tellingly points to the inseparability of body and mind, and of past occasions and immediate experience.[21]

Our experience of the past, moreover, is not totally singular since each occasion in nature is affected by past occasions. All occasions arise from relevant objects and perish into the status of objects for other occasions, but these, analogously to us, "enjoy" their decisive moment of self-attainment as an "emotional unity."[22] Our consciousness itself is not without its analogies in nature. "Consciousness is the acme of emphasis," the selection of objects of concern. Each occasion of experience is concerned with an otherness transcending itself, that is, with an object. Natural occasions are themselves in some sense "concerned" with the objects they "select" as important or necessary for their fulfillment. The process by which concern and selection occur is termed *prehension*, and prehension in some real sense is shared by all entities,[23] human and nonhuman alike.

The notion of *concern* is crucial to Whitehead's theory of knowledge even though it must itself be divested of any suggestion of knowledge. Deriving the notion from Quaker usage, he holds that it helps to clarify both epistemology and the ontological structure behind it. We have seen that he takes the rise of an affective tone originating from things "whose relevance is given" as the basic fact of the existence of every entity in nature. We have seen too that every entity has "concern" for an object. This concern is precisely what makes the object a component in the experience of the entity as subject, with "affective tone" drawn both *from* the object and directed *toward* it. No prehension can be divested of an affective tone or "concern."

In regard to human perception, Whitehead holds that concernedness is the essence of perception. Indeed, significant perception takes place only on the basis of concern, of an affective tone toward what is being perceived.[24] Unless this principle is grasped, Whitehead's theory of knowledge will not be at all appreciated.

It is in conjunction with perception that he states his idea of the ontological status of objects in the world in a decisive way. In an important distinction, he says that the process of perception creates itself, but not the *object* of perception.[25] The object has a unity of its own, expressive of its capacity to generate new occasions for the subject. Viewed abstractly, objects are passive, but viewed in conjunction, "they carry the creative activity which drives the world."[26]

When perception is limited to sensation, the object is reduced to sheer passivity, to a mere recipient of the qualities with which they are associated in sense perception. But Whitehead declares that sense perception, conceived in isolation, *never* enters into human experience. We *accept* the world of objects which is directly presented for our experience even though our habits, states of mind, and modes of behavior all enter into this plain matter-of-fact acceptance. There is even evidence that animals accept the world in this sense, that they make an "immediate assumption of a substantial world around them."[27] The hypothesis of a mere sensationalist perception not only fails to account for our direct observation of the world, it has produced the disastrous notion that events in external nature are "vacuous," wholly devoid of meaning and value;[28] something that Whitehead vehemently opposes.

Exclusive reliance on sense perception, he feels, can only promote a false metaphysic. It results "from high-grade intellectuality" which ignores the instinctive interpretations which govern human and animal life and which "presuppose a contemporary world throbbing with energetic values." It refuses to give credence to the massive insistence of our total experience; it is useful, for certain purposes, to be sure, but a disaster unless we recognize it for what it is—a bare abstraction.[29]

Whitehead's epistemological reconstruction of sensationalism is a recur-

rence to pre-Kantian modes of thought. It is based on the critical repudiation of Kant's doctrine of the objective world as a theoretical construct
from purely subjective experience, a repudiation too of Newton's doctrine that events in nature are void of purpose and intrinsic worth and of
the dualism of Descartes's separation of mind and body. Whitehead believes that the thought of these men is to be held in very high esteem but
that the captivity of philosophy to it has lasted long enough for it to have
performed its proper work.[30] The time has come to move beyond it
toward something more inclusive and congenial to our time.

Toward this end, he freely adopts categories drawn from modern
science on the one hand, but on the other has recourse to what can only
be termed a *radical personalization of nature* as a whole. The personaliz-
ing of events in nature, he believes, is necessitated by a thoroughgoing
acceptance of the subject-object scheme of knowledge, by which he
means not limiting the subjective element to the subject alone but extending it analogously to the object. Nothing else can in his view establish a
real reciprocity between them.

He defends his analogous use of such categories as "feeling," "subjective aim," and "satisfaction" by saying that the reformed subjectivist
principle is an alternative statement of the principle of relativity, which
indicates that "it belongs to the nature of a 'being' that it is a potential for
every 'becoming.' "[31] The subjectivist principle, under his bold interpretation, is that the whole of reality consists of elements disclosed in the
analysis of the subject.

Against the charge that his use of emotional terms in describing nonhuman processes is eccentric, he remarks that "the proper method of
choosing technical terms is to adopt terms from some outstanding exposition of an analogous doctrine." What better outstanding exposition is to
be found than the human experience of knowing something, in which
perception is inevitably clothed with emotion.[32] Not only Bradley,
William James, and G. E. Moore used the term *feeling* in the way
proposed in the philosophy of organism, but Plato himself implied it in
his doctrine of "living emotion." Its germ is present in his insistence that
the whole character is conformed to adequate knowledge, and his refusal
to abstract emotion from intellectual perception by identifying virtue
with knowledge. Each philosophical doctrine, Whitehead concludes, can
be reasonably asked to ground its terminology on its own proper tradition. "If this precaution has been taken, an outcry as to neologisms is a
measure of unconscious dogmatism."[33] While I suspect that this language

masks a deeply mystical regard for nature, it answers his critics well enough.

Turning to the metaphysics, we find that Whitehead's basic premise accords with a strong strand of tradition: some form of *order* is a necessary feature of the world. He does not try to prove this but accepts it as the *given* upon which all experience depends. It is something that is grounded in *faith*, "the faith that at the base of things we shall not find mere arbitrary mystery."[34] His metaphysic is an attempt to discern the order on which the processes of the world depend through a dispassionate consideration of things, antecedently to any special investigation into their details. His analysis is not scientific, though based on scientific principles; it is metaphysical, that is, it is concerned with general concepts that apply not to some aspects of experience but to all of it.[35]

This sounds pretty high-flown, but I am sure that it should not be taken as an indication of Kantian or Hegelian hubris. Whitehead has a good deal of humor and humility both about what is metaphysically possible and his own project, and speaks of "how shallow, puny and imperfect are efforts to sound the depths in nature of things."[36] He goes on to say that in philosophy "the merest hint of dogmatic certainty as to finality of statement is an exhibition of folly."[37] Still, he takes the enterprise with deep seriousness, however tentative it must be.

Following Aristotle (for whom he has great admiration, although he reserves his highest praise for Plato, "the wisest of men"[38]), Whitehead is preeminently a teleological thinker; his concern is with the *nisus*, the driving force, of things. But his view of the nature of things is very different from that of the ancient philosopher. Aristotle held that everything had an unchanging substance, a fixed, permanent underlying reality, together with changing attributes, or qualities that varied. The unchanging substance supported or sustained the changing attributes without itself being subject to change. Whitehead felt that the impact of modern science's emphasis on change had in effect reversed Aristotle's premise. Thus his picture of the world begins with change. The basic component of any given entity is process. *All things are in process and the whole is process.*

In light of this premise a question immediately presents itself: How is our experience of permanence, of stability, to be accounted for? The relation between change and changelessness is of course a fundamental problem of philosophy. In Whitehead's view the chief thing to be avoided in dealing with the question is the Aristotelian bifurcation of reality into that which changes and that which does not change. The notion of "an unchanging subject of change" will no longer serve.[39] If the basic constituent of an entity is without change, there is no logical way, according to Whitehead, to account for change itself. Yet if entities are in themselves continuously changing, they would lack enough identity to be discerned; in short, there would be no entity to change. He responds to this issue by saying that while entities are constituted by process, that is, are not to be taken as the end result of a process but by their very nature *are what they are* by process,[40] they are at the same time "epochal" units of experience. By this term he means that these units possess self-identity or individuality in the sense that, although in process, they are composed of relatively stable or enduring patterns of interacting things which are sufficiently self-contained to be occasions for experience.[41]

Epochality is perhaps one of the weakest of Whitehead's categories. It does serve however to enforce his insistence that there are no static substances; everything is in movement toward its *telos,* in process of becoming. Any given thing, and the world as such, consists of these processes, each of which is unique, complex, and interdependent. Nothing is or happens in and of itself; *all things interact.* Actual entities or actual occasions are the only things with real existence. The phrase *actual entities* applies to everything that is temporal and is also applicable to the divine life. *Actual occasions* refers to the temporal realm and always excludes God from its scope. Hence in separation from actual entities, "there is nothing, merely nonentity—'The rest is silence.' "[42]

There are two species of process in the world, Whitehead maintains, the microscopic and the macroscopic. The first one is described as an actual entity in process of reaching self-identity, of becoming itself as a unit. When it reaches the fulfillment of its subjective aim or its satisfaction, it perishes as an actual entity. But it becomes available for further processes, and these further processes similarly become available for still others. This is the second or the macroscopic form of process.[43]

The idea of the perishing of an actual entity requires, I believe, a further word. Once it reaches fulfillment, an actual entity ceases to be actual in that it has found the end of its striving and is therefore no longer active in self-creativity. It dies in the sense of no longer being an active subjective unit, but in dying and becoming objective material for other units, it remains creative in that it *continues* as an element in the creative process as a whole. This is a very significant ingredient in the system, as we shall see.

The inner striving of an entity toward subjective fulfillment is designated "final causation," an instance of the creativity that underlies and is ingredient to all reality. Objectification, occurring through the satisfaction of an entity's inner aim and consequent demise (without annihilation, again in the sense that it is a datum for other units) is called "efficient causation."[44]

It is important to emphasize that this interpretation of causation indicates that for Whitehead reality as a whole is not only the scene of constant creative activity, it *is* itself this activity. The becoming of an actual entity is not merely a change from one phase to another; it is a process in which one phase becomes the occasion of another *and* in which all phases come together into a unity.[45] Each phase participates in creativity and expresses itself in individual embodiments. It does so through what Whitehead calls "concrescence," a term derived from the familiar Latin verb meaning "growing together."[46] Through the process of concrescence, the universe of many things acquires an individual unity "in a determinate relegation of each item of the 'many' to its subordination in the constitution of the novel 'one.' "[47] In simpler terms, by participation in the creativity that marks all of reality, actual entities both in becoming and in dying are unified, and are expressive of the fact that "the many become one, and are increased by one."[48]

Just how the actual entities receive their subjective aim and how they reach satisfaction or fulfillment are issues with which Whitehead attempts to reckon by positing the idea of "eternal objects" or "forms of definiteness," which give to the entities their aim or directedness. These eternal objects are themselves *given* and as given are potentialities. Once given, however, they constitute the formal structure of actual entities. They are independent of the entities in the world but are not disconnected from them since they are the potential for the forms of everything that comprises the world. Eternal objects might or might not be given, which makes for an element of *indeterminacy* in reality. Some of them are "pure potentiality" and some "real potentiality." The latter are those which structure the forms of things in the world.[49]

Although given, eternal objects do not give themselves apart from the "decision" of an actual entity. Any given entity must "choose" its form from the eternal objects and choose as well what is to satisfy or fulfill the form chosen. The term *decision*, Whitehead insists, does not point to a causal adjunct to the entity; it constitutes its actuality. An actual entity arises *from* decision, and by its existence on the basis of its decision, it provides the basis for decisions by further actual entities. The term *decision* points of course to a certain freedom in all entities. In order to decide, there must be an *aim* the entity seeks to attain. This aim is provided by an eternal object through the entity's prehension of it.[50]

Through prehension, an entity can include as a part of its essence another entity, whether of the same or another type.[51] Prehension, as we have seen, is the activity by which an actual entity effects its own concrescence with other things; to put the matter more simply, it is the activity by which an entity enters into the process of becoming. The essence of an actual entity consists solely in the fact that it is a prehending thing; its nature is to prehend.[52]

In the discussion of Whitehead's theory of knowledge, we noted that prehension is analogous to feeling. We now note that emotional, affective tone is the crux of the prehending process. The matter of feeling is not entered into lightly, for in Whitehead's view "the energetic activity considered in physics is the emotional intensity entertained in life."[53] Emotion, we have seen, is the basic constituent of our experience. It is not a result of reflection on experience, though it is of course admitted that emotion can result from reflection on experience in the case of "exceptional organisms," that is, human beings. But the ground of emotion "is not in the eye of the beholder, but in what is beheld."[54] In the process of prehension therefore an actual entity feels subjectively the "objective feelings" of actual entities or things that have reached fulfillment. These feelings become "immortalized" in that they become a component of new emergent entities.

While the emergent actual entity feels all antecedent actual entities, it cannot include within itself *all* that it feels or prehends. If this were possible, the entity would have no identity, its subjective aim would be destroyed. Thus it has to choose what it is to include.[55]

The process of prehension has two distinct features: one physical and the other conceptual. Physical prehension, in Whitehead's terms, is that by which an entity feels the already fulfilled actual entities and appropriates their feelings, or as much of them it decides to accept, as ingredients of its own life. Conceptual prehension concerns the feeling an entity has for an "eternal object." An eternal object is entailed in the components of every actual entity.[56] By prehending an eternal object, an entity determines the form or subjective aim it seeks to attain.[57] Conceptual prehension pertains to the form an actual entity chooses and physical prehension concerns the antecedent actual entities through which fulfillment is sought. The two are inseparable and constitute two aspects of each actual entity, the physical and the mental pole.[58] Even the most elemental thing in nature has mentality, analogously so with us.

Eternal objects and the conceptual feeling of entities for them are of the first importance: without these objects and their being prehended by things in the world, there would be only a self-perpetuation of forms already existing. There would be no novelty, no advance in the mystery of the creative process.[59]

The process of prehension, however, cannot rest on itself. There must be some regulative principle that orders the process, some nontemporal factor that oversees and guides it. If such a factor exists, it can only be *an actual entity* since all reality is composed of actual entities. But a nontemporal actual entity would be unique; it would be, Whitehead says cumbersomely, "the principle whereby there is initiated a definite outcome from a situation otherwise riddled with ambiguity."[60] This unique actual entity is *God,* from whom "each temporal concrescence receives that initial aim from which its self-causation starts."[61] Since this is so, God is "the aboriginal instance of creativity," and "the aboriginal instance which qualifies its action."[62]

But, we want to ask, if this "aboriginality" is ascribed to God, what function remains for "eternal objects," upon the reality of which Whitehead insists? These objects, he holds, are unconditioned potentiality and are independent of God as such. But since nothing exists apart from actual entities, these objects become actual and effective through God's conceptual prehension of them. Conceptual prehension of actual entities constitutes God's "primordial nature." In the process of prehending the eternal objects conceptually, God orders them in accordance to their relevance to the process of their becoming actual entities in the world.[63] God does not create the eternal objects since the divine nature as an actual entity requires them just as any actual entity requires them, with however the fundamental difference just noted. This difference, I think, requires emphasis: in God's primordial nature there is the complete conceptual evaluation of all eternal objects; upon this evaluation the whole created order of the cosmos hangs.[64]

Since God's primordial nature is composed of conceptual prehension of the eternal objects, it remains in the realm of potentiality. In order to achieve actuality or consciousness in subjective form, God must be subject to the second kind of prehension, similar to the way other actual entities are. This second kind, physical prehension, is the process whereby God becomes actual through prehending the actualities of the evolving cosmos. This process is described as God's "consequent nature." *It is consequent upon the creative advance of the universe.* Since the divine primordial nature is the point of derivation of the movement toward the actualization of all entities, "the directedness of their becoming," the primordial nature issues in the consequent nature.[65]

Like all other actual entities, God's "subjective aim" is ordinated toward "his own satisfaction or fulfillment." As the ground of all possibilities in the world, "he prehends the fulfillment attained by actual entities and, again, by means of this increases his own actuality." This process of divine actualization, it would seem, never ceases; it is everlasting. This matter is ambiguously expressed however and is patient of other interpretations, upon which even veteran Whiteheadians do not seem to agree.[66]

Analogously to all actual entities, the nature of God is dipolar, "the primordial nature is conceptual, the consequent nature is the weaving of God's physical feelings upon his primordial concepts."[67] And because the divine experience is epochal like that of other entities, it is a unity; it possesses self-identity in its consequent nature and includes within that nature the universal process, constituting one interrelated cosmic reality.[68]

Dipolarity in Whitehead's thought should not be understood as *duality.* The divine experience as we have seen, is "epochal." This means that it is not divisible. Dipolarity is "an analytic device" for understanding the nature of God as it is related to the world and as the world is related to it.[69] One aspect of God's reality is that God is "given" for all temporal possibilities of development; a second is that all realized possibilities in the world are data for God's own realization, God's own becoming. These cannot be, on Whitehead's terms, two discrete, separable "natures," but are rather aspects of the one divine creative life. To put it another way, they point to the divine eternality on the one hand and the divine participation in temporality on the other.

It would have been less confusing, as I see it, if Whitehead had spoken not of two natures of God but of one nature in two distinctive modes. This seems to be what he is really talking about, but perhaps he felt that stronger terms were needed in order to give the point its wanted impact. However this may be, his conception of the unity of God, deriving from the primordial and consequent aspects of the divine life, should not be obscured by his discussions of the two natures. Divine dipolarity is qualified by the "epochal" character of all entities, including the highest actual entity—God.

A good deal of the above is pretty dense and difficult perhaps to follow in some of its details. I have tried to point to the simplicity and relevance of Whitehead's conclusions by underscoring crucial issues, though it goes without saying that the details both support and elaborate on the conclusions. While Whitehead's style and use of terms may be daunting to some of us, he is describing matters that concern us in the most concrete sense, that pertain to our day-to-day apprehension of the natural world and the relation of our apprehension of it to the way the natural world presents itself to us. Few writers have provided so inclusive a view of human reality as it relates to all that envelopes us. The manner in which it is expressed may seem prosaic, but in its results it is a broad poetic vision of life combined with analytic acuity of a very high order. And despite sexist language and images used of God, which I have contrived to alter unless directly quoting, Whitehead has given us a view of the divine life that transcends sexism altogether. In his philosophy of organism, the divine life is neither masculine nor feminine but the two in combination. God is "directing Father" and "nurturing Mother" at one and the same time, with each qualifying the other.

CHAPTER 8

Whitehead and Christian Doctrine

IN WHITEHEAD'S SYSTEM marked differences from the classical Christian doctrine of God are everywhere in evidence. These differences form the core of his critique of Christianity and, generally, of religion. This critique is at least as important as the more negative critiques of Marx and Freud. Whitehead's is somewhat less accessible than the sociopolitical and psychological discussions of the other two thinkers because it is explicitly metaphysical and deliberately moral. This is not to deny the metaphysical implications or moral aspects of the Marxian and Freudian analysis, but simply to say that in Whitehead's thought we have the one great metaphysical critique of the Christian doctrine of God in modern times. It is sympathetic and critical at one and the same time, and as such should be accorded as much attention as the other two critiques.

The first and most notable difference from classical Christian thought is Whitehead's insistence that the principle of creativity in universal reality is independent of God, in terms at least of its potentiality. The metaphysical principle of creativity belongs to the nature of things as such; all entities in the cosmos are instances of it. Creativity is "the universal of universals characterizing ultimate matter of fact."[1] It is the final category presupposed in all special categories. God lies within the sphere of special categories and is therefore an instance of it, as is everything else in the creative process.

Another significant difference, closely related to the above, is Whitehead's firm assertion that the "eternal objects" are independent of God. These "timeless, abstract forms of definiteness" belong to the essential nature of things and therefore transcend God, much as the "eternal ideas" or "forms" transcend the demiurge in Plato's thought. Christian theology in the classical age, following the Jewish philosopher Philo of Alexandria, rejected the Platonic doctrine that the eternal ideas were extradeical, that they were in any sense independent of God. Rather, they were intradeical—the eternal ideas of the eternal God, existing solely within the divine mind. The ultimate principle of the cosmos was God, who transcended everything, being transcended by nothing at all.

Whitehead also rejects the *creatio ex nihilo* doctrine of traditional Christian theism. It is around this doctrine that most of his criticism of the Christian conception of God centers, moral as well as metaphysical. He has a great deal to say about it in a number of places and connections. This will be dealt with in course. But before turning directly to it I want to examine more closely the ultimate principle of creativity as related to God in Whitehead's scheme.

Although God is an instance of the principle of creativity, God is notably a very special instance of it. Creativity is the abstract principle of possibility; it has no actuality. It becomes actual in God, and through the divine agency alone it becomes actual in all other entities. If creativity is to reach actuality, it has to do so through the offices of God. This means that no actual world could arise apart from God. And as we have seen, nothing whatever exists apart from actual entities—"The rest is silence."[2] It is clear therefore that God is the possibility for creativity, defined as the abstract principle of possibility, to become actual. If God is the possibility for possibility to find actualization, God is then no mere servant of the principle of creativity; creativity is as much God's servant. This seems warranted by Whitehead's constant affirmation that no actual world whatever could arise apart from God.

This issue finds its chief explication in his description of God's relation to the eternal objects, which have their effectiveness only in relation to the divine life. While they are originally independent of God, they are yet totally dependent on God for their actualization in the world. As the possibility for the possibility of the eternal objects' realization in the world, God's "midwifery" takes on a function transcending any work a midwife performs amongst us. A child may be born quite without the attendance of a midwife, but an eternal object has the possibility of being born into the real world exclusively through God.

Since God is the ground of the possibility for the actual world, there must be an ultimacy about the divine reality. It would therefore be true to say of God, in a variation of Whitehead's description of creativity, that God "is the ultimate principle characterizing all possibilities in the actual world." This much at least the Christian doctrine has declared a necessary affirmation. Anything beyond it more often than not has been thought to pertain to speculative theology. It seems clear that the biblical doctrine asserts little more, though its implications may exceed its assertions.

But Whitehead's interests here lie more in his interpretation of actual occasions in the world process than anything else. He holds that his doctrines of creativity, God, and the eternal objects are necessary for understanding the nature of actual entities. Thus it would be useful to examine this matter in more detail.

The world as a process of transition from one actual occasion to another is dependent on God's provision of an "initial aim" to all emerging occasions, but once this aim has been provided, the occasions become independently self-creative. "All actual entities share with God the characteristic of self-causation" and by token of this every one of them "shares with God the characteristic of transcending all other actual entities, including God."[3] All actual entities are relevant to all others, again including God, but no realized occasion completely determines another. No two patterns are identical and each pattern therefore has a definite uniqueness. In this sense they transcend each other and transcend God. And since God prehends the feelings of all actual occasions in the world, and since God's actuality, or God's "consequent nature," reaches its satisfaction—relative to the given moment of the world's life—through prehension of realized occasions, the world contributes to the divine life, rendering God dependent upon the world for God's own actualization or fulfillment.

This line of reasoning has led Whitehead to say at one point that it "is as true to say that God creates the World, as that the World creates God."[4] Kenneth F. Thompson in a probing discussion of Whitehead's view of God and creation[5] asks aptly whether he could have meant this in quite the way it sounds, going on to indicate a number of his dicta that seem to qualify it. He cannot have intended to imply that the world affects God in the same way and to the same extent that God affects the world. God can be termed the creator of each actual entity in that the subjective aim God affords it for its realization remains the unifying factor of interplay between its physical and conceptual feelings. The conceptual feelings of all things in the world are not only derived from God but reproduce in the subject (the actual entity) the data and value of God's conceptual feelings.[6] While God gives the initial aim to all entities, no entity (nor all entities in combination) gives initial aim to God. This points to God's unique and

115

continuous activity. Although not exclusively creative, God is the creative ground of the world of things.[7]

Creatio ex nihilo is not viable in Whitehead's view in part because of the associations that have grown up around it in Christian tradition. Given the attention he gives these associations, it would seem that they weighed heavily with him, almost equally perhaps with the metaphysical reasons for his negation of the ancient teaching of the church. If considered absolute creator, God will, Whitehead holds, almost inevitably be conceived as absolute sovereign, an omnipotent, despotic agency demanding complete submission—in short a "divine caesar."[8]

This picture of God is thoroughly repugnant to the moral sense, Whitehead holds, and moreover it renders the problem of evil insolvable. The idea of divine omnipotence, implied in the *ex nihilo* doctrine, means that God is the ultimate and determinative reality, that nothing can occur in the universe unless it is divinely willed or allowed. An unqualified omnipotence such as this would entail that God has responsibility for every detail of every happening and is the origin of evil as well as all good.[9] Such a God would not be unqualifiedly good and would not be worthy of worship. In order to be perfectly good, God must in some fundamental sense be limited in power, but that very limitation points to God's perfection of goodness.[10]

The limitation of divine power is found in the creativity immanent in the process of the world itself, there "not accidentally, but by nature," since each actual entity has the power of self-determination within the initial aim given it by God. The "freedom" of each entity to become what it "chooses" to become, again given its form, accounts for evil in the world because the entities do not always fulfill the aim God gives them. The freedom of actual occasions frees God from responsibility for evil. Although implicated in every detail of the world's life, God is not responsible for every detail.[11]

And too, the doctrine of creation out of nothing points to a self-sufficient creator, a God who requires nothing beyond the divine life because this is already perfectly fulfilled. This view implies that God has no real relation to the world. In order to conceive of a real relation of God to the world, Whitehead insists, some idea of reciprocity is necessary. He posits a reciprocity of need, as has been noted. The world needs God as its ground of order. Without order there would be no world, and without God there would be no order since God supplies each entity of the process its form. God needs the world for the satisfaction of God's own "physical feeling." The divine "consequent nature" is constituted by the data the world supplies through fulfilled actual entities. The relation of God to the world is such that "he yearns after concrete fact," both that the entities may reach satisfaction and that this may contribute to God's own life.[12]

Rather than speaking of creation out of nothing, we should say, according to Whitehead, that God "is not *before* all creation, but *with* all creation."[13]

The despotic idea of God entertained in much of Christian tradition, he holds, should be unseated by taking with greater seriousness "the Galilean origin of Christianity," and by using it as the key to understanding the nature of God in relation to the world.[14] If the life of Christ is taken as "a revelation of the nature of God and his agency in the world," then "the decisiveness of a supreme ideal" rather than the "exhibition of over-ruling power" would govern our thought.[15] We would then find it necessary to conceive of God as persuasive agency rather than despotic force.[16] Christian theologians have tried to combine the ideas of divine omnipotence and divine persuasion without significant success; either omnipotence must go, Whitehead believes, or be completely subordinated to the divine persuasive power.

In Whitehead's thought, it is true, God's power is principally persuasive. It is "the lure for feeling," that agency in the world by reason of which purposes are directed toward their proper ends, facts of existence stretched to values of existence, aims extended from values for self to values for others—God "confronts what is actual [in the world] with what is possible for it."[17]

Yet God is more than a persuasive power, even though primarily God is just that. God is the ground antecedent to all transition in the universal process, "the one systematic, complete fact," who conditions every creative act; God's vision determines every possibility of value and nothing whatever can exist apart from the divine provision of an initial aim. As the binding element in the world and the singular universal consciousness and all-embracing love, God is an exceedingly powerful factor in the world's life, even though not all-powerful. Every entity in the world, Whitehead says in a striking phrase, "lives by its incarnation of God in itself." As for God, "he adds himself to the actual ground from which every creative act takes place."[18]

These functions point to the divine initiative, the creative outreach of the divine love, an aspect of Whitehead's doctrine which tends to be obscured by some of his statements, for example, "the power by which God sustains the world is the power of himself as the ideal."[19] Frequently Whitehead seems to be torn between the Aristotelian idea of God as attractive force, as all-drawing Eros, and the Platonic idea of the divine as active force, as a creative agency in the world, working toward every possibility of good. In some instances and for certain purposes, the Aristotelian conception is dominant; in others, the Platonic idea of the demiurge dominates. If Eros marks one aspect of the divine in Whitehead's teaching, Agape marks another. In his view God is ever the concerned God, not simply the loved but decisively the loving God, moving out in care for the world's life. God is the "lure" in the passive sense, but at the same time the active, creative "lurer." God awaits fulfillment from the world and yet is always working for the fulfillment of the world for its own sake, not merely for the sake of the divine life.

God takes knowledge of every fact of the actual world, whether good or evil, and always seeks to overcome evil with good, to meet evil in such a way that it issues in the restoration of good. Even evil, pain, and degradation are not a total loss, for elements of the good exist within them. These elements, Whitehead says, woven "into the rhythm of mortal things" are united with God and thus immortalized. In union with God, they condition God's subsequent action in the world, whether "with enlarged, or diminished, presentation of ideal values."[20] The world makes a difference to *and* in God; it conditions both God's very existence and God's outreach.

Enough has been said of Whitehead's critique of Christian theism and of his own doctrine of God, enough at least for present purposes. We need to make a few more observations however about the general character of his thought before concluding with some comments on his contributions to the problem of nature and grace. The first thing to be observed is that Whitehead's is a "friendly universe," a place in which human beings may feel at home. It is supportive of human activity, aims, and ideals. Social and cultural attainments count for something in the total scheme of things; they are not mere flickers within a vast, uncaring world. Indeed, the possibility of moral and civilized life is grounded in the nature of things. Human beings can know the good because the good is ingredient to life. Knowledge of the good is "given" because the divine aim toward the good is constitutive of our experience. Whenever this constitutive element is thwarted, whether by human beings or other actual entities, it stands under the judgment of the good not attained.[21] Thus Whitehead is far from sanguine about evil; he takes it very seriously indeed.

Another issue to be mentioned here is that a chief interest in the whole range of Whitehead's thought is to further "civilization," by which he means the quality of human life in general, with religion as a crucial dimension in the process. Although he deplores many features of the religious enterprise, he yet holds that religion—the purer the form, the better—is essential for the growth and development of civilized life. The worship of power is a barbarizing force, static doctrinal systems are idolatrous, and in the interests of civilization he subjects both to critical scrutiny. Another and more fundamental reason for his criticisms of them is the centrality of religion in human life. "The religious vision and its history of persistent expansion is our one ground for optimism. Apart from it," he argues, "human life is a flash of occasional enjoyments lighting up a mass of pain and misery, a bagatelle of transient experience."[22] But if religion is to serve its purpose effectively in the drive toward civilization, it must become less insular and strident in its assertions. Religion as "the intuition of holiness" is a value beyond value, but it needs to be reconceived in the light of the best modern thought, scientific and moral as well as philosophical.

"The final principle of religion" as Whitehead conceives it, is that there is "a wisdom in the nature of things, from which flow our direction of practice, and our possibility of the theoretical analysis of fact."[23] This principle is supported by the success of the physical and other theoretical sciences, and above all by our own day to day discernment of ordered relationships. These relationships stretch far beyond anything we can systematically formulate in words. "The formulations are the froth upon the surface," but discernment of the relationships themselves forms for religion "the very substance of existence."[24]

Science has appeared in the modern world, Whitehead says, as "an organized system of thought which in many respects played the part of a theology by reason of the answers which it gave to current theological questions." Above all, "[s]cience suggested a cosmology; and whatever suggests a cosmology, suggests a religion."[25] The religion suggested goes beyond the concerns of existentialist philosophy and theology in that it is grounded in what Whitehead takes to be the metaphysical realities presented by nature, by the actual world. Nature does not accidentally exhibit an order. There is an actual world because there is an order of nature. "If there were no order there would be no world. . . . Since there is a world, we know that there is an order."[26]

He regards this line of reasoning as an extension of Kant's argument for the existence of God. Kant saw the necessity for God on the basis of what he understood to be the moral order and rejected in his scheme the argument from the cosmos, a contingency in part determined by the scientific thinking of his time. With however the emergence of modern science, the cosmological dimension entered into prominence. Whitehead is a cosmological, teleological thinker, joyously so, with no reluctant glance back to the Enlightenment. His teaching finds its foundation in the aesthetic experience, the experience of the order, beauty, and harmony of the cosmos rather than, with Kant, in cognitive and conceptive experience. All order, in his view, is aesthetic order, of which the moral order is an aspect. "The actual world is the outcome of the aesthetic order, and the aesthetic order is derived from the immanence of God."[27] But his respect for Kant is such that he does not attack his thought directly, but merely attempts to go behind it to rescue pre-Kantian categories and to take the Kantian subjectivist principle to its final term, building upon it a far more inclusive metaphysic.

In a fundamental way, Whitehead's vision is a great deal more "existential" than that of Neo-Kantian and existentialist philosophers. These thinkers tend to isolate human experience, whether cognitive, moral, or aesthetic, from its context in life, in the actual world. In Whitehead's process philosophy, the physical world is a community, with human community as a part of it. The whole is bound together. "If you abolish the whole, you abolish its parts; and if you abolish any part, then *that* whole is abolished."[28] Atomic actual entities express individually the genetic unity of the universe.[29] There is no vacuous actuality, devoid of subjective feeling, for apart from the feeling of subjects, "there is nothing, nothing, nothing, bare nothingness."[30]

The difference between organic experience and the inorganic environment is only one of degree. The solidarity of nature is decisive. Experience as a whole is finally derivable from feelings, which are "the 'real' components of actual entities."[31] Our propositions, intellectual beliefs are "only realizable as one sort of 'objective' datum for feelings."[32] Even history is "the record of the expressions of feelings peculiar to humanity."[33] This principle of unified experience in reality is, as we have seen, in Whitehead's view necessary for fruitful metaphysics. Metaphysical theories which admit a disjunction between the components of human experience and the component elements of the external world stamp experience with an air of illusoriness and divorce it from "the community of the external world." It renders the temporal order, as in Kant's *Critique of Pure Reason*, "in its essence, dead, phantasmal, phenomenal," and so in the end "merely experienced," not "known." The very possibility of *knowledge* of things depends, Whitehead avers, "on the interwoven nature of things."[34]

His criticism of the notion following from Newtonian physics, mentioned above, that nature is without value is based on a similar strand of thought. A "dead nature can give no reasons. All ultimate reasons are in terms of aim at value. A dead nature aims at nothing. It is the essence of life that it exists for its own sake, as the intrinsic reaping of value."[35] Values are always embodied, always specific. "There is no such thing as bare value."[36] Every actuality then has its own value. But values pertaining to the various actualities differ in intensity, depth, and importance. There "is a difference of degree which makes all the difference—in effect it is a difference in quality."[37] Nature burst one of its boundaries in the rise from the inorganic to the organic and yet another in the rise of humankind. In humanity the "Rubicon has been crossed."[38]

True as this is, it is quite impossible to draw a fine line between natural reality and human reality. "There is no clear division among genera; there is no clear division among species; there are no clear divisions anywhere."[39] Human experience is an actual entity within the world of actual entities, however distinctive it is. It has its reality only because within the human body there is a vast and complex "society" of actual entities, of "cellular communities," all intrinsically akin to actual entities everywhere occurring, and all completely dependent on them as the environment in which alone human life can exist.

The placing of human history in Whitehead's system can be gathered from the considerations above. It is diametric to that of most contemporary theologians. In the whole of *Process and Reality* there are only three direct references to history as such.[40] Behind this reduction of the status of history is Whitehead's insistence that the subjectivist principle of modern thought, on which the exaltation of history rests, is inadequate. The Kantian metaphysic in his view is a prime instance of the inadequacy of this principle, as we have seen. Kant limited his area of concern to the moral sphere, to specifically human or historical life, abstracting it from the natural world. Whitehead holds that history presupposes a metaphysic of nature, that metaphysical dogmas derived through an interpretation of past history depend on a prior metaphysical interpretation of the present realities of the world confronting us. "You can only interpret the past in terms of the present. The present is all that you have."[41]

A further idea behind the secondary status of history, Whitehead says in a line with less than complete clarity, is that the appeal to history is "to the summits of attainment beyond any immediate clarity in our own individual existence." He goes on, however, to say that the appeal to history is the appeal to authority, which must be submitted in turn to the appeal to reason, "to that ultimate judge, universal and yet individual to each, to which all authority must bow. History has authority so far, and exactly so far, as it admits of some measure of rational interpretation."[42]

Thus he finds it "a curious delusion" that so many Christian thinkers suppose that "the rock upon which our beliefs are founded is an historical investigation."[43] History in and of itself is not the locus of belief, but as a part of a larger whole it provides the key insight into the metaphysical ground of the world in which we live now. The status of life in nature is the great problem of modern thought; it is "the central meeting point of all the strains of systematic thought, humanistic, naturalistic, philosophic."[44]

The unifying thread of Whitehead's thought, as indicated earlier on, is the aesthetic dimension. Beauty, in his view, is the only self-justifying value in the world. By beauty he means "the internal conformation of the various items of experience with each other, for the production of maximum effectiveness." The "teleology of the Universe is directed to the production of Beauty."[45] Any system of things that in any wide sense is beautiful, that is, "aims at and in some way accomplishes the perfections of harmony, is to that extent justified." In the entire range of reality, God is constantly urging all things toward the perfection of beauty. God is "the active entertainment of all ideals, with the urge to their finite realization, each in its due season."[46]

Whitehead's system finds whatever justification it has on the basis of beauty. If beauty is as Whitehead defines it, then his system has much of the beautiful about it. Certainly his unified vision of nature has a great deal to commend itself on these very grounds. And it is at this precise point that his philosophy can make a contribution to contemporary theology of great significance. A nature considered intrinsically valueless, without its own self-justifying beauty, as with the main drift of theology today, is not likely to be loved or even properly respected. When nature is seen as a "community of values," and the values actually resident within it as the indispensable condition for human values, the case is far otherwise. Nature can be loved for its own sake and not simply for our sake. Some such vision seems essential if humanity is to survive as "the summit species" or to survive at all. Such a vision makes for a unified conception of the actual world by sharply curtailing the tendency to bifurcate natural reality and human reality.

What Whitehead has to say about nature is just as important as what he has to say about God. It may prove to be more enduring, at least in respect to the more highly speculative aspects of his theism. But however future generations treat his thought, his understanding of nature, along with those views either similar to or based on it, should it become a major concern of theology, would reduce or at least temper the almost obsessive preoccupation with history that marks so much of modern thought.

The danger is that theology will utilize Whitehead's doctrine of God— as is already widely the case—and rush to the realm of history, to the life and thought of the church, without attending to his doctrine of nature. This would not only be a great loss, it would obviate one of the most important contributions Whitehead could make to theology: some clear-headed, imaginative thought about the actual world in which we live, and so about ourselves *within* the actual world and not abstracted from it.

No one knew better than Whitehead that it is the province of philosophy to suggest, to illuminate the ordinary by probing metaphor and analogy. "Exactness," he once said, "is out of the question. It can only be obtained by some trivial convention."[47] His metaphysical and analogical language may seem anything but clear-headed to some, but upon analysis might be found to be quite tolerable tools for clear-headed thought. The world in his philosophy is such that it can not only be thought but in some real sense comprehended. The marked personalization of nature in his thinking is not born of romantic fervor but of what, if one looks closely at the data, seems to be warranted by the reality before us and of which we are components. Since there is "feeling" in us, since we experience "aims," "satisfactions," and the like, it is reasonable to suppose that these things have a basis in all that produced us. The more this is thought about, the more it seems to be just what Whitehead considered it to be—a necessity of thought. The categories he employed can of course be modified, given more precision here and there, even altered, but something like them may well prove to be essential if justice is to be done to the actualities in the world.

Whitehead's doctrine of nature is much more complicated, and his love of it far deeper, than I have been able to indicate here. This is similarly so of his doctrine of grace, only the bare outlines of which we will be able to consider. Manifestly for Whitehead, nature is not a separate realm from the realm of grace. They are indivisibly one. This does not mean that they are indistinguishable, but that grace operates in and throughout the whole of nature and that nature could not exist apart from grace.

Somewhat curiously, he does not speak directly of grace in *Religion in the Making,* but it is implied on virtually every page as the divine influence immanent in the world, as "the wisdom in the nature of things," making for order and harmony. In another place, however, he brings grace into the forefront of his discussion, speaking of it specifically and in connection with his ongoing critique of traditional Christian views about the nature of God. The Western idea of grace, he says in *Adventures of Ideas,* one of his most compelling and important works, "leans heavily towards the notion of a wholly transcendent God imposing his partial favours on the world." Calvin's version of this idea suggests the Manichean doctrine of a wholly evil material world, "partially rescued by God's arbitrary selection." Indeed, Whitehead says, perhaps less than fairly, the physical world for Calvinism seems "an arbitrary imposition of the will of God." The Augustinian doctrine, the origin of the Western view, took on diverse aspects, some of which derived from the idea of the will of a transcendent God, and some from the nature of an immanent God.[48] The worship of "glory arising from power," so prominent at many points in Augustine's theology and in the subsequent teaching of the Western church, indicates "a barbaric conception of God,"[49] a species of idolatrous symbolism that has degraded the doctrine of grace and the doctrine of the atonement.[50] The anticipation by Plato of a doctrine of grace, as "divine persuasion" and as productive of such order as is possible amid brute forces should form, Whitehead declares, the basis of the "new Reformation" of our time. A doctrine of grace along Platonic lines is required by "our cosmological outlook."[51]

A distinction Whitehead draws between what he terms "the secular functions" of God and those functions that appeal most immediately to the sphere of religion[52] is pertinent to his viewpoint on grace. Many judgments about the divine activity are not, he avers, specifically religious at all. They lie at "a lower level of experience" than religious emotions. "The secularization of the concept of God," he goes on to say, "is at least as important a requisite of thought as is the secularization of other elements of experience." While the concept of God is essential to "religious feeling," such feeling is not an essential element in the concept of God's functions in the universe. "In this respect religious literature has been sadly misleading to philosophic theory, partly by attraction and partly by repulsion." He does not elaborate on the issue but the point is clear. The concept of God does not belong to the religious sphere alone because God's functions pertain to plain, matter-of-fact details, of "appetitions which lie at the base of things," the gradation of which "solves all indeterminations of transition." These are the divine activities of interest to philosophy. But however "secularly conceived" these functions are, under Whitehead's scheme, they are in some fundamental sense of grace, owing to God's provision of initial aims to all actual occasions and providential guidance of the process of the world.

Although one can appreciate Whitehead's effort to show that religion does not have God as captive, the hard and fast distinction he draws here between the religious and secular spheres is a good deal more blurred than his language implies. At almost every other point he denies, really quite vehemently, sharp distinctions such as this, maintaining that neat divisions between realms of experience and levels of existence are not possible. The only plausible explanation I can see for this breach lies in his distrust of dogmatic theology and its exclusivistic tendencies, together with his own habit of limiting religion to emotion—never entirely of course, but markedly and frequently. But whatever its roots may be, the "secular functions" of God are not without religious significance and equally they are not without "an emotional tone" that is religious or quasi-religious in character. Still, what he has to say about the matter commends itself in part. Theologians might well give more consideration to God's functions that do not greatly stir religious feeling and put their findings to apologetic use, though in the recognition that any function of God, in whatever connection and in whatever way discerned, has bearing on the religious dimension of experience.

What Whitehead implies in the distinction is that grace is a twofold reality, the grace present and active in creation and the grace present and active in the religious life of humankind. There cannot be two graces for him just as there cannot be two natures, one human and the other nonhuman. As nature is one organic whole, so grace is in and with the whole. The emphatic note is immanence, but transcendence is a crucial factor, without which no providential guidance of the process, no immanence of grace, would be possible. For not only is God transcendent in primordial nature but in important respects in consequent nature as well.

125

God is transcendent as the eternal evaluation of the world, the wisdom upon which all possible order in the world depends and the judgment under which all disorder in the world stands.[53] God's very dependency on the world for fulfillment is not a reflection of need alone; it is an aspect of grace, God's loving concern and loving direction of all things toward their end in the divine life. The divine life gives itself in grace for the world's life.

There is one final consideration in Whitehead's thought which bespeaks of grace, or at least one of the gracious elements in experience, which needs to be taken into account. It is his concept of peace. Peace is, he says, that "Harmony of Harmonies which calms destructive turbulence and completes civilization." It is not the negative conception of anaesthesia; it is a positive feeling that crowns "the life and motion of the soul." It is "a surpassing of personality," "an inversion of relative values," "a grasp of infinitude," and "an appeal beyond boundaries." The sense of peace "preserves the springs of energy" and at the same time "masters them for true avoidance of paralyzing distraction." It "introduces faith, where reason fails to reveal the details."[54] Moreover, "the experience of Peace is largely beyond the control of purpose. It comes as a gift."[55]

A further fruit of peace is that from it issues "the love of mankind" as such, not simply those people who pertain to us. Yet another is "the understanding of tragedy, and . . . its preservation" at the same time. Amid pain, frustration, and loss, the passing in the world of so much beauty, heroism, and daring, "Peace . . . is the intuition of permanence"; it is the knowledge that the tragic element of the world's life is not in vain. It involves at its core a deep feeling of "an aim in the Universe, winning such triumph as is possible to it." Starting with the dream of youth, it reaps the harvest of tragic beauty, namely, that "suffering attains its end in a Harmony of Harmonies." "The immediate experience of this Final Fact . . . is the sense of Peace."[56]

These mystical sounding phrases are of course just that—reflections of Whitehead's mystical vision of reality and of the transcendent qualities possible to human experience. They form no mere addendum to his metaphysical system; they are ingredient to it throughout. The one supports the other. In his thought he makes provision not only for the grace immanent in entities but also for a grace transcending that in all entities—a grace that is gratuitous, mysterious in character. It is "the peace that passes all understanding" founded upon "the love that will not let us go."

Whitehead does not always speak as a metaphysical thinker; he often speaks as a deeply religious man, combining metaphysics and the "affective tones" of religion in his view of reality. His idea of grace, in its primary sense, is a case in point. His deep attachment to "the revelation given in Jesus of Nazareth," as he termed it, was of critical importance for his understanding of grace, though it was "anticipated" in Plato's thought. The persuasive element so prominent in Jesus' teaching, abetted by that in Plato's, has in Whitehead's thought assumed an almost exclusive status— not totally, as we have seen, but nearly so. Whitehead is right to stress this element as the first sense in which grace is to be understood. But persuasion and coercion need to be viewed more dialectically than he allows, for there is a certain coerciveness in the nature of things. A fish can only be a fish, a human being only a human being. I am not free to become anything I want to become as a human being. I am deeply determined by genetics and, in Tillich's conception, by destiny. The freedom of actual entities is exaggerated in Whitehead's vision, although he is right to point to a certain "freedom" in everything. God however determines the structure of things and does so in such a way that there is an element of coercion about the divine power. Something of coercive power attaches to the divine "judgment" as well, even on Whitehead's terms. Certain aspects of suffering follow from the failure to realize the potential given by God. They are directly consequent upon such failure. Do they not reflect a kind of coerciveness on the part of the orderer of all order? God's power is persuasive, but when persuasion fails, does God not "mandate" and in some sense "exact" the consequences? If such is the case, this mandate and exaction are within "the love that will not let us go," we may believe, since the divine justice is essentially restorative, not punitive.

However this may be, I cannot but hold that Whitehead's emphasis on the divine persuasion, justified as it is in the light of the history of the Christian doctrine of grace, is pressed a little too far. What his thought affords is not a substitute for classical Christian theism; it affords a corrective, a corrective that is among the most searching and challenging to arise in the modern era.

CHAPTER 9

Westermann and the Biblical Witness

I AM NO BIBLICAL SCHOLAR or even a biblical scholar's son, hence much of what I have to say here may prove to be the height of folly, if not downright presumption. I am, however, familiar with the conclusions and suggestions, some of them at least, of biblical scholarship, and it is with these that the theologian is primarily concerned. Like all other serious disciplines, biblical scholarship entails speculative elements, that is, elements not directly derived from the data, but taken to the data through presuppositions entertained by those engaged in the discipline. In what follows, I want to look at some of the conclusions and presuppositions of biblical scholarship, especially those of Claus Westermann, an Old Testament theologian, whose work is germane to the discussion here. First, a few words about presuppositions, their place in scholarly thought, and their critical results.

The interpretation of the past, according to Whitehead, is based on present experience, "since the present is all you have." While this statement has a point, it will not stand by itself. As Whitehead himself said repeatedly, past occurrences in nature continually enter into the formation of present occurrences, and in this sense, have an "immortality" about them. Something similar must be said regarding past occurrences in history. Past events enter into the formation of present events and condition present experience. The present therefore is never merely present. Present experience, moreover, enters into the understanding of the past, so much so that for us the past is never merely past. To say that we are historically and culturally conditioned beings does not mean, as often declared, that we are conditioned simply by the present circumstances of our lives and present hopes of the future. We are conditioned by the past as it bears on present understanding, not merely by past events and the way they were interpreted, but also by past hopes as they entered into past experience and helped form it. Past interpretation of past events and past hopes, then, are ingredient to present experience, and it is only upon such an understanding of present experience that Whitehead's statement will stand. Certainly it is our present experience that we take to the past, but not without what the past itself contributes to present understanding.

Biblical scholars delving into historical texts and artifacts have to project themselves imaginatively back into the past, more or less succeeding in the enterprise. Yet two essential factors are involved, one a good deal more obvious than the other. First, they never leave themselves behind; second, they are themselves already shaped to some considerable extent by the very past interpretation that they are interpreting. No doubt some scholars are more deeply influenced by their immersion in the past than others, but this is not the chief issue involved. What is of moment is not so much the degree to which scholars are influenced by their study of the past as is the character of their present understanding as already shaped by the past, something they ineluctably take to their study of it. Since present understanding is never without the impact of past events and past understanding, all of us are shaped by the past, no matter what our level of knowledge of it might be, though the more extensive that knowledge is, the greater the possibility for its shaping power to penetrate the mind. It is true also that extensive knowledge of the past helps to free us from the spell of the present, but nothing can free us from present understanding as conditioned by the past. While the renunciation of present understanding is possible, any such renunciation is made through an awareness of present understanding; hence present understanding remains a powerful, if largely negative factor. Positive aspects of present understanding remain operative however, inevitably so. The groups who seek to live, as it were, in the biblical age, rejecting the present age as evil, cannot possibly escape all of the forces, pressures, and influences of the present. There is simply no exit from present understanding into a past biblical mentality, or a past mentality of any sort, certainly no total exit.

Biblical scholars have a profound interest in the past, else they would not be biblical scholars. But for many, if not most of them, interest in the past is secondary to interest in truth for the present, not that truth for the present is separate from truth for the past, but that the truth sought is for the benefit of those presently living and those who will live in the coming years. This interest colors the yield of their study of the past; indeed, it significantly contributes to their findings; that is, it determines in part what they are looking for, and subtly (sometimes not so subtly) shapes the character of their conclusions about past historical events. Biblical scholars view the distant past through successively less distant pasts and finally view it in the light of the immediate past as it enters into the formation of present understanding.

An instance of the impact of the immediate past, a past gathering force in the Renaissance and reaching full flower in the Enlightenment, concerns the emphasis on the centrality of history in the biblical witness found in so much of critical scholarship during past decades and on into the present time. It is clear to any student of the Bible that history—events in human experience occurring within the social, political, communal realm—is in the forefront of the biblical writings. This was not lost on the ancient Christian theologians, as evidenced in the writings of Irenaeus, Augustine, and many others. But in modern times the recent past has provided a new and powerful impetus toward focusing upon the historical factor in the Scriptures. The Enlightenment and its aftermath produced not only an emphasis upon history, it also produced a certain understanding of history, one that virtually became an obsession among biblical scholars and theologians. History became an entity unto itself. "God is the God of history" became a byword of critical studies and theology. "God is revealed in history" and, by implication, in nothing else. "Man is a historical being, has his life in history, and can only be understood as such" was another phrase brandished about frequently. This was particularly true in Germanic circles, but these circles widened in time to include almost the whole of Western theological thought.

Nature was "out there," quite apart from history, of use only insofar as it could be made to serve the purposes of history. An animus against nature, already embedded in the tradition, swept the halls of higher learning with a new and driving force. This animus was taken up by biblical scholars and taken to the Scriptures. But that was only the negative side. Positively, they took an understanding of the nature of history derived from Enlightenment thought to the Scriptures, and read them in its terms, not wholly of course, but sufficiently so to make a far-reaching difference in interpretation. This idea of history, verging on dogma, was linear, a line of time in which events occurred on the basis of cause and effect. It was not recognized that this single-track concept of history was far from that of scriptural records. Nor was it recognized that, for the biblical writers, history was not abstracted from nature. Indeed, history and nature, while distinguished in some sense perhaps, were hardly considered two separate realities at all.

Nomadic herdsmen were wont, we can only suppose, to link their tribal histories at every turn to grazing fields, weather and water, to the health of their flocks, to breeding and increase. Their history, familial, communal, and religious as it was, was tied to nature. Tribal wars were a part of their history, but these were fought mostly over fertile plains and the paths to them, over things that pertained to nature and that entered substantially into their history. That they had some sense of transcending nature probably goes without saying, but this sense of transcendence was balanced by a sense of dependence, deep and all-pervasive. Their thoughts and hopes, their very lives, depended on weather and wind, on verdant growth and watering places.

The Exodus is frequently interpreted by modern biblical scholars as though it were an occurrence in history without remainder, overlooking or critically discounting the plagues of locusts, frogs and gnats, the hailstones, rivers of blood, and the rest, directed against the gods of Egypt. These things, however, are ingredient to the story and have a significance all their own. The plagues are sent by the God who delivers the people by means of effective control over the forces of nature. And there is the drying up of the Red Sea, a central feature of the story, which again brings nature and the divine control over it to the fore. Much of biblical scholarship discounts the Red Sea incident and imperceptibly denudes the deliverance of its embeddedness in nature, claiming it for history alone, something more in accordance with the scientific world view. The Red Sea story of course requires critical interpretation. This interpretation, however, should not do violence to the consciousness of the ancients through the notion that their interests were in history shorn of its linkage with nature.

In the wanderings in the wilderness, Yahweh led the people by a cloud, opened the rock and caused the water to flow, fed them from the "high vault" of heaven, thundered the law from the heights of Sinai, and, in due course, brought them into the land of milk and honey, the land promised of old to Abraham and his descendants. Many modern biblical scholars are inclined to demythologize the land or seek to spiritualize it. That land as land, as a piece of property in the midst of nature, is not taken with anything like the same seriousness with which the ancient Jews took it or for that matter with the same seriousness many modern Jews take it. Here the "historical event" of the fulfillment of the promise is of a piece with the gift of the land. It is given substance by means of nature.

That the ancient Hebrews had no word for nature makes no fundamental difference to the issue at hand. Klaus Koch points out that there is no word in the prophets which the dictionary would translate as history. There is, moreover, no specific word in the Old Testament for marriage, or agriculture or religion. "Is this supposed to mean that these areas of life were unknown in Israel?"[1] The same thing applies to the term *nature*. The land may have been considered a part of created reality or perhaps something just there, mysteriously in the possession of Yahweh, yet the land was inseverable from their understanding of their deliverance and calling. It is probably true that in the early period and perhaps much later too, as Claus Westermann holds, "[w]hat is created and what occurs have not yet been separated from one another; the special realm of 'nature' does not yet exist."[2] If no special realm of nature existed for the ancient Hebrews, was there any notion of a special realm of "history"?

Although the idea of movement along the line of time from the Exodus toward an expectation of "the day of the Lord" was developed by the Israelites, they were far too concrete in their thought to discount the impingement of nature upon their lives at every point, including its cyclic rhythms which were wholly decisive for their life in the world.

In modern theological and biblical studies, however, not only has the scriptural testimony about nature been thrust aside, its testimony to creation has been relegated to a quite secondary status. Gerhard von Rad, one of the most influential Old Testament scholars of recent times, has said that creation in the Hebrew Bible is "no more than a starting point" for "the miracle of God's providential care." In Second Isaiah creation is alleged to be but a "magnificent foil for the message of salvation."[3] In genuinely Yahwistic belief, von Rad declares magisterially, the doctrine of creation never attained the stature of a relevant, independent doctrine because of *"the exclusive commitment of Israel's faith to historical salvation."*[4] Von Rad later admitted that biblical scholars were looking at the theological problems of the Old Testament from the one-sided standpoint of a historically conditioned theology, but his earlier work had amply demonstrated how biblical scholarship could be caught up in its own presuppositions.

Koch, noting von Rad's argument that the prophets become comprehensible only when the historical traditions to which they appeal are known and which they see recreated in their eschatology, says bluntly that, according to von Rad, "for the prophets history is *the* divine revelation."[5] While this judgment exaggerates von Rad's position, it does not miss the mark by very far. Yet even during von Rad's heyday, his views did not go unchallenged. Other scholars maintained that neither ancient

Israel nor the prophets had developed a sense of history anything like that with which von Rad credits them, but his was a powerful voice, and, moreover, his writings have the virtue of great clarity and persuasiveness. He was heeded and widely read by many theologians, not least among whom was Jürgen Moltmann, as we have seen, and W. Pannenberg as well.

There is certainly historiography in the Old Testament, Koch says, which shows events developing out of human causes and effects and which can be interpreted in a historical sense. Yet no view of history such as von Rad's can be found in any one of the prophets. For the prophets, divine acts and decrees precede every human action, and while they seem to develop stage by stage, they do not amount to history as we understand it today. What we find in the prophets is *suprahistory* or *metahistory* (Koch's preferred term), something composed of various levels which cannot be clearly divided from one another. Suprahistory "means a 'total' movement running through time, which includes—and also impels—not only the Israelite people but everything that exists between them and the underlying reality of God."[6] While this statement is less than completely clear, it is apparent that Koch's position takes into account the actual data of the prophetic writings much more completely than von Rad's. Koch, however, has nothing to say about the role of nature in prophetic thought. Toward the end of his work on the prophets, he points out that in their writing "there is no question of an antithesis between history and nature."[7] It is a pity that such an important observation is made only in passing and without comment.

Reviewing the prophetic writings for the purposes here, as an amateur, though not an altogether uncritical one, I was struck anew by the numerous references to Yahweh's use of natural forces in implementing judgment and blessing. Some consideration of these references might help to give point to Koch's statement. Natural forces are as much in Yahweh's command as political forces. Though some of the prophets, Ezekiel for example, stress the political arena as the primary means by which Yahweh executes judgment, most of them bring nature to the fore. Even Ezekiel, for whom the sword seems to be the chief instrument of divine judgment, does not neglect to speak of pestilence, and in his image of "the evil arrows of famine" (5:12) combines the martial and the natural. Hosea, while concerned above all else with the nation's harlotry and the Holy One's response to it, yet has some of the best nature imagery in the prophets (e.g., 4:19, "A wind has wrapped them in its wings"; 8:7, "For they sow the wind, and shall reap the whirlwind"; 10:4, "so judgment springs up like poisonous weeds in the furrows of the field"; 10:12, "Sow for yourselves righteousness, reap the fruit of steadfast love"; and 14:5-8, "I will be as the dew to Israel, he shall blossom as the lily . . . his beauty like an olive . . . his fragrance like the wine of Lebanon.") Hosea also pictures natural forces as means of divine retribution: "Therefore, I will take back my grain in its time, and my wine in its season, and I will take away my wool and my flax" (1:9); "Though he may flourish as the reed plant, the east wind, the wind of the Lord, shall come, rising from the wilderness; and his fountain shall dry up, his spring shall be parched" (13:15). Jeremiah declares in what had become a sort of prophetic formula that, in the time of the divine visitation, "there will be no grapes on the vine, no figs on the tree. The leaf will fade and things I have given will be taken away" (8:13). In First Isaiah too the forces of nature are in evidence. Although the sayings there, as in Hosea, are more or less figurative—for example, "Hail shall sweep away the refuge of lies; water will come over the hiding place" (28:17)—it is hard to hold that all of his references to nature were intended to be merely figurative.

In the earlier tradition of Amos's prophecy, there seems to be no suggestion of a figurative usage. The Lord withholds "the rain from the people, withering the fields" (4:7); he smites them "with blight and mildew," with locusts and "pestilence after the manner of Egypt" (4:9, 10). In Haggai, Yahweh smites "with blight and mildew" (2:17). In Habakkuk, when the Lord comes in judgment, "the fig tree will not blossom, the vines will not bear fruit, the olive tree will not grow, and the fields will yield no grain" (3:17). Though Habakkuk uses this formula for purposes of his own, the note of vengeance through nature is nevertheless marked. Zephaniah says that in judgment the Lord "will utterly consume all things from the land" (1:2), and the later chapters of Zechariah, concerned as they are with grace and the coming redemption, also witness to judgment through the use of natural forces. The heathen who do not come up to the feast of Tabernacles, he says, "the Lord will smite with a plague" (14:18).

The entries immediately above have no aim beyond calling attention to an aspect of the prophetic literature that much critical exegesis has tended to ignore or to acknowledge only to discount. Despite the redactional activity evident in the texts, particularly in respect to the doxologies in Amos dealing with the glories of the creator, there is an affirmation of the power of God in nature that can scarcely be obviated. It may be that there was a progressive historicization of nature in Israel's religious life,[8] but this should not be taken to mean that the forces of nature, however historicized, ceased to be a factor in prophetic thought and testimony. Indeed, these forces defied complete historicization; they were beyond any notion of history as a series of "once-and-for-all events" and by their random reoccurrence shattered any conception of historical life as transpiring apart from the natural environment which provided the matter of history.

Koch, noting that Old Testament scholars have attributed to Amos or Jeremiah a fundamental rejection of the cult, remarks that this rejection is coming to be seen as the result of a Protestant prejudice, since manifestly these prophets had deep cultic interests. The antinature stance of much recent theology is similarly behind the tendency to refuse to give due weight to the witness to nature in the biblical writings. Von Rad himself recognized this problem some decades ago: "The greater part of what the Old Testament has to say about what we call nature has simply never been considered."[9] While this constitutes a call for such a consideration, and von Rad himself provided a preliminary sketch in his work on Second Isaiah, not a great deal of work has been done on the issue, certainly not enough.

One very significant development, however, is to be found in the trend represented in the writings of a student of von Rad's, Claus Westermann, regarding the place of creation and blessing in the Old Testament. Continuing von Rad's "traditio-historical" approach and focusing his primary attention on the sources, Westermann's analysis of the creation account in Genesis is among the most complex and inclusive in modern scholarly literature. He begins his discussion of the primeval events in the biblical accounts by setting it within the context of the rich array of similar accounts in the ancient world.[10] While some distinctive features attach to the Genesis story, Westermann notes, divine creation of the world and of humankind is a common theme in the history of nonbiblical religions. Israel's neighbors spoke of a personal-creator divinity for thousands of years before Israelite history began. There was a long history of contact between the creation stories of the Semitic world, including those of Israel. The Genesis writers therefore did not stumble upon the idea of creation and then introduce it into the thought of Israel. J and P worked on the basis of tradition long known in Israel. Although they adapted and reshaped their materials, stories of creation were part of the lore of Israel for hundreds of years before they found their written form in Genesis.

135

The purpose of J and P was to pass on something that they had received that was "not the result of, but prior to, their confession of Yahweh as the savior of Israel."[11] Their intention was not to make the primeval story the beginning of the history of Israel, but to set the primeval story, which Israel shared with its neighbors and predecessors, in the widest context, the beginning of the world and humankind. To state the matter another way, they accepted the story about creation, adapted it and handed it on as a part of the tradition of their own community.[12]

In regard to the status of the divine creation in the traditional self-understanding of Israel, Westermann makes a number of remarks that seem to clarify the issue to some extent. They move in certain instances beyond von Rad's position and are pertinent to our purpose. The Old Testament, he says, does not have a doctrine of creation, "a concept of belief which describes the total relationship of the person of God as faith." There is no passage in which creation or the creator is conceived in terms of belief as such. In the language of the Old Testament, such notions as "belief in the creator" or "creation belief" are not possible because the idea of belief in the creator presumes the possibility of an alternative, that of nonbelief, something *not* possible for the people of the Old Testament. This is the reason why there is no stated concern with a belief in creation. Creation "was a presupposition or just taken for granted" by the ancient world, including Israel.[13] This is the reason that speaking about the creator never became a part of a credo in Israel. The summaries of Israel's faith were limited from beginning to end, as von Rad held, to "the historical credo."[14]

The idea of "the historical credo" has been subjected to a great deal of criticism. Although von Rad has emphasized an important dimension of the way Israel's faith was expressed, it is clear that Israel's theological concerns were not limited to his conception of the "credo."[15] Westermann's acceptance of it seems to fly in the face of much else that he has to say about the character of Old Testament thought,[16] most notably perhaps his dictum that because God is the creator, there is "no sharp division between nature and history." The realms of human life, nature, and cosmos belong together, he holds, in the fact that together they form the *one* realm of creation. "All that happens belongs together in the fact that God acts in it." If however nature and history constitute the one realm of the divine action, how can Westermann say that the acting of God in creation is regarded in the Old Testament "as something essentially different from his saving and judging acts in history."[17] The primeval story has a universal character; it is concerned with the world and humankind as a whole, and is not specifically Israelite. There is no attempt to integrate fully the story of creation with the acts of God in Israel's historical life. Second Isaiah speaks of the creator, Westermann says, not to point to the creation as such, but to place the work of the creator in the context of the present situation of the people in the Babylonian exile. He wants to assure them that deliverance is a possibility and "reminds them of God's work of creation in which this possibility is given."[18]

If the possibility of deliverance lies in the creative power of God, one wants to ask Westermann, does not faith in deliverance entail some kind of faith in God as creator? There is more at work here than simply the mere presupposition that God is the creator. There is active faith in the creative power of God as the ground of deliverance. In the preexilic prophets, Yahweh's creative control of the world and "acts" in history were not seen as essentially different, as we have seen, but of a piece with each other. God's control of nature enters into the prophetic oracles with the force of belief just as surely as what are so frequently and so loosely called divine acts of history. It is true that in Old Testament thought the creative action of God and his action in history were not fully integrated, though Second Isaiah comes close to it, as von Rad suggests: "But for Deutero-Isaiah, the creation does not belong in a category distinct from that of the deliverance of the Red Sea. . . . At this point, the doctrine of creation has been fully absorbed in the complex soteriological belief." "What appears theologically to be two distinct acts are in fact one and the same act of the universal redemptive purpose of God."[19] Schmidt goes somewhat further, holding not only that any opposition between creation and history is inadmissible, but that in fact "Deutero-Isaiah even equates the two. Redemption, like election, is a creative act of Yahweh."[20]

That some such phrase as "We believe in one God, creator of heaven and earth" does not appear in the "credal" statements of Israel, as they are called, scarcely means that faith in the creative power of Yahweh was entirely absent. Faith in Yahweh was faith in the One who ruled over nature and human existence, and whose activity was perceived in both. No such phrase as "We believe in one God, Lord of History" appears in Israel's statements of faith, but it is clear that, for the Israelites, Yahweh was Lord over human existence and was active in human affairs. To be such, Yahweh had also to be Lord over that in which human existence was set, and without which human existence could have no reality at all.

Just because divine creation seems everywhere to have been assumed in the ancient world is not sufficient justification to claim that it was not a belief or faith, however elemental. Westermann quarrels with S. G. F. Brandon's view that ancient Egyptian cosmogenic speculation was one of the "earliest attempts by man to abstract himself from immersion in present experience, and to conceive of the world as having had a beginning, and to make a sustained intellectual effort to account for it."[21] According to Westermann, this point of view obscures the meaning of the stories of origin which "are not the result of an intellectual inquiry into the origin of the here and now. They stem from a concern for security in the face of the existing situation."[22] Only afterwards was intellectual inquiry added. The question of existence, of securing the stability of the world, of life and its framework, takes precedence.[23] Concern for security probably was the primary consideration of the ancients, but could this concern have manifested itself apart from reflection regarding origins, not formal intellectual inquiry, but questioning thought? The emergence of a myth to secure "the existing situation" must have entailed some sort of reflection on the nature of the situation to be secured and also on the nature of the agency or power that was to secure the situation. That the world was created was not known, it was believed. The creation myths are expressions of this belief. Fear probably stood at the base of the development of the myths, but fear was conquered, tempered at least, by the creation stories, which could have arisen only through something like a process of reflection.

Creation, Westermann holds, is never, in the Old Testament, the object of a revelation, is never in any way brought into the context of revelation. To speak of the biblical witness to creation is to make of creation something which of its nature it cannot be. "There was no witness at Creation. Accordingly, there cannot be a witness in any sense to the fact of Creation."[24] Of course there was no witness to *fact* of creation, but there were witnesses to the "existing situation," to adopt the term Westermann uses in regard to the myths designed to secure the stability of the world. The existing situation was a world of relative stability and order. There was evident disorder too, yet no concern about disorder could have arisen apart from a perceived general order. The source of this order was believed to be God, and in this sense there was witness to creation, even faith in a creator. Witness is a tricky word with a large number of connotations. When applied to human response to something alleged to be a divine movement or activity, whether in the natural or historical realm, witness can be understood only in terms of belief or faith. As the outcome of a war may be seen as Yahweh's favor or judgment, so may a famine or a flood. The witness is the same in regard to both; the divine hand is discerned to be at work in them. While events that take place in the social, political, and communal realm give rise to the witness and shape its form, and even enter into its substance, they do not provide that which is essential to witness, and which makes witness what it is—the affirmation of the divine presence and operative power. Historical events are, in this sense, no different from events in nature. The experience of our ancient ancestors of being alive in a wondrous world, menacing but at the same time nurturing, led them to see events in nature as indications of divine favor or judgment, and in due course to witness to the presence and power of the divine in nature as such, and to see it as a divine creation. This is witness just as surely as the witness that Yahweh was implicated in the Exodus. No one witnessed, that is, literally saw, Yahweh leading the people out of Egypt. Yahweh's presence and power were believed to be in and behind the event, and it is this belief that became Israel's witness.

Westermann will allow no witness to creation because he limits revelation—and so, witness and faith—to history, to God in particular acts. This history begins with the Exodus, which determines all that follows in the historical exchange between God and the people of Israel. There is no sign of this exchange in the primeval stories of creation, or any sign of the separation of the spheres of existence that make up the historical state. Every area of existence is related directly to God. There is no separation between the sacred and the profane, that is, no religious area of existence. As a result, Westermann concludes, there was no such thing as revelation in regard to creation.[25]

This scheme is very tidy and support for it can be gleaned from the biblical documents and collateral literature. There are more ragged edges in the development of Israel's historical consciousness, however, than Westermann's neat scheme implies. The Exodus was no doubt pivotal in the process, forging the tribes into a new and closer identity, but the process continued through the conquest of Canaan and the settlement, on down to the establishment of the monarchy. The patriarchal legends, once gathered, were a force in unifying consciousness and establishing identity, less dramatic and less celebrated than the Exodus, yet still a powerful force. The creation myths were themselves a significant factor in the emergence of Israel's historical consciousness and its clarification of belief in Yahweh.

Yahweh was never simply and solely the God whose activity was discerned in particular historical acts. God was behind the power of the wind that swept the desert, the rains from heaven, and the yield of the earth. The creation myths were not something the Israelites had trouble adjusting to a developed sense of history. The creation myths were integral to the movement toward historical consciousness. That the world was created, had a beginning, was a contributing factor to the awareness that time was the arena of historical activity, with space as its horizon.

The creation stories were no more foreign to the ancient forebears of the Israelites than to any other peoples of the Near East. They had lived with them centuries before Yahwistic belief flowered. The adjustment was not that of integrating the creation stories into stories about Yahweh. It was the other way around. The development of belief in Yahweh constituted a new stage in religious consciousness, so powerful that for a time it seemed to blot out all else. In due course, however, the ancient traditions about creation and the tribes, never lost, began to reassert themselves and the new faith had to be drawn into them. No more than a rough, fairly workable unity between the two was achieved until postexilic times, but the religious consciousness, then as now, was able to tolerate less than consistency of thought.

The views sketched out above can claim only probability; certainty here is beyond grasp. They are, however, no less probable than those of Westermann and the historical school, in which probability seems to be raised to the status of dogma.

There is a problem too with Westermann's notion that in the primal stories every area of life is directly related to God; that there is no religious area of existence and hence no such thing as revelation in regard to creation. We have touched on this issue already, but a few further remarks directly related to the view Westermann expresses at this point are necessary. He holds that those among whom the myths of the primeval event developed were in a state of constant communion with the divine, having no sense of a gulf between themselves and God; at the same time, he says that the creation myths arose out of the effort to secure the world. But if anxiety about the security of the world is behind the development of the myths, then there is already a sense of separation from the divine. There are also the cultic practices associated with the endeavor to secure the world, which presumably were engaged in not all of the time but only some of the time. If there were shrines, however crude, where cultic practices occurred, then there was already a separation of the sacred from the profane and thus a "religious area of existence."

Little less difficulty attaches to Westermann's understanding of the way Israel conceived of the sacred. With the qualification to be considered in a moment, he limits the sacred as such to sacred history. Like von Rad, he sees the sacral understanding of the world as nonhistorical, something that has no essential place in the continuous historical exchange between Israel and Yahweh.[26] The sacral view of the world is "mythological." P in the Genesis account demythologizes the heavenly bodies and makes them a part of created reality; there is no longer any possibility for any notion of a divine sun, moon, or world.[27] The primeval story also frees human achievement from the mythological interpretations found in some of the religions surrounding Israel. Human endeavor and progress were desacralized in Israel from the beginning. "Secularized human endeavor and cultural progress retained their link with divine activity because it was God who gave success to humankind . . . but human achievements in civilization do not acquire a divine origin."[28]

The process of desacralization was complete and was, in Westermann's view, one of the fundamental achievements of Israel.[29] It was wrought in reaction to the understanding of sacralized reality in the nature religions of Israel's neighbors. When Israel ceased to be a wandering people and became established in Canaan, a process of what can be called resacralization began in a different way and to a different effect. There were borrowings from the Canaanites, but the controlling conception remained, for the most part, that of P. The land in some sense became sacred, as did the temple and its cult. The Sabbath was sacred; in the Priestly Code God sanctifies the seventh day. "What is being said here," Westermann notes, "is that all time is directed toward the holy time."[30] There is also the tradition of the first fruits belonging to God, as being sacred to God. The kings of Israel were anointed, indicating that political rule and the state itself had something sacred about them even while standing under prophetic judgment. Work was not purely secular. It was divinely appointed and its fulfillment was obedience to the divine command. Westermann deals extraordinarily well with this process in his treatment of blessing.

The problem I find with his thought at this point is that he does not take Israel's resacralization of reality far enough. He excludes the creation as such, at least so far as I am able to determine. Israel desacralized nature, it seems, and left it that way even while resacralizing other and lesser entities. Perhaps this view is connected with Westermann's insistence that creation is not revelatory. To denude creation of that power is to remove it from the sacral. The process of resacralization, however, went beyond Westermann's estimate of it. Although nature was not holy in itself, no more than human work, it was created by the Holy One, bespoke of the holy word or holy act that called it into being and reflected the mind, will, and power of the Holy One. If this is so, and Westermann would have to admit as much, I suppose, then creation was both revelatory and had what might be called a sacral character or, if this says too much, a sacramental character. The distinction between these two terms is less than clear in the dictionary, but the sacral suggests an intrinsic quality in creation while the sacramental points to created entities as means for divine self-disclosure.

The world in its every part was created by the Holy One and every part of it, wind and fire, vapor and drought, could be means by which the divine presence was announced or the divine pleasure effected. These things were not adventitious realities; they were realities in which the divine was known and experienced as near or far. Israel's conception of the God of tremendous majesty and inexhaustible power did not derive from its "historical exchange with God" alone. Irenaeus's insight that the mercy of God is revealed in history and the majesty of God is revealed in nature is applicable here, though there is no ironclad distinction between the two. God is merciful in the majestic reaches of nature and majestic in the depths of mercy. The distinction has point however in that it shows that both nature and history are integral to the divine self-revelation.

Among Westermann's contributions to contemporary theological thought, the chief one perhaps is to be found in his discussion of blessing in the Old Testament. It is at this point that his writings are particularly relevant to the theology of nature and grace. The neglect of the Old Testament concern with blessing by biblical scholars, Westermann holds, can only be the result of a prejudgment, something encountered in the theologies of the Old Testament where blessing is a priori denied all significance. Von Rad's attempt to subsume blessing under salvation is a prime example.[31] The trouble with much Old Testament theology, as Westermann sees it, is that it has limited its concern to the first two chapters of Genesis, to the story of creation and fall into disobedience, failing to see that Genesis 1–11 is a unit and thus that the blessing and the genealogies are integral to the story of creation.

There are critical difficulties with Westermann's treatment of blessing and the genealogies,[32] but what he has to say about them provides an important, if partial, corrective to the *Heilsgeschichte* school of thought, along with a number of highly suggestive insights for theology. The biblical story of creation, according to Westermann, includes not only the origin of the world and humankind; it includes the origin of all aspects of civilization as well. While the Genesis account does not lay great emphasis on the development of civilization, it nevertheless recognizes and preserves the importance of this development, so much so that it is a constituent of the primeval story. The motif of "the progress of civilization" in Genesis, however, is quite different from that found in other religions of the Near East. In the Sumerian myths, it is from the genealogy of the gods that civilization and its benefits take their origin. In the Bible, it is from the genealogy of the human race, from human endeavor and not "divine birth" that civilization arises. There people are not created to minister to the gods but to master, cultivate, and preserve the earth. The discoveries and inventions of civilization are not first prepared by the gods and then given to humanity. "Faced with the mythology of the Ancient Near East, the Bible takes the same stand as does the modern secular historian: all progress in civilization is a human achievement."[33]

For different reasons, this says too much and too little at the same time. Regard to these reasons will be taken a little later. What I want to do at this juncture is to set forth a clear outline of Westermann's concept of blessing and, so far as possible, its consequences for his theology.

The biblical story for Westermann clearly distinguishes between human achievement and the creative action of God. Israel, however, does see a divine activity behind the development of civilization. It is not God's creative action; it is the blessing that God has bestowed on the person as his creature. Disobedience and punishment notwithstanding, humanity in both J and P is left with life and vital power, with the land and its fertility. The story of creation in P is resumed in the form of genealogy, and Genesis 4:17–26 is a part of this story. As generations pass and people develop, they acquire new skills and achievements in civilization. It is the power and the dynamism of the blessing that enables them to "fill the earth and subdue it," to make, discover, and invent through the capacity given by God. "[T]he activity of the God who blesses is the activity of the God who creates."[34]

The blessing of God in Scripture takes different forms. That formulated in Numbers 6:22–27, the Aaronic blessing, according to Westermann, sounds "spiritual" primarily: "The Lord make his face to shine upon you, be gracious unto you . . . and give you peace." However, Deuteronomy 7:13 speaks of blessing as "secular", as this-worldly: "He will love you, bless you and multiply you; he will bless the fruit of your body and the fruit of your ground, your grain and your wine and your oil." In Deuteronomy, Israel's deliverer has become the bestower of blessing. The promise of the land is part of the context of promises of blessing. "This shows that any reduction of Israel's faith to God's acts in history is a basic misinterpretation of that faith."[35]

The blessing had a profound effect on Israel's worship, but Mowinckel was wrong, Westermann contends, to consider blessing as the determinative act for all worship. At the center of Israel's worship was the history of God's dealing with his people, his action of deliverance and covenant with them. Yet God's activity of blessing was given an essential place in worship. A part of every gathering of the community was the blessing of dismissal. Indeed, the whole service was concerned with blessing, with the blessing that the worshipers might take away to their own homes. Wisdom itself should be seen in the context of the bestowal of blessing. Both wisdom and blessing are universal in import. They have no connection with God's actions in history as summarized in the "great credos." Job shows that creation and blessing belong together, and in apocalyptic literature the final state is described in terms of blessing.

While this literature is so intensely dramatic that there is no room for a continuous activity of the bestowal of blessing, in the end-time saving acts are no longer possible, and the end-time is seen as the final state of blessing, something corresponding to a final destruction, from which there is no longer any possibility of deliverance. Eternal peace for all, including animals, prosperity, security, tranquility, and so on are essential features.[36]

In Israel's understanding of God, the power of blessing is brought under the activity of Yahweh. God alone is master of this power and alone disposes of it as creator of heaven and earth. "This vital, effective power that makes the future possible" is understood as "the basic power of 'history'." The blessing given in Genesis 1:28 "means that as long as humankind exists, God will remain effectively at work in them because of this action in creation. . . . It can never fail whenever there is talk of an action of God directed towards humans."[37]

Westermann makes much of the commission to cultivate and maintain the garden in the J account. He brings both under the category of work and spins out a host of speculative theories regarding it. Work grows and branches out with the advancement of humanity and includes the division of labor, which becomes necessary with it. God's blessing, active in success, accompanies this branching out, and all human work can participate in it. "Human technical activity in all its ramifications, natural sciences as well as the humanities in all ramifications can be understood under this commissioning by God."[38] Cultivating and maintaining the earth include, then, both physical and intellectual work. Indeed, intellectual activity, reflection and contemplation belong to all spheres of human life, to living space, to nourishment, to work and community, to coming to terms in the broad sense with every sphere of life. The Old Testament calls this wisdom, something given originally to humankind as a whole.[39]

This same commissioning is what is meant by "dominion over the earth" in the Priestly Code. There is no suggestion, Westermann says in an ecological vein, of arbitrary employment of power, and no textual basis when, in the contemporary discussion about *dominium terrae*, an unscrupulous exploitation of the earth's resources is referred to the granting of dominion in the creation story. "Every form of exploitation of the earth is contempt for God's commission."[40]

The commission determines the theological position of wisdom in the Old Testament, as implied above. The significance of wisdom as an integral part of the Bible resides in "the fact" that it makes clear that the creator gave human beings the capacity to be properly oriented in the world and of mastering the tasks given them. "This requires neither revelation nor theological reflection," Westermann says. "Wisdom is secular or profane."[41] Human beings are progressively to experience the world, preserve and assimilate their experience, learn from their mistakes and mature through false steps. The creator has given the creatures over to themselves in the acquisition and preservation of experience, in insight and knowledge. The creator wants the creatures to be independent. The expansion of wisdom into the sciences is divinely intended and is of a piece with human independence. "[T]he freedom of the sciences" is based on "the will of the creator."[42] It is necessary to note in the same breath, Westermann goes on to say, that wisdom has priority over all the sciences. No science is comprehensive. Wisdom, however, in its original form embraces the whole of human life. Wisdom as a part of the Bible can help counter the centrifugal form of all the sciences with its centripetal force. It can help, moreover, to counter the absolutizing tendency of the sciences with its functional tendency, "which is there only for the sake of man, indeed for the sake of the whole man."[43]

In addition to blessing, commissioning, and wisdom, there are several other features of Westermann's thought that are integral to our purpose here. Among them is his discussion of the condition of humankind before and after the fall into disobedience.[44] The meaning of the phrase "the image and likeness of God" is not a declaration about Adam, "but about an action of God who decides to create man in his own image; an action which is directed to something between God and man." The creator creates a creature that "corresponds to him, to whom he can speak, and who can hear him." The narrative says nothing about humankind as such; it speaks of a creative event. To view it as applying to an individual person has dogged Christian tradition from the outset and has caused confusion at every turn. Irenaeus's distinction between the natural image and the supernatural likeness of God was the progenitor of much speculation on the meaning of the phrase. Before him, Philo, under the influence of Greek philosophy, saw the image and likeness in human spiritual capabilities. This idea became dominant in Christian thought. Augustine saw the image and likeness in soul, memory, intellect, and love. Modern theology, following Schleiermacher, interprets the phrase in terms of moral, religious, and personal life. In the Old Testament, however, there is no "division of the corporal and the spiritual; it speaks only of man as a whole."[45] Karl Barth is quoted with approval. The image of God, Barth says, "consists not in something or other that man is or does. It exists just because man himself . . . exists as a creature of God. He would not be man if he were not God's creature." This statement by itself, Westermann says, begs the question but when placed in the context of the creation event, its meaning becomes clear. Barth rightly describes the image and likeness of God as the "special character of human existence by virtue of which it is as it were a Thou which can be addressed by God and an I which is responsible before God."[46]

Westermann holds that if this explanation corresponds to the text, it has far-reaching consequences. If no particular human quality is indicated in the text, its meaning cuts through all differences between human beings, all differences between religion, and all differences between believers and nonbelievers. Human dignity is found in its very creatureliness.[47]

The text makes it clear, Westermann continues, that only when man and woman are together is the creation of humankind complete. "The narrative of the creation of man reaches its climax in the joyful exclamation with which man welcomes his companion. The being which God has created is only now really man—man in the community."[48] The Yahwist brings together in one sweep the creation of man and woman and their defection. Their disobedience toward God is not the act of an individual, but of the man and the woman together, the two in community.[49]

Regarding what is traditionally called the "fall," Westermann holds that the Old Testament knows nothing of a narrative which says that Adam sank into a state of corruption through disobedience, that from that moment on he was "fallen man."[50] This all-embracing meaning is absent in the text. The significance of the disobedience is limited to the primal event. The command not to eat of the fruit of the tree of the knowledge of good and evil is of special importance in the narrative. Something is entrusted to Adam in the command. The command introduces him to freedom and in the command he can put himself in relationship with the one who commands. "The freedom of this relationship arises only from the command; without it there would be no freedom." The command in the creation narrative has a completely positive meaning. "It is an act of confidence in man in his relationship to God. It takes him seriously as man who can decide in freedom and it opens to him the possibility of loyalty."[51]

The temptation narrative (Gen. 3: 1–7) presents defection as a human phenomenon. "There always has been, there always will be defection." Human beings are such, Westermann insists, that under certain circumstances they can be seduced. The ability to defect and its cause both point to human limitations. "That is what he [man] is, and no ethic, no religion, no political power can alter this situation in any way."[52]

The punishment for disobedience is explusion from the garden. The other so-called punishments are not really punishments. They describe the state of Adam and Eve separated from God; the suffering they point to is not punishment, for suffering always has been and always will be a part of human existence. It belongs to human limitations and indeed to the whole of creation.[53] Nor is work a punishment. Already, Adam and Eve were commanded to till the garden. The encounter with thorns and thistles outside the garden is intended to describe the fact that human work always requires toil and effort; every area of work entails thorns and thistles unavoidably. This is not pessimism, Westermann says; it is sober realism which protects work from dangerous idealizing. "The Creation narrative describes as a state something which is experienced and recognized as belonging to the essence of human existence."[54]

Despite disobedience and punishment, the blessing given with creation remains intact. Those who are now far from God are always blessed by God. Their lives remain open to the future just because of the power of the blessing. Before the expulsion, God clothes Adam and Eve, indicating that they no longer need to feel unmasked or ashamed and that they are accepted in their weakness. God removes from them that constant feeling that they are sinners, not wishing that they be always conscious of the sins.[55]

The loss of the possiblity of being like God does not mean that Adam and Eve are no longer able to reflect something of God's creative power and life; it means simply that they cannot reach to heaven, cannot take over the conditions of the creator. Access to the tree of life, a well-known motif in the Ancient Near East and so in Israel, is forbidden them because wisdom, in the sense of all-embracing knowledge and eternal life, belongs to God alone. Indestructibility is not in view for them. They are "bounded unconditionally by death." Death is not described as a punishment for disobedience, although as alienated from God Adam and Eve are on the way to death. In the context of the narrative, death is "an absolute condition of human life."[56]

So far from being a proper interpretation of Genesis 2–3, what is regarded as the fall in tradition has its origin in late Jewish tradition, Westermann holds, clearly so in the Fourth (Second) Book of Esdras: "O Adam, what have you done? For though it was you who sinned, the fall was not yours alone, but ours also who are your descendants" (7:18). Here Adam is not, as in the Genesis account, seen as a representative of humankind, but as a historical individual whose "fall" was passed on through him to his descendants. Paul's interpretation of the narrative follows late Jewish tradition and "did not have its origin in Paul's encounter with Christ."[57] The development represented in Augustine's thought is based on the quite incorrect presupposition that history begins with the fall and that the "original state" which preceeded the fall was one of ideal innocence quite separate from our present history. It fails to realize that the course of events from the installation in the garden to expulsion from it is meant to be a primeval happening which "explains human existence in its essential elements from man as he actually exists."[58] While the narrative shows the connection between human guilt and limitation through suffering, toil, and death, it does not declare that "the wages of sin is death." The curse touches Adam and Eve, Westermann says in Irenaean fashion, "only in passing." They are alienated from God, but not completely separated from God. Guilt and death belong inseparably to human existence, but Adam and Eve, Westermann says again, remain those whom God cares for, protects, and blesses. "Only the narrative as it runs its course can say this with all its subtlety and nuances; it cannot be compressed into a doctrine."[59]

The story of creation, Westermann says, has a significance for the human race that will always be relevant. In light of the new interpretation being given it (Westermann's, that is), the opposition between the sciences of anthropology, and especially evolutionary science, and church teaching on original justice and original sin becomes obsolete. The Bible knows no "sinless man" or state of innocence. It should therefore no longer be disputed that the theological dimension can exclude the anthropological, psychological, and social dimensions of the explanation of this phenomenon. For all that, the unique and even relevant message of Genesis 2–3 will become clear only when the significance and necessity of scientific research into the beginnings of the human race are fully acknowledged.[60]

Two remarks on Westermann's view of the relation of Adam and Christ will conclude my exposition of his exegetical and theological positions and lead to an assessment of them in terms of the theology of nature and grace. First, there is the firm assurance, according to Westermann, that the message of the New Testament agrees with the creation narrative. Human beings in the Christian Scriptures are seen with all their potentialities and limitations through sin and death. Second, what is characteristic of the Gospel accounts of Jesus is that in his confrontations with others, in his teaching and acting, that which is basically human is completely dominant. There is the question of human beings as creatures who are hungry and thirsty, sick and healthy, creatures in their basic community structures, asking about the meaning of life and fulfillment. "It is perfectly obvious that man presented in the Creation narratives is man who meets us in the Gospels; that the history of the relationship between God and man of the creation story is what the Gospels are talking about."[61]

Westermann's interpretation of the creation story is of course not without its weaknesses and not without its critics. As Brevard Childs notes, Westermann has made a genuine contribution to biblical studies by defending the integrity of the primeval history. Universal history is not, as in von Rad, derivative of Israel's election. Westermann's attempt, however, to substitute an existential interpretation of the opening chapters of Genesis in the place of *Heilsgeschichte* raises, Childs says, a host of new

149

problems. There is no canonical warrant for interpreting these chapters as a description of the quality of life constitutive of being human, for "the point of the paradisal state is to contest the ontological character of human sinfulness."[62]

Childs is highly critical of the so-called kerygmatic exegesis method of interpretation popularized by von Rad and continued by H. W. Wolff, W. Bruegemann, and Westermann. This method attempts to discern the central intention of a writer, usually by means of formulae or themes, and then to link the intention to a reconstruction of a historical situation which allegedly evoked that response. The major concern of those using this method is to combine historical exegesis with theological interpretation, something that, in Childs's view, results in extreme subjectivity and reductionism, and that extends the form-critical method beyond its original function in the effort to provide a theological message. "Often the assumption that the theological point must be related to an original intention within a reconstructed historical context runs directly in the face of the literature's explicit statement of its function within the final form of the biblical text."[63]

In order to appreciate this criticism, it is necessary to know a little something about Childs's own method and approach to the literature. His method, called "canonical," is sharply distinguished from the traditio-critical method in that it seeks to describe the form and function of the Hebrew Bible in its role as Sacred Scripture for Israel, arguing that it cannot be correctly understood unless its role as religious literature is correctly assessed. The canonical method assumes the normative status of the final form of the text of the Bible.[64] Given this approach, Childs holds that the historical-critical method usually fails to understand the peculiar dynamics of Israel's religious literature and loses sight of the fundamental dialectic which lies at the heart of the canonical method, for constitutive of Israel's history is the fact that the literature formed the identity of the religious community, which in turn shaped the community. The historical-critical method assumes the determining force on every biblical text to be political, social, or economical factors which it seeks to establish in disregard of the religious dynamism of the canon.[65]

I do not intend to enter into the disputes between biblical critics. I have no competence for any such engagement, but it seems clear to me that some of the criticisms recorded above do apply to Westermann and that his method has led him into stretching the texts into affirmations that lack sufficient warrant. Yet it is hard to believe that he has failed to understand the dynamic of Israel's religious literature. He has not, most probably, grasped it in the same way and to the same effect he might have done had he employed something like the canonical method and concentrated less on J and P as separate histories. Still, he has perceived the interaction of the two traditions through their redactions, and his thought in its overall character indicates that he has grasped the dynamics of the literature as a comprehensive whole, even though using what might be described as a defective method.

Moreover, it is probably true that there is no strict "canonical warrant" for interpreting the opening chapters of Genesis as a description of the quality of life constitutive of being human. Yet if Westermann had not undertaken his existential interpretation of them, Old Testament theology would be poorer for it. It is quite possibly true that the point of the paradisal state is to contest the ontological character of human sin-fulness—a view that has a great deal of traditional support, exegetical and theological. Not only is Westermann's courageous willingness to challenge it an admirable thing in itself, his own viewpoint is far from insupportable. The writers of the Genesis account may well have been describing the human situation as they saw it. Surely this was at least a part of their intent. It may be too that Westermann takes his descriptive analysis too far and too seriously, but to dismiss it out of hand is another matter. Westermann has not of course perceived the whole truth but he has perceived a part of it.

One of the main problems I find with Westermann's writings has to do with the theological interpretations that are interspersed in the form of excursi and the odd paragraph here and there. *Elements of Old Testament Theology* is essentially an exegetical work, with theological interpretations scattered throughout. Exegesis and theology of course are not separable since theological premises inevitably enter into exegesis and exegesis gives rise to theological interpretation, but the demarcation between textual analysis and theological affirmation is blurred in Westermann's writings to an unwonted extent, making it difficult to determine what Westermann the exegete is saying that the text is saying, and what Westermann the theologian is saying about the text. Although the two cannot be severed, some little indication of what is intended to be primarily exegetical as against what is intended to be primarily theological would have been useful to the reader. Another problem concerns clarity of expression, something that Westermann frequently lacks. It is hard to believe that his translators are altogether to blame for this. Von Rad reads beautifully in translation. If Westermann had von Rad's grace of style and capacity for clear expression, and better translators as well, his influence, both as an exegete and theologian would, I have little doubt, be considerably greater than it is.

By far the most serious problem I have with Westermann has to do with his program of redressing the historical bias of modern theology, his attempt, that is, to strike an effective balance between emphasis on creation and salvation. This attempt, although laudable in itself, is vitiated by his less than complete freedom from captivity to the very historical bias he criticizes. His writings demonstrate that he has fought to break loose from it and that he has done so brilliantly in spots, but the hold of the old school's direction of thought is so powerful a force in his thinking that even as he slips out of it at certain crucial points, he slides back into it almost every time he is moved to speak passionately and thus to show his most firmly held theological and apologetical views. It is precisely at this point that inconsistency and what can only be termed confusion of thought occur in his writings.

Westermann holds, as we have seen, that because God is the creator, there is no sharp division between nature and history in the Old Testament.[66] But by making history revelatory and denying any possibility of revelation through nature, he draws the sharpest division between them that can well be conceived. Revelation is strictly limited to God's historical interchange with his people. Creation is a presupposition; its goal "is not a self-manifestation of God, so that God can be known from his work of creation *(revelatio generalis)*."[67] Having said this, Westermann declares that it was God's judgment that creation is good; it could never be our judgment or arise out of our experience.[68] If this is so, then God has revealed something in creation, namely, that it is good, a judgment alleged to be beyond our ken. I am not at all sure that such a judgment was simply handed over to us from God. If there were no inklings of the good of creation within human consciousness, it is hard to see how it found such wide acceptance. This however is a minor point. My major concern is the declaration that revelation is entirely absent from the creation, a declaration in company with the assertion that we have knowledge of what God thinks about creation, his judgment that it is good, which a fortiori would have to be understood in terms of revelation, one not derivable, on Westermann's terms, from our historical experience.

In his discussion of the theological meaning of the primeval story, Westermann says that the keynote of the Genesis account is "comprehensive talk about reality." There is no attempt to talk about God's "particular acts," which, from the viewpoint of the Old Testament, is what history is all about. "If the primeval event is not to be understood as revelation, if there is nothing in the texts that stems from revelation in itself as such, then the old controversy between *revelatio generalis* and *revelatio specialis* is no more."[69] While one can applaud this effort to resolve an old controversy, one has to question the grounds of the resolution. Revelation consists, according to Westermann, in "individual acts" of God in history. He never states however just what might be entailed in any kind of divine act. It is no easier to define or even describe a divine act in history than a divine act in nature. The historical school makes an enormous presupposition in assuming that it knows what a divine historical act is, that it is something isolatable from the rest of human experience, from experience of the natural realm. To claim that history is the sphere of the divine revelation—that that is where the "action" is—is to limit the operative power of the divine to that which is most amenable to human comprehension, at least to the realm with which we are perforce most familiar. In view of the almost limitless mystery in which we are set, any attempt to reduce the revelatory character of reality to the "historical" segment of experience seems very precarious indeed.

Westermann's judgment on *revelatio generalis* hangs in part on his understanding of natural theology, which seems to be similar to that entertained by the Reformers. If natural theology is not simply an inferential reading of the great appearances of nature, undertaken "objectively" and independently of all other consideration, but is rather a theology of nature, arising from religious experience, with the experience of nature inextricably intertwined, a theology of nature becomes a legitimate and necessary enterprise. It is along such lines that the opposition between general and special revelation, if not conceptually overcome, can at least be reduced to a workable unity. My own view is that there is no historical experience, no religious experience that can be isolated from the experience of nature. If this is so, revelation applies to nature as much as to history; it applies not only to a part of experience, but to all of it.

Westermann wants to keep God out of nature, to the extent at least of maintaining that it is nonrevelatory. He holds that there is no conception of *creatio continua* in the Old Testament. The *otiositas* or rest of God after creation means that God will not intervene in the completed work of creation, will not disturb the established order. "Creation is thus set apart from all that follows as a unique, once and for all event."[70] The creator can no longer intercede in the finished work of creation. God ceases, it would seem, to be creative until the eschaton, at which point God is stirred into creativity once more and forms "a new creation," which consists of the final state of blessing. Meanwhile God is constantly active in history, encountering Israel and demanding response, everywhere intervening and disposing the forces of nature to suit the divine purposes!

Instead of *creatio continua* which, Westermann says, is a contradiction in itself, there is blessing, something not to be confused with preservation. Blessing on creation "is not just the act of preserving it in the state it once reached; it is much rather dynamic, manifold and rich in content." God is acknowledged as creator "precisely in the fact that all that exists and all that happens is explained from him, derived from him, and understood in connection with him. All that happens comes from him and all that happens leads to him."[71]

The doctrine of continual creation has of course been interpreted in a static sense, as has divine preservation, but it has also been seen as the constant activity of God in the creative process, bringing new things out of old things, continually shaping and reshaping the creation. In view of the affirmations of Westermann quoted above, it seems that something like *creatio continua* in this sense is what he wants to affirm. If all that happens comes from God, whether in nature or in history, God is continually active in both, and if the creator, God's activity must be creative. The continual doctrine is not incompatible with the biblical idea of the uniqueness of the "original creation," for continuing creation is wrought on the basis of what was originally established and is constantly reestablished, though always calling forth new possibilities and forming new constellations of reality in the world.

Despite Westermann's affirmations of the intimacy of God's relation with his creation through the dynamic character of blessing, and his assertion that all that happens comes from God, he posits the view that the Bible "takes the same stance as does the modern secular historian: all progress in civilization is a human achievement."[72] Although the blessing is said to be "the power of history," its principal function, other than insuring the structural continuity of life, seems to be to insure the independence of human beings, to insure their freedom of invention and investigation, a part of which is the development and growth of science. We have already noted Westermann's keen desire to show that there need be no opposition between the sciences and biblical religion. This desire finds extensive expression in his writings, so much so that it becomes a marked motif in them.[73] His investment in the freedom of science is so heavy that, on occasion and for certain ends, he tends toward a deistic point of view—namely, God created once and for all, blessed the creation and let it go its own way without intervention. Westermann leans over backwards to establish nature, once created, as a "neutral" realm in which the sciences can be pursued unhindered. The divine hand, it would seem, is raised passively in blessing over nature but is otherwise not actively involved in it.

Westermann's call for a new dialogue between science and biblical religion however is well taken. He insists that P is not presenting his understanding of the beginning of creation as definitive, as rejecting all other explanation. Above all he tries, Westermann notes, to preserve the mystery of creation. There is no one idea of creation in Scripture. The ideas we find there are essentially variable and no one of them can be absolutized. Genesis 1 has grown out of a combination of older and younger strata, "the so-called word account and act-account." While the "ideas about creation have to change . . . this does not mean that the older one is false, and the younger correct." In this we have the justification in our age for a scientific explanation of the origin of the world, a justification recognized from the "beginning to the extent that it does not absolutize itself."[74]

Westermann is sympathetic with those scientists who are derisory of revealed truth in regard to creation. Some of them, Paul Davis notes, regard the whole conception of revealed truth as a positive evil. He quotes H. Bondi in this connection: "Generally the state of mind of a believer in a revelation is the awful arrogance of saying 'I *know*, and those who do not agree with my belief are wrong.' In no other field is such arrogance so widespread, in no other field do people feel so utterly certain of their 'knowledge.' "[75] Westermann deplores this "awful arrogance" as much as any scientist and seeks to undercut it at every point. His dogmatic insistence however that God is revealed or reveals Godself in history and not in nature is but another form of absolutism, one that scientists could be no more happy about than with the absolutist conception of creation. The problem devolves upon what "revealed truth" might mean in the case of history as well as creation. What is revealed, we can only suppose, is that God is active in both, seeking to communicate something of the divine power and life to us, not as an irrevocable and immutable "truth," but as a constant, unrelenting presence and concern, as a presiding and directing force over the whole of reality. Some such notion is essential for

155

theology. Scientists will have a hard time with this most fundamental of all religious beliefs, as apparently some theologians themselves do, Westermann not excepted. The witness of science is not at present disposed in this direction. It has other work to do. While the witness of theology must seek to incorporate and "baptize" the witness of science, it cannot forfeit that which is finally the telling point of its own witness, namely, that God created, creates, and will create, that the ground of nature and history and all their possibilities and occurrences are to be found in God.

Science no more than religion takes place apart from the impact of God upon it. Westermann himself verges on making science revelatory but his insistence that "history" alone yields revelation prohibits him from doing it. Science is for him necessary for the extension of knowledge of origins, the structures of life and anthropology in all its various senses, yet it can tell us nothing of God, the creator of all things. The creator and the creation are here theoretically split: we know that God is creator but not by revelation; we know that there is a creation but the creation is revelatorily silent, speaking not a word of the One who called it into being.

There are all sorts of inconsistencies in Westermann's thought, though certainly no more so than found in the biblical witness itself. It does seem to me however that Westermann frequently wants more from his premises than they can afford. This is especially so of his treatment of blessing. The power of blessing is effective not merely in that it maintains existence; "it is a forward-thrusting, ever pregnant power of becoming."[76] Yet, speaking in a different vein, Westermann describes it as "natural to life, a quiet, continuous, flowing and unnoticed working, realized in a gradual process." Blessing is different from God's saving work in that it is not as the latter experienced in event or in a sequence of events. It therefore has nothing of revelation about it.[77] If blessing is a "quiet, unnoticed working" and is nonrevelatory, how do we know so much about it? Is our knowledge of it an inferential reading of experienced factors in nature, a covert form of natural theology, as it were? Could the perceived structures making for the continuance and progress of life be grasped as coming from divine blessing apart from some revelatory indication that it is so? Westermann seems to interpret the blessing in a less than fully theistic sense, despite passionate outbursts to the contrary. God, we have to say, is not only present and active in every aspect of creation as a flowing, unnoticed force; in all divine activity, God is dynamically communicating something of Godself. Self-communication is a piece with the divine dynamism.

Westermann wants to show that the blessing has to do with the whole of organic life, and theoretically he does so. But practically speaking, he sees it as "the basic power of history." Whenever his theological priorities come to the fore, natural reality is scarcely alluded to. Human interests, human mastery, human investigation, and human prospects occupy his whole field of vision. While this indicates the lingering grip of the historical school on him, it does not obviate his contributions to the theology of nature and grace. He does not speak much of grace, but his discussion of the blessing and the commission to humankind entails the divine self-giving in grace. Indeed, it is manifest that the gracious activity of God is the key to understanding what he is driving at, even though it finds explicit expression only, so far I am able to see, in his treatment of the Psalms.[78] The creation itself is gift, never merely the given. Beyond this, creation is gifted; it contains in itself the continuing power of the divine blessing. Blessed at the beginning, the divine gift of blessing in creation is uninterruptedly operative until its complete fulfillment in the last days.

The endeavor to unify creation and redemption in Westermann's works is vitiated from the start because his basic presuppositions thrust them apart. He apparently does not see that the unifying factor, if there is such, is to be found in the gracious character of the one God, that since both creation and redemption are of grace, both are revelatory. If one is revelatory and the other is not, a cleavage of the most severe and shattering kind results. It is precisely this cleavage that gives rise to the strange inconsistencies in his thought. Nothing is clearer than his desire to provide a unified vision of God's works in creation, blessing, redemption, and fulfillment, but he is unable to achieve it because of a consciousness that, like so many others, has been infected by the bacillus of history, the tendency to compress the divine self-communication into a preconceived mold made up of historical categories.

Confused as it is, Westermann's view is preferable to that of Schmidt who claims, along with many others of the historical school, that "faith in a creator is the consequence . . . of the faith in salvation."[79] Any such view is just too pat, too amenable to the presuppositions of the school of thought in which Westermann has a foot, perhaps a foot and one half of another, and in which Schmidt stands solidly with both feet. The evidence in the text for this pat dictum is a good deal less decisive than can be gathered from much modern scholarship. Moreover it runs counter to common sense. Its power over critical thought for so long a period can be accounted for only by reason of its constant dogmatic declaration and its congruence with a powerful strand in modern thought. The great fact for Israel, as for its neighbors in the Near East, was that there was a world, or at least an environment, mysterious and fecund, and that there were clearly discernible traces of structure and process within both the world and human life. This simply could not have been missed, however preoccupied Israel became with redemption.

Before emancipation, blacks in the South were concerned with freedom above all else. The redemptive power of God was everywhere central in their preaching and spirituals. But the myths of creation, immemorial in their African heritage, fortified by the biblical myth, never allowed them to forget that they were creatures in a world of divine making and that they were formed in the divine image. The *imago Dei* conception played a large part in the hope that sustained them during their subjugation. As already suggested, it was similarly so with Israel. Those in captivity think principally of freedom from captivity, but this does not entirely blot out everything that has hitherto formed consciousness. It is possible on the basis of the history of religions and the biblical witness itself to hold that conceptions of creation were among the earliest and most foundational of beliefs, that creation was the chief work of the divine for humanity since without it nothing else availed.

With the growing recognition that our history, with whatever divine "intervention" or "invasion" within it that there is, portends ceaseless strife and the possible destruction of the human enterprise altogether, it is time to put history in its place, to consider it as an event in the much larger continuum of nature. This recognition might help to divert us from ourselves, from our separate histories and fractiousness, and enable us to attend to that which we all have in common and upon which we all totally depend. If biblical religion has tended to obscure, to obviate some such recognition, so much the worse for biblical religion. I do not think that the biblical witness has necessarily produced this result, but a one-sided focus on the grace of redemption as against the grace of creation has seduced the Christian mind to an excessive glorification of history and to a conception of it as something virtually severed from nature. We are reaping the fruit of this severance in abundance just now. Any force or tendency that serves to expose the fatuousness of this severance should be welcomed with relief and gratitude.

Westermann's work on creation and blessing, although lacking in complete clarity and consistency, is a movement toward this end, even though his discussion of creation and blessing needs to be taken beyond the limits he sets for it. He is a transitional figure, in process of breaking free from the historical school of thought. While not wholly succeeding, he succeeds sufficiently to challenge the old point of view and to suggest, both wittingly and unwittingly, possible alternatives. Whatever else we may think of his position, we should be glad to record that he has given us cause to rethink some of the basic aspects of biblical faith and thought and has given us some useful hints for their reformulation.

Whitehead spoke of the secular functions of God, functions not specifically interesting to the religious temperament but of great importance for the maintenance and furtherance of the world. Westermann's view of the secular character of wisdom and of the blessing in Deuteronomy is not dissimilar in meaning. The blessing insures the seasons, seed time and harvest, the orderly progression of nature. God, we can only suppose, has many functions beyond ministry to human salvation. Whitehead's metaphysics reminds us of this tellingly. Westermann's ideas are vastly more anthropocentric in cast but they do serve to direct attention beyond the immediate interests of human redemption and what is normally associated with the religious sphere of life. Both Whitehead and Westermann are speaking of grace at work in nature and in the natural inclinations of human beings, something distinct, perhaps, but not separate from the grace of salvation. Both, in different ways, provide testimony that the religious temperament as it has developed in the West needs to be expanded, made inclusive of the manifold operations of grace in nature.

Again, Westermann and Whitehead have much to teach us about the acceptance of the limitations given in our creaturehood. It seems to me that Westermann makes a very good case from the standpoint of the biblical witness for his view that there was no "fall" as traditionally conceived, no fall from perfection into imperfection. The creation is intrinsically imperfect as distinguished from the creator, a distinction found in Irenaeus. This means that the whole process of creation with its random pockets of irrationality, of seeming chaos and chance occurrence, is divinely intended. There is, however, within creation enough to suggest the rational, the perfect, enough that pleads for the perfect and inclines the heart not only to long for the perfect but to work for it—precisely on the basis of the perceived imperfection of the world—that faith in the divine perfection, finitely immanent yet infinitely transcendent, finds a kind of justification, however tentative it must be. This notion falls under the category of "theological anthropology," it is true, but I contend that no anthropology, theological or otherwise, can be in the slightest degree realistic unless it reckons with humanity's embeddedness in nature with its imperfections, with its multitudinous expressions of the drive to be and their truncations, with their fall into decay and death and, in the end, their becoming "fertilizer" for the rise of future occurrences.

Religious folk have been known to shout loud protests against the notion that we are fertilizer for the soil. The reductionism in this is patent, but that our experience in our lifespan prepares the ground for future growth should not be derided overmuch. We might gratefully hold that this much is true about us, however much more there may be to the mystery of being human. Derision in the face of this viewpoint might betoken an angelistic notion of our nature, too precious by far in that it obscures our rootedness in the common ground of the earth and so fosters at every turn a false anthroplogy.

If nothing else, our study of Westermann, Whitehead, and the others has demonstrated, I hope, the depth and difficulty of the problem of nature and grace. I hope too that it has highlighted its undeniable centrality in the attempt to reckon with the biblical witness and with Christian faith and thought, today for tomorrow.

CHAPTER 10

The Nature of Grace and the Grace of Nature

IN THE ATTEMPT TO GRASP the implications of historical developments, it is sometimes useful to conjecture what might have happened if events had been other than they were. Suppose for a moment that the Pelagian controversy had never arisen, that Augustine had had no occasion to draw his fateful formula that grace pertains not to the constitution but to the restitution of our nature. Had this been the case, theology in the West would have proceeded, we may imagine, more along the lines of theology in the East, in which the demarcation between nature and grace was much less sharp.

Differences no doubt would have remained. The West before Augustine had already placed a greater emphasis on slavery to sin than was usual in the East, and this emphasis shaped the Western understanding of grace. But without Pelagianism or some such movement, the rift between East and West would have been much less severe and a more positive regard for nature perhaps would have ensued. Augustine himself, in the absence of Pelagianism, might have developed his positive deliverances on creation more fully and deliberately in terms of grace,[1] remaining within the orbit of Eastern influence to the extent at least of not falling prey to the bifurcating tendencies that were present in his own mind and in the North African church.

Conjectures such as these make it possible to surmise that the line drawn between nature and grace in the West, making them not only distinguishable but virtually separate realities or realms, was not an essential implicate of faith. It was rather on the order of an accident of history, something more or less fortuitous.

For all that, the whole drift of the theology of grace in the Western church might have been other than it proved to be if only Pelagius had met with Augustine during his trip to Hippo.[2] To the loss of both men (and perhaps the church at large), Augustine was in Carthage. The two had great respect for each other's character, intelligence, and writings, and if they had met for extended conversation, they might have understood

161

each other better even if not reaching fundamental agreement. The bitterness of the controversy might have been lessened, and perhaps their respective viewpoints would have been seen to have a certain complementarity. Imaginings such as these are not idle. They give further point to the claim that the split, or near split, between nature and grace in Western theology, developed so largely under the influence of Augustine, did not occur by reason of any imperious theological necessity but through circumstance and chance.

Augustine's anti-Pelagian formula had behind it the assumption that conscious appropriation of grace was a condition for grace to be itself. This assumption, never given explicit expression but clearly implied throughout Augustine's anti-Pelagian polemic, is what gives point to the formula and to the theological difficulties it has given rise to in history. It not only had the effect of making nature and grace rivals, it placed limits on the operation of grace itself, limits that are theologically questionable, if not inadmissible. This issue is adverted to again because it bears directly on how grace may be characterized and how far nature may be considered to be of grace.

Can then grace be grace without it being perceived as such, without it being gratefully received? In one sense, this question has to be answered negatively. Grace as the divine self-communication comes to its full term only when it is consciously appropriated, recognized and received in full awareness of its reality. The term *full*, however, raises another question. In whom has grace come to its full term and by whom has it been received in full awareness—Abraham, Moses, the prophets, Buddha, Paul, or Ghandi? Perhaps it came to all these figures in its full term, but did any one of them fully recognize it for what it is?

Christologically it has been affirmed that the fullness of the divine grace was given to Jesus and that he was fully open to it. But was he fully aware of the fullness of divine grace within his life? There are indications in the Gospels that he was not fully aware of it, not all the time at least. The cry of dereliction from the cross seems to indicate something of this sort. But there is another question involved: Could Jesus have been fully human if he had been fully aware of the divine grace operating within his life at every moment? Could he have questioned, doubted, experienced temptation? Could he have drawn back from death, felt forsaken? These questions cannot be answered decisively. They point however to the problem of the language of "full awareness" and the like.

However it was with Jesus and the others, with most of us awareness of divine grace is sporadic at best, coming to us in one situation and not in another, recognized fleetingly, partially, and always imperfectly, frequently not recognized at all for what it is. The conscious appropriation of grace is a relative matter, even for those seasoned in faith and sainted in holiness.

Consciousness, moreover, is not the whole of human reality. It may be the acme of human reality as Whitehead reminds us, but that reality includes a great deal more. Since this is so, we are obliged to inquire about the operation of grace in dimensions of our lives that, to use a conventional phrase, "lie below the threshold of conscious awareness." Are these dimensions of our nature upon which consciousness directly depends outside of the sphere of the activity of grace? If grace finds its limit in consciousness, the complexities of our brain and neural system, the wondrous interaction of the cellular structures that stand at the basis of life would be graceless. If these marvels of precision and functional specialization are outside the sphere of the effective operation of grace, we ask with Tillich, can it be said that grace affects us as we are?

There is also the question of the subliminal mind. Consciousness is a fraction of what constitutes human mentality. To use Coleridge's image, it is "the narrow neck of the bottle," below which lies the swirling mass of unconsciousness, that which shapes and forms us more powerfully perhaps than we can at present begin to estimate. Does grace have nothing to do with the "bottle" itself, with what lies below its "narrow neck"?

The claim sometimes advanced that in affecting consciousness grace reaches into everything upon which consciousness depends no doubt has some truth about it. There is, however, a problem connected with it. The conscious mind does not fully control the unconscious mind. While consciousness serves to check, repress, and direct the subliminal mind at certain crucial points, such control is far from total. Unconsciousness erupts, as it were, from time to time, asserting its power over consciousness.

Is unconsciousness, moreover, altogether dark and dangerous, only a storehouse of basic fears and anxieties? Is it invariably selfish, void of any small impulse toward self-transcendence? Psychology affords no ready answers to these questions. Some strands of it imply however that since unconsciousness is shaped by early childhood experiences, altruistic impulses are for the most part absent from it. But if lacking in such impulses, early childhood experiences are marked with urges toward union with others, love of kind and less kindred objects, with, that is, the bases, the potentialities for altruistic action.

The whole matter of unconsciousness is unavoidably murky and still pretty largely in the assumptive stage in psychology, though it is generally recognized that the notion points to something real in experience: urges well up from within, come unbidden, shape our momentary moods and general outlook, and prompt or move us to act. Action deriving from these urges may be destructive of relationships and even of the self, but on occasion it may be marked by self-transcendence. As often observed, to plunge into a surging river to save a drowning person regardless of danger to self, is more often than not an immediate subliminal response to the situation, rarely a consciously calculated decision. But even if unconsciousness were nothing but a pit of selfishness, would it for that reason have no ground in grace? If it is a precondition for the possibility of conscious response to grace, is it not itself of grace?

The answers given to questions like these will be based on whether grace is considered as that which constitutes nature as well as that which restores or perfects it. In my view there must be an integral relation between the constitution and the restitution of nature. The grace of the one God is operative in both, though operative in different ways and received in different ways, consciously and unconsciously, and biologically as well.

Lionel Tiger, in an amusing but quite suggestive review of *The Biology of Religion* by Vernon Reynolds and Ralph Tanner, seriously contends, so far as I make it out, that religion has an "appreciably genetic" basis.[3] In attempting to account for the tenacious persistence of religion in our society, where powerful intellectual currents militate against it constantly, Tiger suggests—no, more than this, holds—that religions exist because they helped to solve an age-old problem: "What to do with a cerebral cortex that has the capacity to create immobilizing scenarios of disaster and to dwell fruitlessly on the utter meaninglessness of it all." Natural selection responded to this problem "by wiring into our brains a moderate propensity to embrace sunny scenarios even when they are not supported by the facts." People believe things, even though not warranted by reality, which "keep the neurotransmitters from flooding the brain with the paralysis of deep depression. Given this chemically mediated cognitive bias, any system of belief that offers hope, however false, will flourish."[4]

Tiger is an anthropologist with apparently no interest in religion beyond the anthropological level. What he has to say is of theological interest, however, not because his speculation is of use in substantiating a theological issue but because it may serve to illuminate such an issue as the ordination of human beings toward God as a given in the creative process. *Tu fecisti nos ad te,* in Augustine's terms: we are created toward God, created not only by God but for God. This is a theological "fact," something that for theology pertains to our nature as such and is rooted in all that constitutes us as human beings, not excluding, since it is basic to all else, the biological level, though Augustine himself did not well consider this. Tiger may think the drive toward religious understanding is fatuous even though a necessity of nature, but the drive is present, as present as the drive toward scientific self-understanding. Science no less than religion is a defense against meaninglessness, and its technological offspring has produced its share of "sunny scenarios" even "where not supported by the facts." However this may be, the issue here has to do with grace as the basis of the "natural" drive to understand ourselves within the complexities of the nature out of which we have arisen and how to cope with our findings. In Tiger's view "natural selection," in providing for the biological bases of hope, performs a function that might be characterized as "gracious," or something tolerably analogous to it. Hope not only makes life endurable, it provides life with its forward thrust. Hope lies at the bases of science itself, whether hope for growth in scientific understanding or no more than hope for making a reputation through scientific research and discovery. Without hope there would be no scientific advance; without hope there would be no advance in any human enterprise.

Hope then is ingredient to human life and its drive toward the future. If it is the result of natural selection as Tiger holds, all of us are in some sense "religious" since all of us hope, whatever the character of the hope. Tiger is not in this article speaking of the phenomenon of hope as such but of religious hope.[5] Fatuous as religious hope seems to appear to him, it nevertheless is for him a "gift" of nature, and if religious hope is a gift of nature, on his own terms all hope would have to be similarly so.

Minds of a theological bent cannot but see hope as a gift of nature within the continuum of grace. Natural selection is itself a means of grace; that is, grace is operative in natural selection, though not without the randomness and unpredictability that qualify the created entities in which natural selection finds embodiment. More will be said about randomness a little later. My concern here is with the operation of grace within the forms and forces of natural reality. For theology, the mysterious function of natural selection is not, cannot be purely natural, whether in origin or in thrust. Natural selection does not stand upon itself without remainder. Nor does it grope in a void; it "tends" to tend toward something, with whatever great and many mischances and failures. The process is grounded in grace and is guided by grace. Guidance is the word wanted here. The process is guided rather than determined, though some determination is involved: the determination that there be a process and that the process be one toward forms of order, or approximations thereto. But the process is given by grace (and in grace) its own life and its own manner of functioning and with these, the possibility of error and defection. Grace does not dictate, it directs, lures, and woos, allowing the process a certain independence and scope for self-development. Yet as in grace and of grace, the process is never independent of grace, not even in the independence it has in grace. Grace is all-enveloping.[6] Nothing is or happens apart from grace. Grace is God in relation to the world.

In relation to the natural process as a whole, the human enterprise is but a minute fragment. Anthropocentric assertiveness is otiose in the face of this, and anthropocentric interpretations of grace are doubly so. The old conception of grace as *pro nobis* has to give way to an enlarged understanding of grace as universal in scope, limited by nothing outside of itself except the character that created reality has in and by grace. A more rigorously theocentric perspective is called for today in the place of the pinched perspective of former times, which virtually limited grace to the ecclesial reality, to something focused almost exclusively on human needs and human salvation. The theocentric recasting of grace will require and is already requiring painful readjustment, not only in the systematic field but in the pastoral or practical fields, which nourish people at the grass roots on a multitude of ideas and tactics that concentrate on human problems and how to solve them. Grace is available, these perspectives assure us, but as an ecclesial reality, having nothing to do with the world beyond except in so far as it is "taken" to it through Christians and Christian organizations. The human-centeredness of so much that passes for practical theology today spills into prayer groups, whose chief interest often seems to be in self-serving "private" prayer, with little thought of a self-transcending glorification of God. It is imperative, as Whitehead holds, that we learn to see that the divine energies are not focused on us alone. Both theological sanity and realistic humility call for it.

Grace of course has a special bearing upon our lives, for of the creatures, so far as we know, only human beings can respond to grace willingly and live freely in accordance with it. Only human beings can devise theologies of grace, take the experience of grace and use it as an interpretative category for understanding what lies beyond the experience. But peculiar as we are, our peculiarity rests on the no less peculiar operation of grace in all the forms and forces in nature that prepared the way for our advent. This is not to be taken to imply that creation is for us, that the forms and forces of nature were created so that in due course we could arrive upon the scene. Our arrival may have been left to the element of randomness, of unpredictability that God apparently meant to be an ingredient in creation. Not that the emergence of human reality took God by surprise—God provided for the possibility, we may suppose, yet allowed nature to move toward it in the elemental freedom divinely accorded the world, which is the background and basis of our freedom. As human freedom is of grace and its exercise is within the gracious continuum of nature, so the elemental freedom within nature that made human reality a possibility is of grace and is exercised within the graciousness of creation. The forces of nature were, we may again suppose, free enough to make false moves, providing for the rise of creatures, whole species, which did not prove to be capable of survival, whether through some further randomness in creation or through failure to respond or adapt adequately to the given conditions or situation.

Through scientific discoveries and technological developments following from them, the human race may well be poised on self-destruction. This possibility is born of human freedom. However horrible it might prove to be in its consequences, this freedom occurs within the graciousness of creation. That God does not will the immediate extinction of humanity is indicated by what we call the grace of redemption. Nevertheless, the extinction may well happen. Even if the dreaded nuclear holocaust is avoided, other perils may arise in the future. They may stem from further technological developments, from a new ice age threatening to overtake the earth or from a random collision in outer space which might cover the planet with radiation dust, snuffing out life as we know it. Should one or another of these things occur, it too would be of grace, that is, something occurring within the graciousness of creation, which allows randomness of created forms.

Paul's idea that nothing will be lost, that God will be all in all, might prove, if stretched, to be a comfort in the face of such possibilities. It might also be comforting to suppose that as species died out in the past and others arose after them and then perished, some new species might come forth after us, perhaps one freer and more intelligent than we are, and more responsive to the grace of God. Our historical experience, if more than fossils of it survive, might be instructive to some such future species. As each one of us has his or her morning and evening, our species and those, if any, succeeding it will perhaps have theirs too. One may hope that our species will be sufficiently responsive to the grace of God to use responsibly the freedom we have by grace to prevent racial suicide, and so allow more time for the grace in the created process and in the redemptive processes of history to do its work.

It is even conceivable that nuclear armaments are a kind of grace, a sign to us as a race that we must learn to live together or risk perishing altogether. Certainly the grace of creation underlies their development, providing first an atomic structure that can be smashed, then the human drive and ingenuity to smash it, and finally and decisively the human freedom to use the result for good or ill. To hold that nuclear armaments are a sign of grace has at least one quite positive merit: it points with great force to grace as something which is implicated in every development, that nothing whatever takes place apart from grace, not entirely so.

A theocentric view of grace and a realistic reckoning with the freedom given us in grace will reinforce what we already suspect but are loathe to admit, namely, that the world is not ours; it has not been given to us, nor was it created for us alone. It has an independence from us and the power to exist quite apart from us. If our race perishes, the processes of nature will continue much as though we had never been. The world is not calculable in terms of human purposes, not even in terms of revelation and the faith deriving from it. In revelation God remains precisely God, remains infinite mystery. The mystery is disclosed in revelation but not resolved; if anything, it is heightened.

Within the divine mystery are mysteries, the greatest of which is creative grace, the will of love out of which the worlds were formed and are continued in existence. Every occurrence has its basis in this mystery, including of course our history and such redemptive processes as it contains. Redemption therefore should be understood as an aspect of the divine creative activity. It should be so with us today regardless of the order of thought that pertained in the generations of the biblical writers and the early church theologians, and that continues to shape thought in the present. A transcendence of this order of thought is now not only theologically desirable, it is necessary in view of what we know about ourselves and our situation in the world today, and by proper regard for the theocentric thrust of theology itself. This view would not demean the grace of redemption but give it its wonted setting, include it within the context of creation, apart from which no word of redemptive grace could be heard at any time or in any place.

A more theocentric view would serve to temper, even significantly modify, the presumption concealed, and often only too apparent, in a number of Christian claims in respect to redemptive grace itself. *Extra ecclesiam nulla salus* may no longer be an official teaching of the Roman Catholic Church, but its force lingers on in the pulpits and pews of many parishes here and abroad. The sense of the teaching is especially strong in some of the non-Roman fundamentalist groups, and suggestions of it persistently cling to the outlook of people who belong to mainline Protestant churches, clerical as well as lay. Preaching and teaching generally proceed upon the notion that the grace of redemption belongs to the church or to specifically Christian spheres of influence alone. Theologians and missionaries belonging to both Catholic and Protestant churches have been endeavoring to lessen the force of exclusivist doctrines of grace for some time now, especially during the past two decades. Whether through modification or denial of such doctrines, these theologians call for a more universalistic understanding of grace, as do many missionaries working among non-Christian people. Their call has not yet made much headway at the grass-roots level, but there are signs that, abetted by an awareness and generalized knowledge of the great non-Christian religions on the part of an increasing number of people today, it is beginning to make an impact.

Among those theologians concerned with the issue, John Hick is a prominent figure. His call for "a global theology" is essentially a radical recasting of the doctrine of grace, making it inclusive of the salvific features of all religions. Rather than placing Christianity at the center, Hick says, God must be placed at the center. The affirmations of the various religions present partial accounts, different asepcts of a more complex ultimate reality. He holds that the time is ripe for attempting a "Copernican" theology, for shifting from a "Ptolemaic" standpoint, from the picture of the religious life of humankind as centering upon and culminating in one's own religion to one in which all religions are seen as significant contributions to theological understanding.[7] Hick is not concerned with the possibility of a global *religion* which, he observes, will never come about so long as there is a wide variety of different styles of human existence. His concern is with a global *theology*, a comprehensive theology growing out of a comparison of the theological viewpoints of different religious faiths.

Hick's program is not dissimilar to Wilfred Cantwell Smith's as set forth in *Toward a World Theology*, a perspicacious work dealing with the similarities, convergence, and overlappings of religious stories, myths, and viewpoints of religions the world over and the possibility of a theology of comparative religions. The basic perspective of the work is theocentric: "If Christians insist that Christ is the center of their lives, it is time we rediscover that God is the center of the universe."[8] In my view perspectives such as these point toward the future path of systematic theology, a path it perforce must take.

Although Hick does not have much to say about the grace of nature, a complaint easily raised regarding Smith too, what he says about the grace of redemption implies a more wholistic context, one inclusive of the grounds in creation for the hope of salvation. A more explicit, though more cautiously expressed view is found in the recent writing of James M. Gustafson, an ethicist who finds the basis of ethical thought and theory in theology at every turn. "The first ethical question is never, 'What ought we to do?'; it is 'What is God doing?' "[9] Ethics done in this way is theocentric in principle, Gustafson says. One of the great difficulties with the Christian tradition is, in his view, "the anthropocentric centering of value, enforced by the view that the divine intention is finally focused on our species." When the span of space and time within which the emergence of human life as scientifically explained is taken into account theologically, "a self- and species-interested conviction that the whole has come into being for our sake" is undercut.[10] Gustafson makes it clear that although we are curiously unique creatures in that we can raise the question of our place and value in the world, this fact does not necessarily constitute us as the focus of all value. While he does not speak directly of the doctrine of nature and grace, that doctrine is presupposed in much that he has to say. Far more than Hick or Smith, he realizes that nature *and* grace are at the center of theological concern.

The stance taken here is similar, though with a more decisive emphasis on the grace of nature. With Hick and Smith I am in general agreement, though in one important respect I find it necessary to differ with Smith, though the difference may be marginal. Smith holds that faith is a foundational category for all religions, and indeed for all human life. Few would want to cavil at this, but he goes further, maintaining that faith will be central to the theology of the future, by which he means the theology of comparative religions. It is his descriptive analyses of faith that give rise to the difficulty I have with his position. Faith, he says at one point, is "the relation of man to God, the human response to the divine, the divine gift to man."[11] At another he speaks of faith as "a global human quality" which in the religious history of the world "is a record of God's loving, creative, inspiring dealings with recalcitrant and sinful but not unresponsive men and women."[12] It seems to me that Smith speaks of faith as though it were grace or else moves from one to the other without sufficiently indicating the transition. The two are not identical. Faith is a human response to the divine self-communication in grace. Although faith may be truly termed a divine gift, the divine gift per se is grace, with faith as a means to appropriate the gift. Smith's desire to be theocentric might be better served by focusing on grace rather than faith. Faith is a human phenomenon, whatever the element of gift; grace is God in self-giving and love, the appropriation of which is ancillary to the gift. Grace therefore is a more theocentric category than faith and one better able, I should think, to meet the demands of comparative theology. For phenomenological purposes faith might be more serviceable, but Smith proposes a theological comparison of religions. Grace is essentially theological. It has anthropological dimensions but God is its paramount, really its sole term of reference. If we are serious about a *theology* of religions, should we not place our stress on grace, the operative power of God in relation to the world and to us?[13]

In most of the great religions of the world grace is not a dominant theme and in some it is thematically absent. That knowledge of grace, its conscious objectification, is not a constitutive factor in the self-understanding of most of the world's religions is not to say that there is not experience of grace within them. If grace is absent from them, then God is gracious in relationship to only a fragment of those created and ordinated toward the divine life. The response to grace differs as widely as the cultural contexts in which it is received, we may suppose, but the impact of grace is present and active in all religious responses to the problems and promise of the human condition.

Grace is a biblical category, one that has become a distinctive, if not the distinctive motif of Christianity. To apply the idea of grace to other religions can be an imperialist ploy, an endeavor to grab all of them, conceptually at least, into the Christian net, claiming that there is an implicit Christianity in the non-Christian religions simply waiting to be

crowned and consummated when confronted with the articulation of
grace known and proclaimed in Christianity. It need not and should not
be seen in this way. In looking at another religion and trying to gain
insight into its meaning, Christians must inevitably employ that which is
the key to their own religious self-understanding. Not that this is sufficient for understanding another religion; hard theoretical work and practical study, along with sympathetic regard and self-transcendence, are
necessary if one is to enter into the intricacies of another religion, its
cultural matrix and myriad subtleties that contribute to its ceremonial
forms and living expressions. However true this is, Christians cannot
think that the basic experience entailed in their religion has no relevance
to other religions. By the same token, Christians should readily admit
that the foundational experiences in other religions are not without relevance to their own. Those of other religions seeking to reach insight into
Christianity will necessarily use their own basic experience in the effort.

The use of the category grace by Christians, then, in trying to grasp the
meaning of another religion need not and ought not to be confused with
imperialist aggression. It should be understood as an outcome of the
universalist impulse of Christianity, a very different thing from imperialism. If grace is the key to Christian reality, it has to be in some sense a
universal reality, operative at all levels of existence and certainly in the
higher reaches of the religious life the world over, however obscured by
religious practices and beliefs.

The systematic devaluation of non-Christian religions, so insistently
pursued by Christian thinkers until lately, is now, we may hope, a thing
of the past. What is needed is a means of positively evaluating them. Their
character as interpretations of existence and as religious responses to the
plight and promise of humankind will be found in their own intrinsic
structures of worship and conviction. But from a specifically Christian
perspective, they will be evaluated in terms of whatever signs and symbols, forms and forces betoken the manifestation of divine grace. Again,
this will not be an alien importation into them if grace is indeed universal
in scope, if grace is God in relation to the world and to the human race.
As God has many names, so grace has many different designations. But it
is grace in each case, the divine endeavor to communicate itself to human
beings in varied circumstances and cultural conditions.

This principle applies to Judaism as well as to any other religion.
Jewish thinkers do not speak of grace very much. In my experience, they
speak of it quite sparingly, if at all, in part perhaps because it has become

so entrenched in Christian thought, and in part because some Christian conceptions of grace are couched in terms of power that diminish human responsibility and independent action beyond all possibility of acceptance. Still, grace as divine gift and self-revelation is a prominent feature in Jewish tradition and in Jewish thought and worship today. The covenant is given, Torah is given, the land is given, wisdom is given, blessing is given, and life itself is given. The foundational principle of Judaism finds its locus in divine grace. Human action and obedience arising out of the freedom given in grace are in response to the gracious gifts of God and are expressions of love to the loving creator of all and the One who is believed to have called and to call the Jewish people to a special witness among the nations. Legalism and legalistic practice, however episodically rife or currently real in Jewish religious life, have not and do not obviate the grace that lies at the foundation of Judaism and informs it throughout. Perhaps they express it. At all events, there is no possibility of understanding either the ancient religion of the Jews or Judaism as it has developed in history without recourse to the doctrine of grace.

Christians will evaluate Judaism as they evaluate any other religion—what is there within it of grace? This does not mean that nothing else is of value in Judaism. Christian evaluation of Judaism does not constitute the value of Judaism. Judaism has its own intrinsic value as a distinct religion with its own integrity, its own depths and horizons, theological and ethical ranges of thought, suffering and endurance, vision and hope that are beyond the ken of Christianity. This is something that Christians have not yet learned to accept and appreciate. The proper posture of the Christian before Judaism is one of grateful awe. Such a posture does not rule out critical regard, but any criticism that is leveled against it should be accompanied with appreciation of the first order, together with penitence for the treatment Jews have received at the hands of Christians down through the centuries.

Special appreciation should be accorded the development of the universal character of the divine outreach in early Jewish tradition and its maintenance on down to the present, no small achievement in view of the defeat and persecution the Jewish people have suffered throughout their long history. This universalism has a specificity about it that is lacking in much Christian thought, in which triumphalism tends to be confused with universalism. In Judaic thought the Noachic covenant was and is taken with a seriousness not common among Christians, at least until quite recently. The Noachic covenant is with the whole of humanity, disclosing the divine care and concern for the earth, its people and all other creatures. The retention of the world in being is for all people, as is the blessing from creation at the beginning. With all the tribalistic features of the religion of the Jews, it nevertheless articulated in an explicit fashion one of the most universalistic theological views to be found in religious literature. The leitmotif of this universalism finds its source in ideas and notions that pertain to divine grace and that can be grasped and understood only in the light of an objectified doctrine of grace.

But in Judaism grace is conceived in particularistic terms too, more characteristically so perhaps than in universalistic terms. The premise of special election or chosenness has been a central feature of Jewish religion for thousands of years. The conviction that Israel was God's beloved, that God had singled out the Israelites for special demands and for a special testing, provided hope and assurance in times of difficulty and thus in all probability was the ground for Jewish survival. The Israelites, however, understood the impact of their own free will. They chose God as God chose them. According to the Midrash, they were not the only people who were given the chance of election. The opportunity to accept the gift of the Torah was given to every nation. This was the reason that the Torah was given in the desert, in a place accessible to all. Only Israel said yes to God: "All that the Lord has spoken, we will do."[14] The scriptural witness though makes it clear that the people of Israel from Sinai onwards believed that they were elected, were uniquely under God's care and love. This belief continues in force today for the greater part of the Jewish community.

In orthodox Christianity the idea of divine election received a heightened emphasis. From the people of Israel sprang the Christ, the one elected to be the sole savior of the world. Israel was elected under this view for the coming of the definitively elected one, after the coming of whom the election of Israel passed through him to the Christian community, the new Israel after the Spirit, not the flesh.

Particularity is a marked feature of biblical religion and is a thorny problem for theology. Particularity, however, is not limited to biblical religion. All religions are particular. Each has its distinctive gifts and peculiar modes of thought and practice. Beyond this, particularity is a marked feature of history and indeed of nature itself. Why was the human race "chosen" to become the dominant species on earth? Was it chosen; did not randomness play a part in the process? Why was the world "chosen" out of the other planets of the solar system to be the sole place where life, at least as we know it, develops and thrives? The possibilities for these things were of grace, we may suppose, but were they divinely decreed in such a way that no other possibilities were possible?

When the matter of particularity is taken to history, it is on less speculative grounds. Why, for example, did Plato and the particularity of Platonism arise in ancient Greece and nowhere else? Why did the compassionate teaching of Guatama Buddha take its specific form as one particular man meditated under a particular bo tree in ancient India? Why did Isaac Newton and not some clever Chinese discover the law of gravity? Why did the theory of relativity await the coming of Einstein? Cultural developments of course stood behind the particular figures in history but these developments were themselves particular. They occurred in one milieu and not another, through one set of circumstances and not another.

Particularity belongs to the essence of history. Some events have a particularity about them that prove determinative of the way history unfolds and the way it is understood. Many particularities contribute to the determinative particularity, and each has its own decisiveness in the determination of the events that prove to be particularly decisive. The Christ event was particularly decisive in determining the course of Western culture and self-understanding, not only in terms of the dominance of Christianity as a religion but in preparing for the rise of science. Unforeseen as it was and unwelcomed as well by many Christians, science arose under the particular aegis of Christianity, with of course the convergence of other particular influences, Greek and Islamic, and more remotely Chinese.

The particularity of the Christ event has behind it the particularity of the Hebrew tradition, apart from which it would be totally unintelligible. The Hebrew tradition has behind it the particularities of the Ancient Near Eastern world and and its religions, in terms of which it developed its own particularity and apart from which it would be difficult to determine what all the fuss was about. When the so-called scandal of particularity associated with the Christ event is considered in relation to these particularities and to the particularities that mark historical life as such, just how scandalous is it? It is scandalous for dogma but not for history.

Here again absolutist claims for the Christ event present themselves, and again we must ask whether such claims are absolutely essential for Christian thought, for Christian consciousness to be itself. Absolutistic claims are common enough in religions the world over, but in few if any of them do these claims reach the pitch—often shrill in extreme—that they reach in Christian tradition. Such claims are born of deep devotion and exclusive allegiance and are probably their inevitable concomitant. In their extreme forms, they also reflect imperialism, a drive toward world conquest. As such they are not immune to theological criticism. Does the whole foundation of Christian conviction and life depend upon them? Will all crumble and fall if absolutist standards are subjected to critical scrutiny and shown to be questionable? Many will feel that this is so and will defend these standards with any and every argument at hand, no matter how specious. Others, wishing to remain within the Christian embrace but finding absolutism impossible to maintain, will attempt to interpret Christian claims in the light of the plethora of particularities of history and the grace of God believed to be behind and in them all.

Particularities find their roots in separate histories, tribal propensities, cultural ties, and communal bonds. They are normally linked with the grace of redemption, the special gift to the tribe or larger grouping that ministers to salvation, resignation, wholeness, or whatever. Commonalities on the other hand, at least the more obvious ones, are linked with the grace of nature, those gifts to humankind at large. The question is whether concentration on particularities, normally the rule in religious dialogues, does not need to be veered more toward commonalities. However deep the historical and cultural differences between Christians and Jews, or between Christians and members of other religions, they have more in common than any difference in belief or practice or view of the world can erase. All are human beings together, are alike nourished by the earth, have the same essential needs and will for survival, require community and space for development, love their progeny, share at least some of the same hopes and dreams, and face an identical demise. These commonalities are so common that they are usually overlooked. All also live in the environment of grace, in that which is formative of the commonalities. Nothing is so basic as what human beings have in common. So long as we focus our attention upon our separate histories, differences will loom so large that they will blot out the deep things we have together as human beings. Human commonalities should not be taken for granted. In order to serve for the peace and survival of our race, they need to be attended to consciously, with all deliberation.

Kipling's "East is East and West is West, and never the twain shall meet" loses force when considered in light of the basic structures of human life and human needs. This is not said in the interest of minimizing the great differences that exist between cultures and the barriers to understanding that they pose; it is said to indicate that cultural differences, however profound, do not obviate the basic affinities that pertain through nature.

There are also cultural and historical affinities between East and West that language like Kipling's obscures. Serious theoretical study of Far Eastern religions by Western thinkers has not only disclosed the cleavages between Eastern and Western consciousness and contributed to dissatisfaction with the exploitative tendencies in Western thought, it has sent these thinkers scurrying back to their own tradition in search for trends within it that run counter to the dominancies of Western cultural life. The dominant notes in Eastern culture find echoes in the minor notes of Western culture. It is equally so the other way round.

Jonathan Spence in a review of Guy S. Alittos's *The Last Confucian: Liang Shu-ming and the Chinese Dilemma of Modernity*[15] points to a situation that illustrates this thesis. Lian Shu-ming's most famous work, *Eastern and Western Culture*, first published in 1931, presented a desperate dilemma. In order to survive, China had to westernize itself, yet the range of values and perspectives inherent in Chinese cultural life transcended what the West had to offer. Bereft of such values as those found in China, how could the people of the West, Lian Shu-ming asked, enjoy the powers their modes of thought had enabled them to grasp. To Westerners "it appears," he went on to say, "that nature is indifferent toward people and so they in turn are even more ruthless toward nature, until they have lost entirely their former feelings toward a humanized universe." True as this charge was, Liang Shu-ming saw only the currents of thought that dominated Western culture, not those that ran in a counter direction. By the same token, he did not take into account the undercurrents in Chinese culture that made forms of westernization possible.[16]

We are living in a world that is moving toward a more unified form of life. While cultural and religious differences remain deep, already the world is potentially one from the standpoint of technology. In the future, perhaps the near future, technological unity is likely to become a realized fact. Behind technology is the science that gave it birth. Science more than any other single enterprise transcends cultural boundaries, providing a common thread of identity between cultures and a powerful thrust toward greater unity of understanding and purpose.

Religion lags behind science in drawing the peoples of the earth together. Historically, religion has been among the most divisive agencies in human society, fostering in Bernard Lonergan's fine phrase, "exultant destructiveness."[17] Within its manifold forms, however, religion has a potentiality for serving the world as a unifying force that could equal and maybe go beyond the service that science performs now and will perform in the future. Before this can happen a momentous change in the self-understanding of the religions of the world will have to take place. For one thing each of the great religions of the world will have to recognize that the others are not going away. Hinduism, Buddhism, Islam, Judaism, and Christianity are here to stay, and quite probably Marxism as well.

Christianity tends yet to think that God has promised it the world, even as it is steadily losing ground in the very culture it spawned. It has not yet seen that confrontation with the world religions is not quite on a par with confrontation in the early ages of our era with the mystery religions and decayed state religions of the Mediterranean basin. Missionary success in the ancient world and indeed present success in parts of the world such as Africa cannot be used as an accurate means for predicting future success in respect, say, to a religion so deeply entrenched and deeply effective as Buddhism.

In the Japanese islands, Christianity does poorly. There has been a Christian presence there for centuries, yet less than one percent of the population is Christian, though the Christian influence among the Japanese far exceeds this statistic. As the most westernized of Asian states, attitudes and ideas fostered by Christianity in part have found a place in the Japanese mind, not however without being subjected to Japanization. The Japanese on the whole are probably impervious to conversion in the formal sense, though open to views that might be useful to them and that can be assimilated into their diverse and rich cultural tradition.

Something of the character and savor of Christianity has penetrated into the cultural and religious life of other societies in the East. Religions that tended to despair of the conditions of life now seek to improve them, not only sponsoring hospitals and orphanages along with their Christian counterparts, but actively endeavoring to alter social structures that enslave and impoverish, though such influences derive from Marxism as well as Christianity. Christian "works of charity" have been imitated, at first perhaps in order to curb the competition, but as time passed such imitation became a part of normal procedure. Christian impact of this kind was unintended for the most part. Hospitals and orphanages were established under Christian aegis for two reasons: (1) they were needed and (2) they served as visible signs of the benefits Christianity could provide "heathen lands," and so were important features of the missionary enterprise. That the "heathen" would build similar institutions of their own was almost certainly not envisaged and most probably not welcomed overmuch. Yet however fortuitous, there was an outreach here, as effective in its own way as actual conversions to Christianity.

Until recently Christianity has not been much affected by other religions. With the dawn and then acute interest in ecology and a justified fear of nuclear disaster, the situation changed and with many fruitful results. One of these results derived from detailed studies of Taoism, focusing particularly on its meditative approach to nature. Such studies have had a transforming effect upon the minds of the Christians engaged in them, forcibly indicating that Taoism and other non-Christian religions have something to say to Christianity, something that needs to be heard and reckoned with, and that pertains moreover to the foundational doctrine of nature and grace. What they have to say is often hidden and obscure, and subject to misinterpretation and falsification owing to the filtering mechanisms of Western mentality. But with patience and sympathic concern their lessons can be garnered, and indeed are being garnered.[18]

It is not at all likely that the widely varying views within world religions can be drawn into anything approaching a unified whole. Any such expectation would be excessive and unrealistic. Nor should this be the aim in view. Sharp differences will remain. These very differences may be seen to hold insights that are complementary, means by which the religious consciousness of one group may be challenged and stretched by another, opening up new horizons regarding the nature of grace and the grace of nature. The process entails negative poles as well as positive poles. Negativities toward the idea of grace and negativities toward nature can be as instructive as positive responses. They can discipline affirmations and help to clarify, sharpen, and perhaps modify them. If the religions of the world, however, are indeed responses to the human predicament under the impact of divine grace, positive emphases will be in evidence, awaiting both critical regard and grateful appropriation.

Just as the study of the religions of the world can expand our understanding of the nature of grace, the scientific study of the creative processes of the world can similarly enlarge our understanding of the grace of nature. Owing to an unfortunate history of relationship and to intransigence on the part of theology and lately on the part of science, theology at present is not in a position to do much for science. The old image of science as the enemy is disappearing from the minds of theologians, many of whom have come to regard it as a friend. Suspicion is still rife however and where suspicion is absent, indifference is often the rule. Thinly veiled hostility to science can be discerned even in the works of theologians who formally approve the scientific enterprise and actively utilize its findings in their theological construction. This hostility is occasioned of course by the splendid achievements of science, its very success. The world today is largely the world that science has made. The voice of theology in the midst of the victorious cries of science has been reduced to an emphysemic whisper. The once so-called queen of the sciences is scarcely even a duchess today. Except in fairly rare instances, it is now a discipline for those in the lowest ranks of the professional peerage. In the face of this, pique has arisen among theologians, a pique which lies behind and in part accounts for their hostility to science. Displacement is never easily accepted. Some theologians feel more acutely displaced than others, but a sense of it lurks about in the minds of most, spilling over often as not into their writings. Plain envy not infrequently appears in what they have to say about science, occasionally blatant but usually covert.

Ignorance of science, particularly in its theoretical aspects and reaches, is endemic among theologians. This ignorance seems to pervade the clerical mind generally. Bona fide scientists are rarely found among the clergy; when found, they are likely to be eyed suspiciously if not with hostility, as in the case of Teilhard de Chardin. Part of the difficulty lies in the nature of theological education, where emphasis on the method and theory of the natural sciences receives scant attention, if any at all. Another difficulty lies in the mental bent of those who normally opt for theological education. Candidates for the ordained ministry for the most part have literary and historical interests, though some few with philosophical training still appear at seminary doors. The number of candidates with training or degrees in the social sciences is increasing; while this is an encouraging sign, the number of those schooled in the natural sciences remains very few indeed.

The displacement of theology by science accounts for this paucity of scientifically trained candidates for ministry to an extent hardly to be overestimated. The professional scientific community is among the largest, most cohesive, and rewarding in the world today. It cannot but attract highly gifted and intelligent young people in great numbers. In the days of Thomas Aquinas the church was the central and most inclusive of institutions. It was big business, the biggest of all, the most cohesive, successful, and rewarding community in the Middle Ages, with immense intellectual credibility and scope for the gifted and intelligent. Would someone like Saint Thomas, someone with his gifts and powers, choosing a career today, be likely to opt for a position in the church as theologian, or would he not be attracted to the scientific community or one of its technological offshoots? The question of course cannot be answered; it has point simply because, if nothing else, it can be asked.

A further difficulty has to do with admission policies in seminaries. The seminary in which I teach places little stock in the quantitative part of the Graduate Record Examination, required for admission. The verbal score weighs at least twice as heavily. Applicants with low scores on the quantitative part of the exam will be admitted if their verbal score is sufficiently high to give them an acceptable average. I do not know whether this policy is widespread in seminaries that require the GRE, but strongly suspect that it is. This policy reflects two things: (1) the curriculum is practically devoid of any consideration of the principles of natural science, and (2) those undertaking the curriculum are further entrenched in the nonquantitative, nonscientific mentality they brought to the seminary. The historical, sociological, psychological, and theological sciences are taught with some rigor, and through them something of the methods and aims of the "hard" sciences are operatively present, but scarcely enough to give the student any comprehensive grasp of them.

In view of the dominance of science in our culture, a first call on theological education should be disciplined concern with the sciences, with both the methodology and philosophy of science. At present only half the mind of theological students is being trained in the seminaries. The scientific side is left undeveloped, left to grope its way without the help so urgently needed for ministry in a culture in which science is the chief determinative factor.

Theoretical science and the scientific enterprise generally deal with nature, the forms and forces in the natural realm. Theological education and the Christian church generally tend to be locked into concern for history, the movements and agencies in the historical realm considered to be of grace. The rift between the two realms is thus maintained and strengthened. The onus to construct some sort of bridge between them falls on theology.

An active and knowledgeable appreciation of scientific understanding is essential for the Christian mission, not the whole of it, to be sure, but a crucial part of it in the world we live in today. Those who are to hear the Christian message are imbued with awe of science and its powers, and are enthralled with its technological by-products; they may know about science only by hearsay, but one thing they know and affirm—science is important, both for our knowledge of ourselves and of the world. Many of these people yet have a predisposition toward religion, toward the Christian faith itself. But their minds are deeply divided between allegiance to science and allegiance to religion. More often than not, it is the divided mind to which the proclamation is addressed. Again more often than not, the divided mind is the purveyor of the proclamation, whether from pulpit or lectern. Theological education, with scientific understanding as one of its core features, could do more than a little toward the unification of the minds of the clergy and the minds of those who hear them.

"Truth is one as God is one" is an old adage that needs to be taken more seriously than it commonly is. It behooves Christian theology to recognize and welcome truth from all quarters, among which science is today without parallel. The governing assumptions of the age have their basis in scientific categories, and all of us share in the scientific enterprise insofar as those governing assumptions are our assumptions. Sharing actively and sharing passively, however, are quite different things. Passive sharing has too long been the rule among theologians and leaders in religious life. Explicit and glad recognition of the scientific impulse and proclivity as something belonging intrinsically to being human, and so in a fundamental sense as something reflecting the divine grace, will, and mind, would be a propitious beginning. It would be useful also to recognize that any agency in the world that moves humankind toward cooperation and mutuality as the scientific enterprise manifestly does, even if not unambiguously, must have behind it the operative power of grace. Some thought might be given as well to the possibility that the dominance of science in our time is itself of grace, the given in terms of which theology must work.

The divine mind, if nature tells us anything about it, is supremely mathematical. Given the intricate structure of the simplest cells found in nature and in human nature, this would have to be so if God is creator. And all of us are scientists in that we think and behave scientifically, whether at a prodigiously low level or a very high level. All of us are mathematicians too. Practically everything we do has a mathematical component, from laying out a garden, hanging a picture on a wall, designing a dwelling, making clothing, marking time, constructing plans for social life and its betterment, making machines, planning wars or divising nuclear armaments. We are confronted everywhere with multiplicity, from atomic to cosmic structures, and everywhere we feel the need to enumerate in order to know and in some sense control what we know. The scientific establishment, like the religious establishment, concentrates and intensifies a dimension of life common to all of us. Higher mathematics focuses and brings to great sophistication something that is essentially human, that pertains to our very being in the world, our relation to each other and to the world itself. The scientific, the mathematical bent resident within us and constituent of our reality and activity, must bespeak of the image of God in us.

If it be protested that *imago Dei* is principally found in love, two things (notice the numerical entry) have to be said in response. First, love as humanly known is not without a numerical aspect. We give and take in marriage because we love this one person in a way that we normally love no others; we love a number of things more than we love other things; we love the numberless stars of night; we love the many in the one and the one in the many. Second, while love pertains to every activity in life—the scientists love their particular scientific disciplines and the mathematicians love their mathematical theories and outcomes, else there would be no pursuit of them—it has special relevance to the religious realm of life, where it is emphasized, articulated, and treasured in a way seldom found in other realms. Love, however, is a basic human response, found in all realms of life.

The Christian doctrine of God as love, as self-giving in creation and redemption, has an irreducibly mathematical basis. The natural world is such that creatures able to respond to the love of God have emerged from it, with mathematically structured DNA systems. The natural world and the intricate functioning of the billions of brain cells in human beings are essential to redemption, found centrally for Christians in the one Christ. The mathematical is part and parcel of the *logos* of being, and is therefore inextricably bound up with the *logos* of love. In love God structures natural reality and human reality in a manner (or in manners) that provides for the possibility for the conscious appropriation of the divine life, for Christians again, in the one Christ and his many members in the church.

A number of hopeful signs for the growth of interchange between the scientific and theological communities are afoot just now. One is that the scientific community is less triumphal than in previous decades. It seems more willing to recognize the limitations inherent in scientific knowledge and the affinities in the varying modes of human knowledge to an extent uncommon in the past. Another is the establishment of such institutions as the Luce Center of Theological Inquiry in Princeton. The Luce Center, opened in 1984, invites scholars from around the world and from various disciplines to spend uninterrupted periods of study and research in order to help theology speak to the intellectual requirements of the day and of coming decades.[19] While no immediate results are to be expected from its work, the center is emblematic of a new direction in theology that can be and, one hopes, will be productive of a closer tie between theology and the sciences, perhaps even a new alliance between them and a new, more unified understanding of the relation of nature and grace. One may hope that in time those at the center and places silmilar to it will be able to speak not only of grace in the traditional sense but of mathematical grace, of grace within the scientific realm, or at least of the grace of nature and its structures and forces. The center, in order to be effective, will require some such unifying theological vision, one that affirms the scientific bent in human beings and the scientific enterprise, and recognizes their signifi-cance for understanding and deepening the classical doctrine of *imago Dei* and the gracious elements of nature that provide for it.

Samuel Shem in a recent novel makes much of Isaiah Berlin's *The Hedgehog and the Fox*. Fine, Shem's main character, who seeks a unitary inner vision, a means of making order out of chaos, is discovered to be a hedgehog (like Plato, Dante, Pascal, Dostoevsky, Proust, and many Ger-mans). His soulmate and lover, Stephanie, is a fox, one who accepts the variety of the world (like Aristotle, Homer, Shakespeare, Joyce, and many Mediterraneans). John, a close friend and confidant of both, opines that he (like Tolstoy) sees only the many while searching to see the one, that he is a fox yearning to be a hedgehog.[20] There is point in this distinction, to be sure, but while some of us are more like foxes than hedgehogs and contrariwise, it remains true that the one is sought only on the basis of the many and the many are recognized on the basis of the sense of an encompassing unity. I am a fox and a hedgehog, sometimes more one than the other, as I would guess most of us are in day-to-day life. Yet I need a unifying vision of life and a living out of the vision. I want nature and grace, key categories for me, to be brought into at least a functional unity, with the bearing of each upon the other reaching enough clarity for me to affirm and be able to defend the view that all is of God and God is in all.

The statement "all is of God and God is in all" is not to be taken as

184

positing a formal monistic point of view. It simply says with Augustine at the conclusion of *De vera religione* that God is the One "of whom are all things, by whom are all things, in whom are all things." As argued above, the world does exist independently from God. But if God is God, this independence cannot be absolute, it can only be relative, something accorded to the world by grace, by leave of the divine creative will of love. Within the world are similarly independent forces, the seminal wills in inorganic entities, more manifestly in organic life, and finally will as experienced and known in human life. These independencies again are not outside of the sphere of grace. They are grounded in grace and provisioned by grace. They are, in other words, possibilities through the gracious action of God. If they are considered outside of the sphere of grace in terms of their origin and even their broad effects, there is a split in reality that makes nature and grace irrelative, something I take to be theologically inadmissible.

Dualism and monism constitute a fundamental dichotomy. Neither one, so far as I can see, has a complete edge on truth. Both say things that ring true in our experience, and we need to try to use the insights afforded by both as effectively as we can, allowing biblical faith in God's grace to season and crown the mix. In this work I have called for a functional unity of nature and grace. Such a unity is not to be confused with identity. We distinguish between nature and grace in our own experience of re-calcitrant wills wooed by the divine will of love, of the passions and aberrations of social life in the face of ameliorating forces and of the devastating powers and processes of nature alongside its hospitality to human life. Frequently our experience leads us to the point of separating nature from grace, making an explicit duality of them. But if there is any such thing as the grace of nature—and I think that there is—this duality presses the matter much too far, throwing us back to the *gratia non tollit naturam sed perficit* formula with its implication that nature is one thing, grace quite another.

Theologians and philosophers, for a variety of reasons and experiences, have of course different intellectual proclivities and psychological tendencies. Some thinkers tend toward dualism, others toward monism, with many variations in between. These tendencies, shaped and furthered by the turns and events of life, can be raised to ontological status. For my part, I would no more want to raise monism to such a status than I would dualism. I insist with the best of dualists that there are independencies of and in the world. On the other hand, I have to insist that these independencies are created and so finally dependent on the grace of God.

Rather than duality, it might be more serviceable to speak of the bipolarity of nature and grace, of two poles within the one created order. This image has some merit, but it might easily mislead the mind into distancing nature from grace as from the north and south poles of the earth. If however the poles of the earth are understood not simply as different sides of the planet but as interconnected and equally essential configurations for its inhabitability, for the emergence and nurture of life, the image might further us.

The relation of nature and grace is one of the final mysteries of theology. The considerations in this work have not been put forward as a solution to this supremely complex problem. I have simply tried through these studies, quite limited and hardly taking into account all the literature on the issue or issues related to it,[21] to suggest some possibilities for theological reflection that might lead toward a more integral perspective on the matter. While it seems clear to me that the old duality will not serve in our time, it is less clear what alternative or alternatives might emerge. Chances are good however that emergent views will take the relation of nature and grace to be less divisible than in the theologies of the past. If it should prove too much to claim that grace is present and active in the whole creation, microorganistically as well as macrocosmically, the question might well arise whether theology has anywhere to go beyond its present impasse.

It is manifest that the redemptive processes of our history are as a moment in the vast reaches of the history of nature. Without nature and its processes, there would be nothing in our history, nothing at all. This fact constrains us to do whatever we can to see to it that nature becomes an urgent, central concern in theology. We are, I believe, called upon to see nature in the light of grace and grace in the light of nature, not as divorcible, not as idéntical, but as inseparably related and indeed as intertwined in creation. We need to see the physical world as a community with the human community as part of it, and to see the whole as not only in grace, but of grace.

Notes

Chapter 1. Augustine and the West

1. *Nature and Grace* 12. All translations are from Whitney J. Oates, ed., *Basic Writings of St. Augustine* (New York: Random House, 1948), vols. 1 and 2, unless otherwise noted.

2. *On the Spirit and the Letter* 47.

3. *Retractions* 68, 63, trans. M. I. Bogan, in *Fathers of the Church* (Washington, D.C.: Catholic University Press, 1968), vol. 60. Also see *Letter* cxxxiii and cxlv, trans. J. G. Cunningham, in Philip Schaff, ed., *Nicene and Post-Nicene Fathers of the Church* (Buffalo, NY: Christian Literature Company, 1886), vol. 1, for a discussion of the relation of grace and will.

4. *Predestination of the Saints* 10. In *On the Spirit and the Letter* 42, however, he quotes one of his earlier tracts, *De peccat. meritis* ii. 7: "I should have no doubt that free will is of grace—that is, it has its place among the gifts of God—not only as to its existence, but also in respect of its goodness." This viewpoint diminishes in force the deeper Augustine gets into controversy with the Pelagians.

5. *Nature and Grace* 12: "He, Pelagius, has not posited anything as we wish to have understood by grace. . . . This is a topic which is concerned about the cure, not the constitution of natural functions."

6. *City of God* XIII.13, trans. Marcus Dods, Modern Library ed. (New York: Random House, 1958).

7. Ibid. XIII. 24.

8. Ibid. XI. 21, 22.

9. See *Confessions* I.ii.2, II.ii.3, ed. E. B. Pusey (London: J. M. Dent, 1950). Note especially III.v.2: "But you were more inward to me than my inward parts"; IV.iv.7: "But behold you were close on the steps of your fugitives"; V.ii.2: "And you were before me, though I had gone away from you."

10. *Nature and Grace* 54.

11. *Predestination of the Saints* 19.

12. "I should have no doubt that free will is of grace." See n. 4 above.

13. *On the Grace of Christ* 25. The intimately interior quality of grace is perhaps best demonstrated in Augustine's virtual equation of it with the operation of the Holy Spirit within the human mind and heart in *On the Spirit and the Letter* 36: "What then is God's law written by God Himself in the hearts of men, but the very presence of the Holy Spirit."

14. *On the Profit of Believing* 34.

15. *On the Nature of the Good* 3–5 and throughout, but note particularly 13, in which the rapturous tone reaches its peak: "all things both great and small . . . whether spiritual or corporeal, every measure, every form, every order . . . are from the Lord God." Also see *The City of God* xxi. 4, where he exhibits a keen appreciation for natural facts.

16. *City of God* xxii. 24: "What wonderful—one might say stupefying—advances has human industry made in the arts of weaving and building, of agriculture and navigation! With what endless variety are designs in pottery, painting, and sculpture produced, and with what skill executed!" This is only a sample. Augustine goes in a similar vein at great length.

17. *Enchiridion* 9.

18. *Confessions* X.xxxv.55; V.iv.7. Also see *Morals of the Catholic Church* 21 and *The Literal Meaning of Genesis* I.ii.33 (trans. John H. Taylor [New York: Newman Press, 1982], vol. 1), in which Augustine displays much interest in the scientific theories of his time.

19. *St. Augustine on the Psalms*, trans. S. Hebgin and F. Corrigan, in Johannes Quaster and Walter Burkhardt, eds., *Ancient Christian Writers* (London: Longmans, Green, 1960), vol. 1, pp. 230ff. In the case of Ps. 19, ibid., pp. 183–85, the glory the heavens show forth is said to be that "glory of God by which we have been saved, by which we have been created in good works." Indeed, "The heavens are the saints, poised above the earth, bearing the Lord." Following this, Augustine enters, as if by title, "Yet the sky, too, after its fashion, has proclaimed the glory of Christ." The whole thrust of the discussion pertains to the grace of redemption with minimal regard for creation.

20. *Confessions* X.vi.9, n.l. p. 228.

21. Ibid., X.vi.8–10, the whole of which is concerned to make this clear.

22. *On the Spirit and the Letter* v. 36.

23. *Grace and Free Will* 44, 45; *Predestination of the Saints* 23.

24. *Grace and Free Will* 41, 43, is among the most direct statements of this doctrine.

25. *Confessions* XIII.ix.10. Also see *City of God* xi.28.

26. Ibid., II.vi.14; see also *Morals of the Catholic Church* 12.

27. *Letter* cxlv. 3.7; lxxxii. 20 (to Jerome); xcii. 1 (to Italica); clxxxviii. 1.3 (to Juliana); clxxxix. 2 (to Boniface); *Enchiridion* 117; *On Forgiveness of Sin and Baptism* 11, 27; *Nature and Grace* 18, 49, 67, 79; *On the Spirit and the Letter* 6, 56, 60, and *On Original Sin* 28.

28. *On the Trinity* xv. 17, 26.

29. *On Grace and Free Will* 25.

30. Ibid.

31. *On the Trinity* iv. 1.

32. George S. Hendry, *Theology of Nature* (Philadelphia: Westminster, 1980),

p. 17. Hendry quotes Luther's exposition of the first article of the Creed in his Small Catechism of 1529 where creation is merged with providence *pro me* ("I believe that God has created me and all that exists; that he has given me and still sustains body and soul, all my limbs and senses, my reason and all faculties of mind . . . that he provides me . . . with all the necessities of life, protects me from all danger and preserves me from all evil.") and comments thus: "The simple piety of this statement conceals a presumption and impiety, for it makes it appear that the entire furniture of creation has been put there for my sake." He goes on to point to the Heidelberg Catechism's two separate questions on creation and providence (Qq. 26, 27) and notes that both are answered in terms of providence: "There is no suggestion that the world of nature might have any theological significance apart from its providential service to man."

33. See *On the Teacher* xiii. 13 and 24; *City of God* xi. 26: "I am most certain that I am, and that I know and delight in this . . . if I am deceived, I am . . . as I know that I am, so I know this also, that I know." Descartes says that he had not been previously aware of such statements as these and that while the principle may be identical with his own, the consequences which he adduces from it, and its position as the ground of a philosophical system, make the characteristic difference between Augustine and himself. See John Veitch, ed. and trans., *The Method, Meditations and Selections from the Principles of Descartes*, 12th ed. (Edinburgh and London: W. Blackwood, 1899), p. 164. Veitch himself adds that Descartes belonged to a school of nonreading philosophers and cared little for what had been said before. Despite these disclaimers, it is hard to believe that any educated person of Descartes's time was unfamiliar with *De civitate dei*, and even harder to believe that any such person was not aware that "someone" had previously posited the views we know to be Augustine's. The resemblance between Descartes's words and Augustine's is too striking to be purely coincidental. Even the *si fallor sum* argument finds expression in Descartes's *Meditations* 6 (Veitch ed., p. 161): "Even if what I imagine is untrue, still I imagine."

34. *Meditations on the First Philosophy* 6 (Veitch ed., p. 164). Descartes was not able to state very "clearly and distinctly" how "extended substances" and "thinking substances" were related, especially in the case of human thought and the human brain, and resorted to the grace of God as that which provided the link between them. The implications of this solution were left undeveloped. Also see *The Principles of Philosophy* 5 (Veitch ed., pp. 233–34), for further discussions of the mind-body duality.

35. Carl J. Friedrich, ed., *Immanuel Kant's Moral and Political Philosophy* (New York: Modern Library, 1949), pp. xxiv, xl.

36. Karl Löwith, *Nature, History and Existentialism*, ed. Arnold Levison (Evanston: Northwestern University Press, 1966), p. 201. Cited as Löwith hereafter. Löwith goes on to note that Hegel, to make his point even sharper, remarked that all the wonders of starlight are nothing in comparison with the

most criminal thought of a human being because only man as *spirit* knows himself. An example of Hegel's theoretical development of man as spirit is found in his *Lectures on the Philosophy of Religion*, ed. E. B. Speirs (London: K. Paul, Trench and Trubner, 1895; trans. of 2nd German ed.), vol. 3, pp. 42ff.

37. H. R. Mackintosh and J. S. Stewart, eds., *The Christian Faith* (New York: Harper & Row, 1963; trans. of 2nd German ed.), vol. 1, p. 234.

38. Ibid., I, p. 262.

39. H. R. Mackintosh and A. B. Macaulay, eds., *The Christian Doctrine of Justification and Reconciliation* (New York: Charles Scribner's Sons, 1900), p. 20.

40. Ibid., pp. 609ff., 612.

41. R. W. Stewart, ed., *The Communion of the Christian with God* (London: Williams and Norgate, 1903; trans. of 2nd German ed.), p. 20. Also see his lectures posthumously trans. and ed. Nathaniel Micklem and Kenneth Saunders, *Systematic Theology* (London: Allen and Unwin, 1927), esp. pp. 21–33.

42. *The Communion of the Christian with God*, p. 32.

43. Löwith, pp. 105–6. "It is not a 'failure of nerve' (as has been suggested) which brought existentialism into existence. What failed us was not our nerve, but rather our belief in a divinely ordered universe in which man could feel himself at home. . . . No social order of whatever kind, not even order in the universe, can substitute for this. Hence, we have indeed 'to be,' or exist, in all those descriptive terms of sheer factuality, contingency, and absurdity which existentialism has brought to light."

44. Ibid., p. 104.

45. Ibid.

46. *Philosophical Fragments*, trans. David F. Swensen, (Princeton: Princeton University Press, 1936), pp. 51, 87: "If the contemporary generation had left behind them nothing but the words, 'we have believed that in such and such a year God appeared among us in the humble figure of a servant, that He lived and taught in our community, and finally died,' it would be more than enough."

47. *Capital*, Engels ed. (New York: Humbladt, 1908; trans. of 3rd German Edition), i, pp. 4, 12.

48. Löwith, pp. 141–42.

49. *Basic Questions in Theology* (London: SCM Press, 1971), vol. 1, p. 102.

50. Löwith's *Nature, History and Existentialism* was a chief inspirant and source for this study. I owe much to the insights and deliberations of this book, the significance of which, it seems to me, has not been sufficiently recognized. The idea of discussing nature and history in relation to grace is my own. Löwith has nothing to say about Augustine or grace and his critical remarks about some of the writers I deal with, e.g., Kant, Hegel, Kierkegaard, and Marx, do not have the same purpose as that developed above.

Chapter 2. Irenaeus and the East

1. *Against Heresies* II. i. 1. The actual title of this tract, Irenaeus's major work, is *A Refutation and Subversion of Knowledge Falsely So Called*. The text used here

is Alexander Roberts and James Donaldson, eds., *Ante-Nicene Fathers* (Boston: Christian Literature Company, 1885), vol. 1, compared with the Cambridge edition of W. Harvey, 1857. On the quotation in my text, see further J. Armitage Robinson, ed., *St. Irenaeus: The Demonstration of the Apostolic Preaching* (New York: Macmillan, 1920), pp. 4, 6; cited afterwards as *Apostolic Preaching*. Irenaeus's chief complaint about Gnosticism throughout is that "it splits God in two."

2. *Against Heresies* III. xxv. 5. See H. B. Timothy, *The Early Christian Apologists and Greek Philosophy* (Assen: Van Gorcum, 1973), p. 83, who points out that Irenaeus was not so strictly biblical as often claimed.

3. *Against Heresies* III. xvi. 6.

4. Ibid., II. xxviii. 2; II. ii. 4.

5. Ibid., II. xxviii. 2.

6. Ibid., II. xxvi. 1: "It is therefore better and more profitable to belong to the simple and unlettered class, and by means of love to attain to nearness of God, than, by imagining ourselves learned and skillful, to be found blasphemous."

7. Ibid., V. xvi. 1; IV. xvii. 1.

8. Ibid., IV. xx. 1.

9. Ibid., II. xxviii. 5; see Richard A. Norris, *God and World in Early Christian Theology* (New York: Seabury, 1965), p. 88.

10. *Against Heresies* II. xxviii. 5.

11. Ibid., IV. xx. 3.

12. Ibid., V. vi. 6.

13. Ibid., III. xv. 6, 7; xiv. 7; xx. 4.

14. Ibid., IV. xx. 7.

15. Ibid., IV.xxxiii. 4; V.vi. 1.

16. Ibid., IV. xxxviii. 1; see *Apostolic Preaching* 14, where Irenaeus speaks more strongly on the matter of the innocence of Adam and Eve before the fall. "At that time entire, preserving their own nature," they had "no comprehension and understanding of things that are base."

17. *Against Heresies* III. xii. 13.

18. Ibid., III. xxiii. 8.

19. Ibid., III. xxiii. 3; *Apostolic Preaching* 16.

20. *Against Heresies* III. xxiii. 5; IV. xl. 3.

21. Ibid. In the *Apostolic Preaching* 17ff., the effect of the curse upon the ground is more prominent than in *Against Heresies,* but the note of compassion is everywhere present.

22. Ibid., III. xxiii. 6.

23. Ibid., III. xx, 1.

24. *Apostolic Preaching* 37; *Against Heresies* III. xxiii. 7.

25. Ibid.; *Apostolic Preaching* 97.

26. *Against Heresies* III. xxiii. 1; V. xxi. 3.

27. Ibid., III. xxiii, 2–4.

28. Ibid., V. xxvi. 1–2. John Lawson, *The Biblical Theology of St. Irenaeus* (London: Epworth Press, 1948), p. 216, holds that Irenaeus does not teach original sin "in the proper sense of the word." Original sin for him is grievous disbelief, not that which occasions guilt. It is not easy to assent to this view entirely since for Irenaeus Adam is responsible for his loss of life and must therefore be in some sense guilty.

29. *Against Heresies* V. i. 3.

30. Ibid., V. iii. 3.

31. Ibid., V. vi. 1; V. xvi. 2. See Lawson, pp. 200ff., on this issue.

32. Ibid., IV. xxii. 2.

33. Ibid., III. xxv. 1.

34. Irenaeus is not completely consistent in affirming this. In the *Apostolic Preaching* 5, he says that "the whole creation is embraced by the Spirit of God" and that "the Word is universally extended in all the world" (101). Yet at another point (89) he speaks of a "wilderness and a waterless place" as "at first the calling of the Gentiles: for the Word had not passed through them, nor given them the Holy Spirit to drink." Though he goes on to speak of a new calling and change of heart, indicating that he has reference here to redemption, at the same time he seems to say that the Gentiles were without the Word and Spirit before called to redemption, which denies one of his general theological premises. In *Against Heresies* II. ix. 1, and III. xvi. 6, for example, he is more consistent.

35. *Against Heresies* IV. xxi. 4. See Lawson, p. 234, on the distinction between the moral and ceremonial law.

36. *Against Heresies* IV. ii. 3.

37. Ibid., IV. xii. 4.

38. Ibid., III. v. 2.

39. Ibid., IV. xxviii. 3.

40. Ibid., V. xxiv. 2.

41. Ibid., III. xxiv. 1.

42. Ibid., V. xxvi. 2.

43. Ibid., V. ii. 2–3.

44. Ibid., V. vi. 1; V. xvi. 2.

45. Ibid., V. ix. 4; V. xii. 1; V. xiv. 4.

46. Ibid., V. xxxvi. 1.

47. Ibid., V. xxxvi. 3.

48. Ibid., V. xxxiii, 3; V. xxxv. 2.

49. Ibid., IV. xxxviii. 1, 3, and 4.

50. Ibid., V. xxxvi. 2–3.

51. Ibid., III. xxi. 10.

52. Ibid., V. xix. 1; IV. v. 1.

53. Ibid., IV. xxxviii. 1.

54. But see Gustaf Wingren, *Man and the Incarnation: A Study in the Biblical Theology of Irenaeus* (London: Oliver and Boyd, 1959), p. 47, who says that Irenaeus held that Christ was the "purpose of creation" as well as its "primary cause," citing *Against Heresies* III. xxxii. 1. I cannot locate the exact citation. It might be anyway that Wingren is providing an interpretation for one of the many statements Irenaeus makes that imply this.

55. *Against Heresies* III. xviii. 6 and xxi. 9.

56. Ibid., IV. xviii. 4, citing Mk. 4:28.

57. Ibid., II. xxviii. 2. It is a curious fact that Augustine demonstrates a vastly greater interest in created entities than Irenaeus though his doctrinal evaluation of them in terms of grace is much less high.

58. Gregory of Nyssa *Oration on Baptism* 46; Basil *Against Eunomius* 39, cited in Nicholas N. Glaubokowsky, "Grace in the Greek Fathers," in W. T. Whitley, ed., *The Doctrine of Grace* (London: SCM Press, 1932), pp. 66–67, cited afterwards as Glaubokowsky. This article, although somewhat euphoric, is a fine discussion and summary of the idea of grace in the Eastern tradition.

59. *Homilies on the Gospel of John* 14.2, in Glaubokowsky, pp. 63–64.

60. Gregory of Nyssa *Orations on the Great Catechism* 34; Gregory the Theologian *Orations on Holy Baptism* 40.7, and Macarius of Egypt, *Homily* 16.4, in Glaubokowsky, pp. 72–73.

61. *Orations on the Great Catechism* 8, in Glaubokowsky, p. 72.

62. John of Damascus *The Orthodox Faith* 2.30, in Glaubokowsky, p. 82.

63. *Against Eunomius* 5, in Glaubokowsky, p. 67.

64. *Against Heresies* V. xii. 6.

65. "The Desanctification of Nature," in Derek Baker, ed., *Sanctity and Secularity* (Oxford: Basil Blackwell, 1973), pp. 1–2. Also see John Meyerdorff, *Living Tradition: Orthodox Witness in a Changing World* (Crestwood, NY: St. Vladimir Press, 1978), for a critical discussion of the dichotomy of nature and grace in Augustine.

66. "The Desanctification of Nature," p. 3.

67. Ibid., p. 4.

68. Gregory Nazianzus *Oration* xxviii. 29, cited in D. S. Wallace-Hadrill, *The Greek Patristic View of Nature* (Manchester: University of Manchester Press, 1968), p. 4.

69. *Hexaemenon* ix.1.188c–189a, cited in Wallace-Hadrill, p. 7.

70. *Oration* ii. 22, in Philip Schaft and Henry Ware, eds., *A Select Library of Nicene and Post-Nicene Fathers*, 2nd series, vol. 7, trans. Charles Gordon Browne and James Edward Swallow (Grand Rapids: Eerdmans, 1955).

71. Wallace-Hadrill, p. 36: "Nature was of great importance to the fathers, but almost always for some reason other than the pursuit of scientific knowledge."

72. J. T. Nielsen, *Adam and Christ in the Theology of Irenaeus of Lyons*

(Assen: Van Gorcum, 1968), pp. 62, 8, 76. Lawson, p. 216, tends to agree with Nielson, but Wingren, pp. 52ff., presents a more balanced view.

73. N. P. Williams, *The Grace of God* (London: Longmans, Green, 1930), pp. 15–16.

Chapter 3. Tillich and the Multidimensional Unity of Life

1. *Systematic Theology* (Chicago: University of Chicago Press, 1963), vol. 3, p. 18.

2. "Autobiographical Reflections," Charles W. Kegley and Robert W. Bretall, eds., *The Theology of Paul Tillich* (New York: Macmillan, 1961), pp. 4–5.

3. *The Protestant Era* (Chicago: University of Chicago Press, 1948), pp. 102–3. The whole section on "Nature and Sacrament," pp. 94ff., is relevant to the situation today.

4. *Systematic Theology* (Chicago: University of Chicago Press, 1951), vol. 1, p. 131.

5. Ibid., pp. 81–82; cf. further, pp. 75–79. Tillich bases this view on Nicolaus Cusanus's *docta ignorantia*.

6. Ibid., p. 94.

7. Ibid., pp. 108–11.

8. Ibid., p. 118.

9. *Systematic Theology*, vol. 3, pp. 12–15.

10. Ibid., p. 19.

11. Ibid., pp. 20–21.

12. Ibid., p. 21.

13. Ibid., p. 24.

14. Ibid., p. 38.

15. Ibid., p. 39.

16. Ibid., pp. 40–41. Tillich notes here that "community itself is a phenomenon of life which has analogies in all realms. It is implied by the polarity of individualization and participation. Neither pole is actual without the other."

17. Ibid., p. 26.

18. Ibid.

19. Ibid., pp. 26–27. These conclusions are derived from an analysis of cognitive and moral acts. A sentence illustrating the trend of thought is this: "The transcendence of the center over the psychological material makes the cognitive act possible, and such an act is a manifestation of spirit."

20. Ibid., pp. 27–28.

21. Ibid., pp. 34 and 74.

22. Ibid., pp. 34–35.

23. Ibid., p. 36.

24. Ibid., pp. 53–54.

25. Ibid.

26. Ibid., p. 200.

27. Ibid., pp. 84–85: "Spirit and man are bound to each other, and only in man does the universe reach up to an anticipatory and fragmentary fulfilment."

28. Ibid., p. 305.

29. Ibid., p. 307.

30. Ibid., p. 108.

31. Ibid., p. 118.

32. Ibid., pp. 359, 375, 377.

33. Ibid., p. 401.

34. Ibid., p. 399: "For God cannot deny himself, and everything positive is an expression of being itself. And since there is nothing merely negative (the negative lives from the positive it distorts) nothing that has being can be ultimately annihilated."

35. *Perspectives on Nineteenth and Twentieth Century Protestant Thought* (London: SCM Press, 1967), p. 126.

36. Ibid.

37. Ibid., p. 162.

38. *Systematic Theology*, vol. 1, p. 176. "There are microcosmic qualities in every being but man alone is *microcosmos*." The use of the metaphor of "level" is, as noted above, rejected in the third volume.

39. Ibid., p. 261.

40. Ibid., p. 176.

41. Ibid., pp. 176–77. Tillich goes on to speak of the necessity of the self's encounter with other selves in terms of resistance in order to prevent every self from trying to make itself absolute. "The individual discovers himself through this resistance. If he does not want to destroy the other person, he must enter into communion with him. In the resistance of the other person, the person is born. . . . Individualization and participation are interdependent on all levels of being."

42. *Systematic Theology* (Chicago: University of Chicago Press, 1957), vol. 2, p. 43.

43. Ibid., pp. 95–96.

44. Ibid., p. 96. Tillich speaks here to the possibility of the manifestation of grace in "other worlds," making two major points: (1) "Man cannot claim to occupy the only possible place for Incarnation"; and (2) "The manifestation of saving power in one place implies that saving power is operating in all places. . . . The Messiah as the bearer of the New Being presupposes that 'God loves the universe,' even though in the appearance of the Christ he actualized this love for historical man alone."

45. Ibid., p. 100.

46. *Systematic Theology*, vol. 1, p. 285.

47. Ibid.

48. Cf. *The Protestant Era*, pp. 132ff., and esp. pp. 207–9, which deal with the concept of a *Gestalt* of grace; see further, *Systematic Theology*, vol. 1, pp. 258, 285, and in vol. 2, pp. 48–49, 125, and 177–79, which concern "justification by grace through faith."

49. *Systematic Theology*, vol. 3, p. 274.

50. Ibid.

51. Ibid. "The very term 'grace' indicates that it is not the product of any act of good will on the part of him who receives it but that it is given gratuitously, without merit." Note further, p. 112: "Man in his self-transcendence can reach for it [the Spiritual Presence], but man cannot grasp it unless he is first grasped by it."

52. *Systematic Theology*, vol. 1, p. 250.

53. *Systematic Theology*, vol. 3, p. 275.

54. Ibid., p. 276.

55. Cf. Stephen Jay Gould, "The Importance of Trifles," *Natural History*, vol. 91, no. 4 (April 1982): 16ff., for an intriguing account of Darwin's close observation of worms.

56. *Systematic Theology*, vol. 1, p. 258.

57. Ibid., pp. 263–64.

58. Ibid., p. 252.

59. Ibid., pp. 134–35. The entire section should be read for several reasons: (1) to discern the finer nuances of thought, (2) to note Tillich's passion regarding the matter, and (3) to sense something of his struggle for clarity. Also see his discussion of the issue in *Christianity and the Encounter of World Religions* (New York: Columbia University Press, 1963), p. 81f.

60. Cf. *The Future of Religions* (New York: Harper & Row, 1966), pp. 31, 80ff.

61. Ibid., p. 81.

62. Alexander J. McKelway, *The Systematic Theology of Paul Tillich* (New York: Dell Publishing Co., 1964), p. 96.

63. Ibid., p. 177.

64. *What Is Religion* (New York: Harper & Row, 1969), p. 174.

65. Ibid.

66. Ibid., pp. 174–75. Also see, *Perspectives on Nineteenth and Twentieth Century Thought*, p. 35f.

67. *Systematic Theology*, vol. 3, p. 5.

68. Kegley and Bretall, op. cit., pp. 63–64. Also see *Systematic Theology*, vol. 3, p. 74, where Tillich addresses the ecological problem directly.

Chapter 4. Rahner on Nature and Grace and Related Issues

1. "Nature and Grace," *Theological Investigations* (New York: Seabury, 1966), vol. 4, p. 183; trans. from *Schriften zur Theologie*, IV (Einsiedeln: Verlagsanstalt Benziger and Co., A. G.) by Kevin Smyth. All volumes of the *Theological Investigations* (hereafter, T.I.) were first published in German by Benziger, begin-

ning with vol. 1 in 1954, and in English by Darton, Longmans and Todd, from 1961–79. The American edition, Seabury Press (vol. 1, 1974; vol. 2, 1975; vol. 7, n.d., first published by Darton, Longmans and Todd, 1971; vol. 8, 1977; vol. 9, n.d., first published by Darton, Longmans and Todd, 1972; vol. 10, 1977; vol. 11, n.d., first published by Darton, Longmans and Todd, 1974; vol. 12, 1974; vol. 13, 1975; vol. 14, 1976, and vol. 16, 1979), was used here. Translations were by Cornelius Ernst Kruger (vols. 3, 6), Kevin Smyth (vol. 4), David Bourke (vols. 7, 8, 9, 10, 11, 12, 13), Graham Harrison (vol. 9), and David Moreland (vol. 16).

2. "Concerning the Relationship between Nature and Grace," (hereafter abbreviated "Concerning Nature and Grace"), T.I., vol. 1, p. 300; "Some Implications of the Scholastic Concept of Uncreated Grace," T.I., vol. 1, p. 334; "Nature and Grace," T.I., vol. 4, p. 175; "God communicates himself to man in his own proper reality."

3. "Concerning Nature and Grace," T.I., vol. 1, p. 302. See "Nature and Grace," T.I., vol. 4, p. 178.

4. "Concerning Nature and Grace," T.I., vol. 1, p. 303.

5. "Nature and Grace," T.I., vol. 4, pp. 183–84.

6. Ibid. Juan Alfaro, "Nature and Grace" in Karl Rahner et al., eds., *Sacramentum Mundi: An Encyclopedia of Theology* (New York: Herder and Herder, 1968), vol. 4, p. 177, puts it this way: "All dualism between nature and grace is radically eliminated because human beings do not exist except as intrinsically ordained by grace to the vision of God as their end, the only final end of their nature."

7. "Concerning Nature and Grace," T.I., vol. 1, p. 315. In his article "Grace," *Sacramentum Mundi*, vol. 2, p. 417, Rahner says that nature "is that reality which the divine self-communication creatively posits for itself as its possible partner in such a way that in relation to it that communication can and does remain what it is: a free and loving favor." The possibility of partnership here mentioned poses a certain dualistic element, one that may be unavoidable, even if it is simply moral.

8. "Nature and Grace," *Sacramentum Mundi*, vol. 2, pp. 412, 417.

9. "Questions of the Controversial Theology of Justification," T.I., vol. 4, pp. 213–14.

10. Ibid., p. 216. If communication of the Spirit is grace in the "strictest sense," was the "brooding" of the Spirit over the waters at creation grace in an "imprecise" or "vague" or "unstrict" sense?

11. Ibid., pp. 212–14; "Concerning Nature and Grace," T.I., vol. 1, p. 311.

12. "Grace," *Sacramentum Mundi*, vol. 2, pp. 416–17.

13. "Concerning Nature and Grace," T.I., vol. 1, p. 310. The term *unexacted* is not fortunate. *Gratuity* is on all counts preferable.

14. "Grace," *Sacramentum Mundi*, vol. 2, pp. 416–17.

15. "Questions on the Controversial Theology of Justification," T.I., vol. 4, pp. 216, 217–18.

16. See "Philosophy and Theology," T.I., vol. 6, pp. 72, 74.

17. Ibid., p. 75. This same principle is developed in Rahner's understanding of the relation of revelation and faith. Faith as the reception of revelation is already theology, inchoate as it might be. Although itself strictly a divine gift, faith must be received and experienced in a definable individuality and historical situation. One cannot hear a truth without assimilating it, confronting it with the rest of one's mind and consciousness. In this sense Rahner says, in "Theology in the New Testament," T.I., vol. 5, p. 28, that theology "begins already in the first moment of hearing itself."

18. "Theology and Anthropology," T.I., vol. 9, pp. 35ff; "Nature and Grace," T.I., vol. 4, pp. 169–70.

19. "History of the World and Salvation History," T.I., vol. 5, p. 97; "Philosophy and Theology," T.I., vol. 6, p. 76; "The Church, the Churches and Religion," T.I., vol. 10, p. 39: "The whole salvation history and revelation history of mankind is coexistent with the history of mankind as personal and spiritual and with all that is morally good in this." Cf. his *Foundations of Christian Faith* (New York: Crossroad, 1978), pp. 138ff; originally published in German in 1976. This volume incorporates material from T.I. and includes some new material as well. It serves as a reasonably good introduction to Rahner's thought.

20. Cf. "Philosophy and Theology," T.I., vol. 6, p. 81.

21. Ibid., p. 79.

22. Ibid., pp. 77–78; cf. Karl Rahner and Joseph Ratzinger, *Revelation and Tradition* (New York: Herder and Herder, 1966), p. 22.

23. "*Theos* in the New Testament," T.I., vol. 1, p. 98; "Observations on the Problem of the 'Anonymous Christian,'" T.I., vol. 14, p. 280.

24. Ibid., pp. 289–90.

25. Ibid., p. 291.

26. "Anonymous Christians," T.I., vol. 6, pp. 391ff.

27. "Observations on the Problem of Anonymous Christians," T.I., vol. 14, pp. 281ff.; cf. "Atheism and Implicit Christianity," T.I., vol. 9, pp. 149, 152.

28. "Anonymous Christians," T.I., vol. 6, pp. 392, 394. Rahner here repeats the view expressed throughout his essays that "although capable of hearing the divine call and positively expecting it, no one has the least right to demand it." Human openness for grace, though itself of grace in the sense of the grace of creation, is not to be confused with salvific grace, which is divine self-bestowal, and perforce utterly gratuitous.

29. "Anonymous Christianity and the Missionary Task of the Church," T.I., vol. 12, p. 174.

30. This is true of his discussions of atheism and secularism. Cf. "Atheism and Implicit Christianity," T.I., vol. 9, pp. 145ff., and "Considerations on Secularization and Atheism," T.I., vol. 11, pp. 167ff.

31. "Anonymous Christianity and the Missionary Task of the Church," T.I.,

vol. 12, pp. 173–75; "Thoughts on the Possibility of Belief Today," T.I., vol. 5, pp. 9–11.

32. "Christianity and Non-Christian Religions," T.I., vol. 5, pp. 23ff. The social dimension of life becomes more and more prominent in Rahner's thought as the *Theological Investigations* proceed, perhaps through the influence of thinkers like Johann Baptist Metz.

33. Ibid., p. 133.

34. "Concerning Nature and Grace," T.I., vol. 1, p. 307.

35. "Nature and Grace," T.I., vol. 4, p. 177.

36. "The Concept of Mystery," T.I., vol. 4, p. 69. It is said here that "incarnation and grace belong to the primordial mystery of God."

37. "Christology within an Evolutionary View of the World," T.I., vol. 5, pp. 180f.

38. Cf. Anne Carr, *The Theological Method of Karl Rahner* (Missoula, MT: Scholars Press, 1977), p. 145, for a discussion of this issue.

39. "On the Theology of the Incarnation," T.I., vol. 4.

40. Ibid., pp. 107, 109–10, 117.

41. Ibid., pp. 111–13. Some of Rahner's critics point out that grace given in Christ seems different only in degree from that available to all. I am not concerned to defend or refute Rahner's view in this immediate context, but it does seem to me that he posits on one fundamental level a difference in kind. Jesus the man, he says, not merely *was* of decisive importance for our salvation by his past acts and the cross, he is *now* and for all eternity the *permanent openness* for our finite being to the infinite God. The Word in his humanity is the necessary mediator of all salvation for the Word remains eternally Christ. Cf. "The Humanity of Christ," T.I., vol. 3, pp. 46ff. That Christ is uniquely savior and eternally the Word would seem to indicate a difference in kind and not degree only.

42. "The Eternal Significance of the Humanity of Jesus for Our Relationship with God," T.I., vol. 3, p. 43.

42. Ibid.

43. "The Incarnation," *Sacramentum Mundi*, vol. 3, pp. 110–11.

44. "On the Theology of the Incarnation," T.I., vol. 4, p. 119.

45. "The Secret of Life," T.I., vol. 6, p. 142.

46. "On the Unity of Spirit and Matter," T.I., vol. 6, p. 171. This tract, along with that referred to in n. 45 above, is crucial for understanding Rahner's general theological position as well as his view of the relation of nature and grace. Although all said here is said elsewhere in a multitude of ways, it finds a brevity and clarity in this piece not always found in his other writings.

47. Ibid., p. 161; also see "The Secret of Life," T.I., vol. 6, p. 144.

48. "The Unity of Spirit and Matter," T.I., vol. 6, pp. 168–69.

49. "Christology within an Evolutionary View of the World," T.I., vol. 5, p. 164.

50. "The Unity of Spirit and Matter," T.I., vol. 6, p. 175.

51. "Christology in the Setting of Modern Man's Understanding of Himself and His World," T.I., vol. 11, p. 219.

52. Ibid., pp. 219–20.

53. "Christology within an Evolutionary View of the World," T.I., vol. 5, p. 178.

54. Ibid., p. 176.

55. "The Secret of Life," T.I., vol. 6, p. 149.

56. "Christology in the Setting of Modern Man," T.I., vol. 11, p. 228.

57. Ibid., p. 227.

58. Ibid., p. 228.

59. "The Eternal Significance of the Humanity of Jesus for Our Relationship with God," T.I., vol. 3, pp. 44–45.

60. "Christology in the Setting of Modern Man," T.I., vol. 11, p. 228, 229.

61. "The Concept of Mystery in Catholic Theology," T.I., vol. 4, pp. 64–72. The *mysteria stricte dicta* are given as Trinity, incarnation and the divinization of man, and grace and glory. Rahner sometimes speaks of them as "God as he is himself" (Trinity) the incarnate Lord, and grace and glory (or the beatific vision) or as the single mystery of God in incarnation and grace, with the Trinity as what the incarnation means. He never includes creation as such.

62. Ibid., pp. 49–50, 52. The comment in the text is not to be taken as a criticism of Rahner's use of the "whither" in terms of the experience of transcendence as the limitless openness of the subject itself or as the anticipatory grasp that exceeds all determinable objectification. It is the directional suggestion of the term itself that is the issue here.

63. Friedrich Schleiermacher, *The Christian Faith* (New York: Harper & Row, 1963), vol. 1, pp. 16–17.

64. "Philosophy and Theology," T.I., vol. 6, p. 79; italics mine.

65. Cf. "Theological Considerations Concerning the Moment of Death," T.I., vol. 11, p. 318; "Ideas for a Theology of Death," T.I., vol. 13, p. 170f.; "Death," *Sacramentum Mundi*, vol. 2, and *On the Theology of Death* (New York: Herder and Herder, 1961), p. 20: "The fundamental moral decision made by a man in the mundane temporality of his bodily existence, is rendered definite and final by death." John Hick, *Death and Eternal Life* (New York: Harper & Row, 1976), pp. 228–35, contains a discussion of Rahner's theology of death.

66. The language of "the absolute embodiment of God in Christ" presents a number of logical and theological problems and in my view it should be avoided, from both lectern and pulpit. "On the Theology of the Incarnation," T.I., vol. 4, p. 117, points to the kind of language that is needed; notably, that in the act of incarnation God remains infinite, but gives the finite an infinite depth.

67. Cf. *The Dynamics of Faith* (New York: Harper & Row, 1957), pp. 73–74, 125; *The Future of Religions* (New York: Harper & Row, 1966), p. 81.

Chapter 5. Metz and the Social Dimension of Grace

1. Metz develops these ideas in a number of contexts: see esp. *Theology of the World*, trans. W. G. Doepel (New York: Seabury, 1973), pp. 13ff., 81f. (German ed., 1968), which, incidentally, is dedicated to Karl Rahner; *Faith in History and Society*, trans. David Smith (New York: Seabury, 1979), pp. 34f., 46ff., and 100–108 (German ed., 1977); also see "The Church's Social Function in the Light of a Political Theology," in *Faith in the World of Politics, Concilium* 36 (New York: Paulist Press, 1968), pp. 3ff., and *The Emergent Church*, trans. Peter Mann (New York: Crossroad), pp. 67ff. (German ed., 1980). Roger Dick Johns, *Man in the World: The Political Theology of Johann Baptist Metz* (Missoula, MT: Scholars Press, 1976), a very good overview of and critical account of Metz's thought, treats these issues in some detail, pp. 87ff., 121ff.

2. Cf. *Theology of the World*, p. 52f.; Johns, *Man in the World*, pp. 100–102, 105f.

3. *Theology of the World*, pp. 88–89.

4. Ibid., p. 96.

5. Jack Healy, "The Development of the Doctrine of Grace and Some Implications for It in the Light of Contemporary Thought" (S.T.M. thesis, General Theological Seminary, 1972), pp. 58ff., deals with Metz's view of grace effectively and at some length.

6. *Theology of the World*, pp. 109, 119.

7. Ibid., p. 89.

8. Ibid., pp. 149–50.

9. *Faith in History and Society*, p. 62. And note this remark on the same page: "Any existential and personal theology that claims to understand human existence, but not as a political problem in the widest sense, is an abstract theology with regard to the existential situation of the individual."

10. *Faith in History and Society*, p. 89.

11. *Theology of the World*, p. 94.

12. Ibid.

13. Cf. Johns, *Man in the World*, pp. 157ff., for a searching account of a number of critical analyses of Metz's theology.

14. *Theology of the World*, p. 38; cf. pp. 61, 85, 146–47.

15. Ibid., pp. 40–41.

16. Ibid., p. 35; cf. Johns, *Man in the World*, p. 93.

17. *Faith in History and Society*, pp. 106f.

18. Ibid., pp. 110–11. "Our idea of history is also unilaterally affected by a screening out of the importance of suffering. We tend, consciously or unconsciously, to define history as the history of what has prevailed."

19. Ibid., p. 107. Metz holds that this argument would seem "to be emphatically confirmed by modern science and especially by the anthropologically ori-

ented branches of science such as human biology." This is a large claim, the evidence for which is considerably less decisive than Metz implies.

20. Ibid., p. 108.

21. Ibid. "The essential dynamics of history consist of the memory of suffering as a negative consciousness of future freedom and as a stimulus to overcome suffering within the framework of that freedom," Metz says here. "The history of freedom is therefore—subject to the assumed alienation of man and nature—only possible as a history of suffering." While due account must be taken of the suffering occasioned by nature, whether "alienated" or not, the greater source of human suffering is history itself. Metz tends to lay too much at nature's door at this juncture. Had he been a little more "dialectical" here, he would have considered suffering *from* nature and suffering *in* history less one-sidedly perhaps.

22. Although Metz attempts to form "a theological enlightenment of the Enlightenment" (*Faith in History and Society*, p. 34) and succeeds to a great extent in doing so, he remains captive to the historical perspectives that derive from the Enlightenment. His analysis of "the human situation" proceeds on the basis of the far from identical twins of the Enlightenment: the evolutionary interpretation of the world which has been abetted by the interest of Western middle-class society on the one hand and the historical and materialist interpretation on the other. Critically rejecting the former for the most part, and critically "baptizing" the latter, he yet stays within the peculiarly Western mentality that lies behind both, taking no regard of the myriad manifestations of religious life and interpretation beyond the confines of this mentality. The "global perspective" he seeks therefore eludes him. It is true that the historical horizon of Western thought is of global importance and that it constitutes the West's greatest contribution to human thought as a whole, but it is questionable whether in itself it is capable of supporting a global interpretation of life. The chances are very good that it will be tempered and perhaps even transformed by the very cultural and social forces across the world that it influences. But Metz does not look beyond the parameters of the Western church. This is given point by his remark (ibid., p. 4) that his analysis may not be applicable to the church in Latin America. "We can no longer simply go on exporting our western theology to the countries of Latin America, where there are now hardly any customers who are sufficiently interested to buy it," and his further remark that what is important for Western theologians is "to try to see their theology within the context of world-wide processes and to take seriously the fact that it is conditioned by its situation within the particular context of middle-class, Central European society."

This is well and truly said, of course, but it bespeaks of a set of mind that allows for no attempt to break out of limitations. Metz's theology is very "in-house." Had he proved more open to influences outside the borders of his own immediate setting, he might well have achieved a more global horizon and one more suited to an analysis of "the human situation." As it is, his thought is far more parochial than he would likely admit. And despite all his disclaimers, he more often than not speaks of the Western perspective as though it were global.

One of the conservative criticisms of Metz's thinking is that it represents "a new integralism," that is, the view "that the world is to take shape only under the direct or indirect action of the church." Johns, *Man in the World*, p. 162, quotes Waldeman Molinski's comment regarding the relation of faith and the world in an integralist interpretation: "Integralism is . . . the effort to explain or master reality exclusively in the light of faith, instead of regarding faith as the key which makes the understanding or mastery of the world possible, but does not itself try to achieve it" ("Integralism," *Sacramentum Mundi*, vol. 3, p. 151, is the reference given). Johns holds that Metz has not altogether abandoned the position implicit in an integralist theology. His understanding of the world is "still largely shaped by an attempt to master it 'in the light of faith,' rather than by the use of faith 'as the key which makes the understanding or mastery of the world possible.'" He concludes by noting that in spite of Metz's advocacy of anthropocentricity and secularization, he "still looks out at the world from the windows of the church." This is a just criticism. I would want to add, however, that the windows are stained with the deep colors of a central European experience still overly confident in its own method and approach.

Chapter 6. Moltmann and the Ultimate Future

1. *Theology of Hope*, trans. Margaret Kohl (London: SCM Press, 1967), German ed., 1965; *The Crucified God*, trans. R. A. Wilson and John Bowden (New York: Harper & Row, 1974), German ed., 1973; *The Church in the Power of the Spirit*, trans. James W. Leitch (London: SCM Press, 1977), German ed., 1975.

2. *The Future of Creation*, trans. Margaret Kohl (Philadelphia: Fortress, 1979), German ed., 1977.

3. Many years ago I had the pleasure of introducing Moltmann to a group of theologians and theological students. He spoke brilliantly about the recovery of the eschatological frame of theology and of history as the arena of serious theological reflection. When he had finished his address, one of the students raised his hand and asked, "But what about nature, Dr. Moltmann; where does it fit in?" Silence fell for a space, and then Moltmann replied that he was just beginning to consider the matter and would be forming his view in due course. *The Theology of Hope*, pp. 89ff., provides a significant and illuminating account of his considerations regarding natural theology, which he says, "is a halo," "a reflection of the future light of God in the inadequate material of present reality." The world must be demonstrated from God, "not God from the world" (pp. 90–91). Also see *The Crucified God*, pp. 210ff., for a discussion of the principle of analogy and the difference between natural theology and a theology of the cross; see further *The Church in the Power of the Spirit*, pp. 157f. and 174f., where

Moltmann, influenced by ecology and process thought, has developed a relatively positive theory of nature. In a recent work, *The Trinity and the Kingdom of God*, trans. Margaret Kohl (London: SCM Press, 1981), pp. 98–99, 120ff. (German ed., 1980), he exhibits perhaps a greater openness to process theology, particularly pertaining to God's increase of riches through his relation to the world. Note also the approbative use of the term *panentheism*, pp. 106ff. See n. 33 below for my comments on his most recent work on creation.

4. *The Future of Creation*, p. 58; note also this remark: "The Christian hope for the ultimate future must not surrender itself to 'the higher sanctities' of hope for what is developing now. That would be a betrayal of the cross and of those for whom the crucified Jesus called his brethren." See further, pp. 53–55.

5. Ibid., p. 115; cf. *The Crucified God*, p. 335.

6. Moltmann cites von Rad, *Old Testament Theology* and Kohler's work of the same title. No attempt will be made to deal with this issue at present since it will be considered in a subsequent chapter.

7. *The Future of Creation*, p. 118.

8. Ibid., pp. 118–19.

9. Ibid., p. 117. Thomas Aquinas, *Summa Theologia* I, qu. 90, art. 3.2 is cited: "*Finis rerum respondit principio, Deus erim principium et finis rerum. Ergo et existus rerum a principio respondet reductioni rerum in finem,*" as is a similar remark from *Comm. in Sent.* I, distinct. 14, qu. 2, art. 2, which indicates that Thomas's conception of time had a circular structure.

10. *The Future of Creation*, pp. 117–18. Rudolf Bultmann, *Glauben und Verstehen* 3 (Tübingen, 1960), pp. 29, 26, is cited.

11. *The Future of Creation*, p. 125.

12. E.g., ibid., pp. 116: "Belief in creation repeats the judgment of the Creator over his creation: 'Behold it was very good.' Unfortunately man cannot, like his Creator, rest at this point. For experience tells him, 'Behold, it is unfortunately not very good.'" One can appreciate Moltmann's view that creation must be understood as *creatio mutabilis*, as perfectable, not perfect, but to term it "not very good" is already to have relegated it to the realm of secondary concern.

13. One of the most effective critical considerations of the futurist school of thought is Dietrich Ritschl, *Memory and Hope: A Study in the Presence of Christ* (New York: Macmillan, 1967). The title is a brilliant stroke, at once instructive and indicative of the author's own approach.

14. *The Future of Creation*, p. 125. Note here, however, the reference to "the hidden, anticipatory indwelling of God."

15. Ibid., p. 128, quoted from W. Heisenberg, *The Physicist's Conception of Nature* (New York: Hutchinson and Harcourt Brace, 1958), p. 29.

16. *The Future of Creation*, p. 129; *The Church in the Power of the Spirit*, p. 175.

17. *The Future of Creation*, p. 130.

18. Ibid., p. 129. The use of Rom. 8:18–24 as a systematic principle in futurist eschatology is just about as questionable as basing a whole kenotic Christology on Phil. 2:5–11. Paul's view that "the whole creation groans and travails" is poetic symbolization, not a systematic theological utterance.

19. Ibid., p. 117. Mircea Eliade, *The Myth of the Eternal Return* (New York: Rutledge and Kegan Paul, 1955), is cited as a descriptive analysis.

20. *The Future of Creation*, pp. 168–69.

21. Ibid., p. 171.

22. Ibid., pp. 163–64.

23. Cf. the discussion in *The Church in the Power of the Spirit*, pp. 134ff., the whole theme of which is stated on p. 135: "Israel is Christianity's original, enduring and final partner in history."

24. *The Future of Creation*, p. i.

25. Ibid., pp. 57–58.

26. Ibid., p. 53. Such a statement, made variously throughout the work, seems to jar badly with the following declaration: "It is essential to learn to distinguish the desired future and the planned and calculated future, first in order to expose the wishes hidden behind the future which is planned and calculated today, and to enquire into the interests and relationships of power, and, secondly, in order to formulate the true desires of all men and women and to bring them to effect." This appears only a few pages later (p. 58). Statements of this kind quoted in the text are not conspicuous in *The Church in the Power of the Spirit* where Moltmann is seen at his most open and generous toward the Jews and the non-Christian religions. Cf. pp. 154–60, for a criticism of "the absolutism of the church" and "the absolutism of the faith." "Christianity has to renounce its exclusive claim and also its inclusive claim" (p. 158).

27. *The Future of Creation*, p. 53, also see p. 78.

28. Ibid., p. 79.

29. Ibid., p. 78. F. W. J. Schelling, *On Human Freedom* (Chicago: Open Court, 1936), p. 50 is cited.

30. *The Future of Creation*, p. 125.

31. Ibid., p. 78. In *The Crucified God*, pp. 26ff., a fuller and more balanced treatment of the dialectical principle of knowledge is given, though in company with such statements as this: "If like is known only by like, then the Son of God would have had to remain in heaven, because he would be unrecognizable by anything earthly" (p. 27). Taken strictly, this does away with the *imago dei* doctrine as well as the principle of analogy. But it is just following this remark that Moltmann admits, it seems, a limited validity to the *analogia entis* in saying that "the analogical principle of knowledge is one-sided if it is not supplemented by the dialectic principle of knowledge."

32. *The Future of Creation*, pp. 78–79.

33. Moltmann himself demonstrates a shift in this direction in his Gifford

Lectures, published after the completion of the above study as *God in Creation: A New Theology of Creation and the Spirit of God*, trans. Margaret Kohl (San Francisco: Harper & Row, 1985), German ed., 1985. While the lines of thought in this ample and very systematic discussion are for the most part recognizably continuous with those we have reviewed, it contains a number of marked differences in emphasis and interpretation. Among these differences we find a far greater openness to the immanence of God in the world (pp. 11ff. and throughout), to evolution as a concept of divine self-movement in creation (pp. 185ff.), and to the intrinsic value of created nature (pp. 37ff.). Limits are also set to "the historicization of the World" and a positive sense in which creation is the framework of history is entered (p. 57). Throughout the conception of grace is enlarged in company with a more generous estimation of nature. I am glad to note here what I take to be significant developments and moderations in Moltmann's perspective.

Chapter 7. Whitehead on Nature and the Nature of Divine Life

1. *Process and Reality* (New York: Macmillan, 1929), p. vi.
2. For expanded treatments see, for example, A. H. Johnson, *Whitehead's Theory of Reality* (Boston: Beacon Press, 1952); Ivor Leclere, *Whitehead's Metaphysics* (New York: Macmillan, 1958); William Christian, *An Interpretation of Whitehead's Metaphysics* (New Haven: Yale University Press, 1959); Kenneth F. Thompson, Jr., *Whitehead's Philosophy of Religion* (The Hague and Paris: Mouton, 1971); John W. Lango, *Whitehead's Ontology* (Albany, NY: State University of New York Press, 1972), and Elizabeth M. Kraus, *The Metaphysics of Experience, A Companion to Whitehead's Process and Reality* (New York: Fordham University Press, 1979).
3. *Adventures of Ideas* (New York: Macmillan, 1922), p. 210. All science, philosophy, religion, all explanations, require concepts finding their origin in this mystery.
4. *Process and Reality*, p. 408.
5. Ibid. Note further in the same work, p. 245, the remark that "organic philosophy holds that consciousness only arises in a late derivative phase of complex integration." The "elements of our experience which stand out clearly and distinctly in our consciousness are not its basic facts; they are the derivative modifications which arise in the process."
6. *Modes of Thought* (New York: Macmillan, 1938), p. 41.
7. Ibid., pp. 181–82.
8. Ibid., p. 223.
9. Ibid., p. 219; *Process and Reality*, p. 247: "The separation of the emotional experience from the presentational intuition is a high abstraction of thought. . . . The primitive experience is emotional feelings, felt in its relevance to a world beyond."

10. *Process and Reality*, p. 248; see further, *Modes of Thought*, p. 219, and *Adventures of Ideas*, p. 226.

11. *Adventures of Ideas*, pp. 244–45.

12. *Process and Reality*, pp. 238ff., 252–53.

13. *Process and Reality*, p. 253.

14. Ibid. Whitehead's discussion of epistemological issues is more ample in this massive work of course, but those sections (scattered) dealing with them in *Modes of Thought* and *Adventures of Ideas* have a directness and clarity about them less present in the larger work. For summary statements of the ontological principle, see *Process and Reality*, pp. 36–39, and esp. p. 373.

15. *Adventures of Ideas*, p. 237.

16. Ibid., p. 241.

17. Ibid., pp. 241–43.

18. Ibid., pp. 243–44.

19. Ibid., pp. 239–40.

20. Ibid., p. 241: "Our consciousness of . . .self-identity . . . is nothing other than knowledge of a special strand of unity within the general unity of nature."

21. *Process and Reality*, p. 365.

22. *Adventures of Ideas*, p. 227.

23. Ibid., pp. 226–27; *Process and Reality*, pp. 35, 335ff.

24. *Adventures of Ideas*, pp. 226, 231.

25. Ibid., pp. 227, 230.

26. Ibid., pp. 230–31.

27. Ibid., p. 279.

28. *Process and Reality*, pp. 253–54.

29. *Adventures of Ideas*, pp. 281–82.

30. *Process and Reality*, pp. vi–viii.

31. Ibid., p. 252.

32. *Adventures of Ideas*, pp. 297–99.

33. Ibid., p. 301.

34. *Science and the Modern World* (New York: Macmillan, 1925), p. 20. Whitehead goes on to say at this point that this "faith in the order of nature . . . cannot be justified by any direct inspection. . . . It springs from the nature of things as disclosed in our own immediate present experience. To experience this faith is to know that our experience, dim and fragmentary as it is, yet sounds the utmost depths of reality: to know that detached details merely in order to be themselves demand that they should find themselves in a system of things."

35. Ibid., p. 27.

36. *Process and Reality*, pp. v–vi.

37. Ibid., p. x.

38. See *Adventures of Ideas*, p. 205.

39. *Process and Reality*, pp. 43, 65.

40. Ibid., pp. 34–35, 53.

41. Ibid., pp. 38–39, 421. Tillich's remarks about process thought are instructive at this point. In *Systematic Theology* (Chicago: University of Chicago Press, 1951), vol. 1, p. 167, he says: "As long as there is experience in any definite sense of the word, there is a structure of experience which can be recognized within the process of experiencing and which can be elaborated critically. Process philosophy is justified in its attempt to dissolve everything which seems to be static. But it would become absurd if it tried to dissolve the structure of process into a process." Again, a few lines later: "Human nature changes in *history*. The structure of a being *which has history* underlies all historical changes." On p. 181, he notes further that a "process philosophy which sacrifices the persisting identity of that which is in process sacrifices the process itself, its continuity, the relation of what is conditioned to its conditions, the inner aim *(telos)* which makes a process a whole." Whitehead does not sacrifice the identity of what is in process. He preserves identity through the use of the concept of the epochality of actual occasions, but it remains questionable whether this concept is strong enough to do justice to the structures of being within becoming entities. Tillich's stress is on being as comprising becoming; Whitehead's is on becoming as embracing being. Both are probably right but neither is wholly right. The truth of the matter may lie somewhere in the mysterious realm between the two. Although designed to point to the unity of experience and to the freedom of the process of becoming enjoyed by actual occasions, the category of the "epochal" says too little about the first and too much about the second.

42. *Process and Reality*, pp. 135, 68.

43. Ibid., pp. 43–44.

44. Ibid., p. 44: "Actuality in perishing acquires objectivity, while it loses subjective immediacy. It loses the final causation which is its internal principle of unrest, and acquires efficient causation whereby it is a ground of obligation characterizing creativity."

45. *Science and the Modern World*, p. 158. See *Process and Reality*, pp. 27, 29, 71, 79–80.

46. *Adventures of Ideas*, p. 303.

47. *Process and Reality*, p. 31.

48. Ibid., p. 32.

49. *Science and the Modern World*, p. 229; *Process and Reality*, pp. 34ff., 68, 70, 280.

50. Ibid., pp. 29–30.

51. See *Adventures of Ideas*, p. 300.

52. *Process and Reality*, p. 65.

53. *Modes of Thought*, p. 232.

54. Ibid., p. 214.

55. *Process and Reality*, p. 337.

56. Ibid., p. 70.

57. Ibid., pp. 63–64.

58. Ibid., p. 379. Whitehead is prepared to admit, on the basis of these two poles of the experience of every actual entity, that there is a certain dualism about reality. Indeed, there are lots of dualisms in each actual entity through its physical inheritance and its mental reaction. The world is not merely physical and not merely mental. Each final actuality is both physical and mental (see pp. 72, 165, 366).

59. Ibid., pp. 335–36.

60. Ibid., p. 523.

61. Ibid., p. 374.

62. Ibid., p. 344.

63. Ibid., p. 46.

64. Ibid., p. 47.

65. Ibid., pp. 134, 524, 527.

66. Ibid., pp. 527–30. The argument here is not easy to follow.

67. Ibid., p. 524.

68. Ibid.

69. Ibid. The quotations from the 1925 Macmillan edition of *Process and Reality*, used in this and the next chapter, have been compared with the corrected edition by David Ray Griffin and Donald W. Sherburn (New York: Free Press, 1978). No significant differences were noted.

Chapter 8. Whitehead and Christian Doctrine

1. *Process and Reality* (New York: Macmillan, 1929), p. 31.

2. Ibid., p. 68.

3. Ibid., p. 339.

4. Ibid., p. 528.

5. Kenneth Frank Thompson, *Whitehead's Philosophy of Religion* (The Hague and Paris: Mouton, 1971), pp. 102ff.

6. Ibid., pp. 125ff.

7. Ibid.

8. *Process and Reality*, p. 520.

9. *Adventures of Ideas* (New York: Macmillan, 1933), p. 217; see further, *Religion in the Making* (New York: Macmillan, 1926), pp. 154, 157; *Process and Reality*, p. 517.

10. See *Religion in the Making*, p. 153.

11. *Adventures of Ideas*, p. 217; also see *Religion in the Making*, pp. 154, 157, and *Process and Reality*, p. 517.

12. Ibid., pp. 524–25.

13. Ibid., p. 521. Whitehead's italics.

14. Ibid., p. 520.

15. *Adventures of Ideas,* p. 214; *Religion in the Making,* p. 57.

16. *Adventures of Ideas,* p. 217.

17. *Religion in the Making,* p. 158.

18. Ibid., pp. 154, 158–59.

19. Ibid., p. 156.

20. Ibid., p. 159.

21. *Process and Reality,* p. 525; *Religion in the Making,* p. 119.

22. *Science and the Modern World* (New York: Macmillan, 1925), p. 275; see A. H. Johnson, *Whitehead's Philosophy of Civilization* (New York: Dover Publications, 1962), pp. 46ff.

23. *Religion in the Making,* p. 143.

24. Ibid.

25. Ibid., p. 141.

26. Ibid., p. 104.

27. Ibid., p. 105.

28. *Process and Reality,* p. 442.

29. Ibid., p. 438.

30. Ibid., p. 254.

31. Ibid., p. 287.

32. Ibid.

33. *Modes of Thought* (New York: Macmillan, 1938), p. 37.

34. *Process and Reality,* p. 289.

35. *Modes of Thought,* p. 184.

36. *Religion in the Making,* p. 103.

37. *Process and Reality,* p. 271.

38. *Modes of Thought,* p. 38.

39. Ibid., p. 21.

40. *Process and Reality,* pp. 74, 75, 254.

41. *Religion in the Making,* p. 84. Whitehead means here that insofar as we have the past, we have it in the present or not at all. He recognizes of course that, as stated in *Adventures of Ideas,* p. 232, "we can discern no clear-cut sense perception wholly concerned with present fact."

42. Ibid., pp. 207–8.

43. *Religion in the Making,* p. 84.

44. *Modes of Thought,* p. 202.

45. *Adventures of Ideas,* p. 341.

46. Ibid., p. 357.

47. *Modes of Thought,* p. 30.

48. *Adventures of Ideas,* pp. 166–67.

49. *Religion in the Making,* p. 55.

50. *Adventures of Ideas,* p. 218.

51. Ibid., pp. 205–6.

52. *Process and Reality,* pp. 315–16.
53. See esp. *Religion in the Making,* pp. 123ff.
54. *Adventures of Ideas,* p. 367.
55. Ibid., p. 368.
56. Ibid., pp. 368–81.

Chapter 9. Westermann and the Biblical Witness

1. Klaus Koch, *The Prophets: The Assyrian Period,* trans. Margaret Kohl (Philadelphia: Fortress, 1983), vol. 1, p. 144 (German ed., 1978).

2. Claus Westermann, *The Praise of God in the Psalms,* trans. Keith R.. Grim (Atlanta: John Knox Press, 1965), p. 127 (German ed., 1961). This remark is made in regard to a group of psalms in which "the praise of the Creator passes directly into praise of the Lord of history." The conception however has broader application.

3. Gerhard von Rad, "The Theological Problem of the Old Testament Doctrine of Creation," in *The Problem of the Hexateuch and Other Essays,* trans. E. W. T. Dillon (London: Oliver and Boyd, 1966), pp. 134, 136, 138 (German ed., 1936).

4. Ibid., p. 142. Italics mine. In his *Old Testament Theology,* trans. D. M. G. Stalker (New York: Harper & Row, 1962), vol. 1, p. 106 (German ed., 1957), von Rad says similarly that "the Old Testament writings confine themselves to representing Jahweh's relationship to Israel and the world in one aspect only, namely as a continuing divine activity in history." Later on this view finds modification in an addition (pp. 114f.) to the first edition in which von Rad states: "It will certainly not be possible for us to confine our theological work to testifying to the divine historical acts. Other things as well took place for Israel in the orbit of these acts of God." But notwithstanding this modification, he allowed the statement made on p. 106 to remain unchanged, indicating apparently that this was where his chief sympathies lay.

5. *The Prophets,* vol. 1, p. 144. Koch is quite ascerbic in commenting on von Rad's position at this point. The reason perhaps is in part because he and von Rad employ the same sort of methodology, the form-critical, and reach different results.

6. Ibid., p. 145. "In Isaiah, as in Amos and Hosea too, suprahistory is composed of various levels which cannot be clearly divided from one another."

7. *The Prophets: The Babylonian and Persian Periods,* trans. Margaret Kohl (Philadelphia: Fortress, 1982), vol. 2, p. 197 (German ed., 1978).

8. Cf. Werner H. Schmidt, *The Faith of the Old Testament,* trans. John Sturdy (Philadelphia: Westminister, 1983), p. 119 (German ed., 1968).

9. "Some Aspects of the Old Testament World-View," in *The Problem of the Hexateuch and other Essays,* p. 144.

10. Claus Westermann, *Genesis 1–11,* trans. John J. Scullion (Minneapolis: Augsburg, 1984), pp. 19ff. (German ed., 1974).

11. Ibid., p. 64. Schmidt, *The Faith of the Old Testament*, p. 175, follows the view of von Rad more closely here than Westermann's: "The confession of faith in a creator is rather the consequence than the presupposition of faith in salvation." Von Rad, however, will not allow creation a place in the "historical credo" of Israel and Westermann disallows, as will be noted shortly, "faith in a creator."

12. *Genesis 1–11*, pp. 64–65. "The primeval stories . . . look back into primeval times where the present world and everything in it had its origin. Israel shared the retrospective view with her neighbors and her predecessors, with all humanity. . . . In interpreting them, one must never lose sight of this aspect of retrospection which they share with so significant a circle of human traditions."

13. Ibid., p. 42–43. Oversimplification is of course a danger here. The creation stories for J and P, Westermann holds, had a dual intention, really looked in two ways. First, they looked back into the primeval times for the origin of the present world. Second, they looked forward to the history of Israel with the primeval stories as a prologue to the history of the interaction of God with Israel. The texts now speak through the medium of history for there is no cultic actualization of creation anew. "[R]ather God's action, which Israel has experienced in its history, is extended to the whole of history and to the whole world" (p. 65).

14. "Creation and History in the Old Testament," in Vilmos Vajta, ed., *The Gospel and Human Destiny* (Minneapolis: Augsburg, 1971), p. 17.

15. Cf. D. G. Spriggs, *Two Old Testament Theologies,* (London: SCM Press, 1974), pp. 53–55, 101–2. This work, a comparison of the theologies of W. Eichrodt, and Gerhard von Rad, provides a good summary of both von Rad's contribution to Old Testament studies and critical assessments of them. A typical critical comment is that quoted from R. C. Dentan, *Journal of Biblical Literature* 82 (1963): 106: "While it is true that a concern with God's action in history is uniquely characteristic of OT religion, it by no means follows that the 'theology' of the OT can, or should be discussed only in these terms." Dentan's own view, to be found in his *The Knowledge of God in Ancient Israel* (New York: Seabury, 1968), pp. 61–65, is that Israel's credo expanded through its history, finally to include belief in God as creator. Indeed, with Second Isaiah, "for the first time, the belief in God as creator of heaven and earth became the *first* article of Israel's creed. The story of creation had long stood at the beginning of her historical traditions; it was now to become the point of departure as well." Younger scholars tend to be more severe in their criticism, e.g., Brevard S. Childs, *Introduction to the Old Testament as Scripture* (Philadelphia: Fortress, 1979), p. 75, says that critical theories like von Rad's credo simply "bear less and less weight."

16. Note especially "Creation and History in the Old Testament," *The Gospel and Human Destiny,* p. 24: "The acting of God in creation and his acting in history stand in relation to one another in the Old Testament; the one is not without the other. . . . Both belong so closely together that God's divinity can

only be seen in both together; were God's acting limited to mankind, he would lose his divinity for the Old Testament way of thinking."

17. Ibid., pp. 15, 23.

18. Ibid., p. 21; "In order to gain attention for this message of salvation, in order to render faith in deliverance possible, the horizon of this saving act is widened all the way to the universal work of the creator God."

19. "The Theological Problem of the Old Testament Doctrine of Creation," p. 136.

20. Schmidt, *The Faith of the Old Testament*, p. 177.

21. *Genesis 1–11*, p. 21. The reference given for the quotation from Brandon is *Creation Legends of the Ancient Near East* (London, 1963), p. 65.

22. *Genesis 1–11*, p. 21.

23. Although I do not want to press this issue overmuch, I do think that Brandon's thesis that the creation stories arose as an answer of the human spirit about the question of the origins of the world has some truth about it and therefore should not be summarily dismissed. One can only suppose that the growth of the early creation myths was accompanied by some measure of curiosity and thought about the matter of origins.

24. *Creation*, trans. John J. Scullion (Philadelphia: Fortress, 1974), p. 114 (German ed., 1971).

25. *Genesis 1–11*, pp. 175, 601; *Creation*, p. 114: In the Old Testament, Westermann says here, "Creation is never the object of revelation and it is never in any way brought into the context of revelation."

26. Cf. Spriggs, *Two Old Testament Theologies*, pp. 45ff., for a good account of von Rad's view.

27. *Genesis 1–11*, p. 598.

28. Ibid., p. 67.

29. Cf. *Creation*, p. 44; *Genesis 1–11*, pp. 25–26, 67, 176.

30. Ibid., p. 599.

31. *Blessing*, trans. Keith Crim (Philadelphia: Fortress, 1978), p. 16 (German ed., 1968): "He [von Rad] assumed that God's saving deeds and his acts of blessing together constitute God's activity as savior."

32. Childs, *Old Testament as Scripture*, p. 142: "in Westermann's huge commentary on Gen. 1–11 all the problems inherent in the traditio-critical method reached their zenith, but in a complexity which threatened to devour exegesis." See further the remarks on pp. 144–45 and p. 153. Norman K. Gottwald, *The Hebrew Bible—A Socio-Literary Introduction* (Philadelphia: Fortress, 1985), pp. 22ff., notes that while the historical-critical method is not a sufficient paradigm for understanding the Hebrew Bible, its contributions have been such that it is utilized by biblical scholars of all methodological persuasions. His own book "attempts to orient the reader to a critical understanding of the Hebrew Bible and to the current state of biblical studies as an intellectual and sociocultural practice.

It underlines the expanding range of choices in methods of biblical study now available, a range far wider than at anytime in the long history of biblical interpretation" (p. xxvii). Gottwald's "common-sense reflection" on the various approaches to the Hebrew Bible and methods for its study (pp. 31ff.) is a thorough and artful presentation of the options.

33. *Genesis 1–11*, pp. 60–61.

34. Ibid., p. 62; cf. "Creation and History in the Old Testament," *The Gospel and Human Destiny*, p. 30; *Creation*, pp. 50, 54.

35. *Blessing*, pp. 45–47.

36. Ibid., p. 64.

37. *Genesis 1–11*, p. 161. On blessing in the Christian setting, see the discussion in *Blessing*, pp. 117ff. "A purely Christian blessing, that is, a blessing that arose *de novo* on the basis of the Christ event," Westermann says, "does not exist. Blessing was a part of the inheritance that Jesus and his community and the entire New Testament received from the past. Blessing has a prehistory that reaches back beyond the Old Testament and Semitic high religions into primitive religions." Note should be taken of Westermann's entries here about the relation of blessing and proclamation. Although not pertinent to our discussion, they are of more than passing interest.

38. *Elements of Old Testament Theology*, trans. Douglas W. Stott (Atlanta: John Knox Press, 1982), p. 99 (German ed., 1978). Cited hereafter as *Elements*.

39. Ibid.

40. Ibid.

41. Ibid., p. 100.

42. Ibid. See further *Creation*, p. 79; *Genesis 1–11*, pp. 176, 603.

43. *Elements*, p. 101. Westermann might better have said that "wisdom is there" not only for the sake of "man," or indeed for the sake of "the whole man," but for the sake of the earth. The commission is to cultivate and maintain the earth, hence it is to human beings not simply for their own sake but the sake of that of which they are a part.

44. *Creation*, pp. 57ff.; also *Elements*, pp. 118ff.; *Genesis 1–11*, pp. 178ff., pp. 237ff.

45. *Creation*, p. 57.

46. Ibid. The reference given is *Kirchliche Dogmatik*, 3, 1, pp. 204ff.

47. *Creation*, p. 60: "God, by creating man in his own image, has given man his human dignity. The secular notion of the dignity of man has retained something of the religious spirit right up to the present day. It is normally used in a solemn context, and not at all in everyday speech. This cannot be otherwise because the notion retains its religious roots even in the secularized world. If one really means that dignity belongs to man as such, to the whole human race, and thereby to each individual who belongs to the human race, then this can be said only from outside the ambit of the human race."

48. Ibid., p. 87; *Genesis 1–11*, pp. 231–32.
49. *Creation*, p. 73.
50. Ibid., p. 89; *Genesis 1–11*, pp. 275–77.
51. *Creation*, p. 91.
52. Ibid., p. 92. This line is repeated almost verbatim in *Elements*, p. 97. In *Genesis 1–11*, p. 605, the matter is expressed thus: "No political, social, theological or ecclesiastical adaptation can in any way alter the fact that a person grows up with an inclination to evil and that the creator will suffer it and will not change it."
53. *Creation*, p. 100.
54. Ibid., p. 103; cf. *Genesis 1–11*, pp. 66, 602.
55. *Creation*, p. 104.
56. Ibid., p. 107.
57. Ibid., p. 108.
58. Ibid., p. 109: "There is but one question which determines the course of the narrative: why is man, created by God, a man who is limited by death, suffering, toil and sin? The narrative is not really answering the question of the origin of man, but the question of man experienced as ambivalent."
59. Ibid.
60. Ibid., pp. 110–11.
61. Ibid., p. 112. Part 6 of *Elements*, pp. 217ff., is a fairly extended discussion of the whole matter of the relation of Old Testament thought and Jesus Christ.
62. *Old Testament as Scripture*, pp. 154–55.
63. Ibid., pp. 74–75.
64. Ibid., pp. 16, 75.
65. Ibid., p. 41. The issue, Childs says, "is not whether or not an Old Testament Introduction should be historical, but the nature of the historical categories being applied."
66. "Creation and History in the Old Testament," p. 23.
67. *Genesis 1–11*, pp. 175, 601.
68. Ibid., pp. 174–75. In *Creation*, pp. 60–64, Westermann discusses this issue at some length. Creation is good, he says, because it is suited for the purpose for which it is created, that is, because it corresponds to its goal. It is not created "for man because man is a part of it." Its goodness consists in the divine intention for it, something not announced in the creation story itself. For the priestly tradition this goodness "is not something which man notices in the works of God; it is not a judgement which man exercises." It will not disappear because "in the eyes of man there is much in the works of Creation that is not good, much that is incomprehensible, much that appears savage and senseless." Against this background only does creation have meaning. Its context and meaning is that God is the creator, and only the creator can say that it is good. By token of this "man is freed from passing judgement on the whole, he is freed from swaying from positive to negative." The announcement that the creation is good in the eyes of

God "makes possible a full, unfettered joy in the gifts of Creation, a revelling in the limitless forces given to nature . . . and an immersion in the fullness and abundance that belong to Creation" (p. 62). This is well said but it raises even more acutely the question I have asked in the text: If creation is nonrevelatory, how do we know that its context and meaning is in God the creator; how do we know that in the eyes of God, it is "very good" unless in some sense this has been vouchsafed to us through revelation?

69. *Genesis 1–11*, p. 601.

70. Ibid., p. 167; *Elements*, p. 94; "Creation and History in the Old Testament," p. 23.

71. Ibid., pp. 23–24.

72. *Genesis 1–11*, p. 61.

73. Cf. *Elements*, pp. 100–101; *Genesis 1–11*, pp. 176, 603; *Creation*, p. 79.

74. *Elements*, p. 90.

75. *God and the New Physics* (New York: Simon and Schuster, 1983), p. 6. The reference given is "Religion is a Good Thing," in R. Duncan and M. Weston-Smith, eds., *Lying Truths* (New York: Pergamon, 1979).

76. *Creation*, p. 55.

77. *Blessing*, p. 13. Yet "the one who blesses is the one who is present" (p. 8). We have to ask whether the divine presence is nonrevelatory. How could it be known unless in some sense revealed?

78. *The Praise of God in the Psalms*, p. 134: "God's grace is at work when he looks into the depths, saves, redeems, and heals. . . . But it is also at work there where he sustains his creation and gives bread to the hungry." Westermann makes this entry in passing and does not integrate it into his general discussion of either creation or blessing. He tends to assume a doctrine of grace without providing any systematic consideration of its implications for the activity of God in creation or benediction.

79. See Schmidt's extended argument for this view, *The Faith of the Old Testament*, pp. 175ff.

Chapter 10. The Nature of Grace and the Grace of Nature

1. As noted above, Augustine's idea of grace was far more inclusive than his characteristic definitions of grace. An excellent article dealing with this issue is S. J. Grabowski, "St. Augustine and the Presence of God," *Theological Studies*, vol. 13 (1952): 336–58.

2. I have read this observation in several places but am unable to locate sources. The observations were concerned with the nature of grace and not with the relation of nature and grace.

3. "The Survival of the Faithful," *The Sciences*, March/April 1985, pp. 61–63.

4. Ibid., p. 63.

5. Tiger has recently written a book entitled *Optimism: The Biology of Hope*,

which no doubt deals with the ranges of hope more fully than his review. My comments are based entirely on what he has to say in his article in *The Sciences* about Reynolds and Tanner, *The Biology of Religion* (London: Longmans, 1985).

6. There is a long tradition in Christian theology which holds that to claim that everything is of grace is tantamount to saying that nothing is distinctively of grace. This point of view has as its motivating power to uphold the specific character of grace as experienced and known in the Christian community. But the specificity of grace in the Christian community is not threatened by a wider view. To extend the idea of grace beyond the Christian ecclesial reality is not to derogate from the grace known and experienced there. It is to deepen it, to give it its needed ground in reality as a whole.

7. *Death and Eternal Life* (New York: Harper & Row, 1976), pp. 30–31.

8. *Toward a World Theology*, (Philadelphia: Westminster, 1981), p. 177.

9. *Ethics from a Theocentric Perspective* (Chicago: University of Chicago Press, 1981), vol. 1, p. 30.

10. Ibid., pp. 267, 268. Also see vol. 2 (Chicago: University of Chicago Press, 1984), p. 5, where Gustafson says, among other things, that "the problem with western moral tradition is that it has descriptions of man which, because of the distinctive features of humanity, place man at the center of all valuation, or as the ultimate value, and see all things in the service of man."

11. *Toward a World Theology*, p. 115.

12. Ibid., p. 171.

13. Smith deals with the matter of faith in an early work, *The Meaning and End of Religion* (1962; New York: Harper & Row, 1978), in which "faith" and the "cumulative tradition," the mass of overt objective data that forms the historical deposit of the past of a religious community, are said to be the notions by which it is possible to conceptualize all that has happened in the religious life of humankind. Faith, however, is here described as "the impingement of the transcendent" (p. 156). In *Faith and Belief* (Princeton: Princeton University Press, 1979) faith is termed "man's responsive involvement in the activity of God's dealing with humankind: that on-going and multi-faceted activity," and again as "man's participation" in the divine activity (p. 140). It seems clear that here again we have not simple faith but grace as the term of faith. Although Smith for methodological reasons does not use the word *grace*, the idea of grace is present throughout. It is my view that both term and idea might usefully be employed in a Christian theology of religions. Faith is a Christian category no less than grace and requires the category of grace for its adequate description. John Hick in Frank Whaling, ed., *The World's Religious Traditions: Essays in Honor of Wilfred Cantrell Smith* (New York: Crossroad, 1984), p. 148, complains that the word *faith* is more at home in the Semitic than the Indian family of traditions and is hardly ideal to point to what Smith calls "that something of vital religious significance" in all religions, but he himself goes on to describe positive faith as "openness to the

Divine which gradually transforms us and which is called salvation or liberation or enlightment" and which "is essentially the same within the different religious contexts within which it occurs." While Hick does not use the word *grace*, his description of faith entails the idea of grace as background and as agency.

14. *The Torah: A Modern Commentary* (New York: Union of American Hebrew Congregations, 1981), pp. 526–27.

15. *New York Times Book Review*, 12 August 1979, p. 11. The book was published by the University of California Press, Berkeley, 1979.

16. We have now in the West an enormously increased reverence for nature in company with the conviction that nature is completely indifferent to human aims and purposes. Thus Stephen J. Gould writes in "This View of Life," *Natural History*, 16 September 1984, p. 14: "The human mind delights in finding pattern— so much so that we often mistake coincidence or forced analogy for profound meaning. No other habit of thought lies so deeply within the soul of a small creature trying to make sense of a world not constructed for it." To give an added punch to his remark, he quotes the *Rubaiyat*:

Into this Universe, and not knowing
Nor whence, like water willy-nilly flowing.

17. *Method in Theology* (New York: Herder and Herder, 1972), p. 111.

18. The following works are illustrative of this trend: John Hick and Hasan Askari, eds., *The Experience of Religious Diversity* (Dorset, England: Gowen, 1985), is a fine discussion of the theological dimensions of dialogue among Buddhists, Christians, Hindus, Jews, and Muslims, useful on all counts but particularly so perhaps in regard to the dialogue among Christians, Jews, and Muslims. Raimundo Pannikkar has dealt with the principles of interreligious dialogue in a number of works. *The Intrareligious Dialogue* (New York: Paulist Press, 1978) is a succinct and accessible statement of them. A better known and more penetrating work by Pannikkar is *The Unknown Christ of Hinduism;* rev. and enl. ed. (Maryknoll, NY: Orbis, 1981), first published in 1964 in London by Darton, Longman and Todd, which concludes with the view, argued throughout, that whatever "God does *ab extra* happens through Christ. Thus recognizing the presence of God in other religions is equivalent to proclaiming the presence of Christ in them." This position is similar to Rahner's. For other views see Gordon Rupp, *Beyond Existentialism and Zen: Religion in a Pluralistic World* (New York: Oxford University Press, 1979); Huston Smith, *Forgotten Truth: The Primordial Tradition* (New York: Harper & Row, 1976); and Owen Thomas, ed., *Attitudes Towards Other Religions* (New York, Harper & Row, 1969), reissued by the University Press of America in 1986.

19. Kenneth A. Briggs, "New Center Dedicated in Princeton," *New York Times*, 16 October 1984.

20. *Fine* (New York: St. Martin's Press, 1985), p. 33.

21. It will perhaps appear strange to some readers that throughout the text I have made little mention of theologians in my own tradition. This has been by design, not neglect. It would be invidious however to fail to note my deep indebtedness to a number of Anglican thinkers and schools of thought and I want to do so here. First among them perhaps are the Cambridge Platonists, especially Henry More (1614–87) and Benjamin Whichcote (d. 1683), who refused to see nature as dead matter and placed a very high value on the forms and forces of natural life, as evidenced by their doctrine of "plastic nature." The following quotation from Whichcote, *Moral and Religious Aphorisms* (London, 1753), no. 109, shows that the Cambridge Platonists would allow no opposition between nature and grace: "God hath set up two lights to enlighten us on our way: the light of reason, which is the light of his creation, and the light of Scripture, which is after-revelation from him. Let us make use of these two lights and suffer neither to be put out." Similar views can be found in the writings of Ralph Cudsworth (1617–88) and Nathanael Culverwel (1618–51), as well as in two Oxford scholars influenced by the Cambridge group, John Norris and Joseph Glenvill. A decisive influence is that of Samuel Taylor Coleridge, the great nineteenth-century poet and theologian who inherited much from the Cambridge Platonists and whose estimate of nature was perhaps even higher than theirs. Although he owed a great deal to Schelling's *Natur-Philosophen* and the romantic movement on the Continent, Coleridge's mature theological views were given distinctive shape through his study of thinkers within his own tradition. Thus in his *Notes on Henry More* in W. C. T. Shedd, ed., *The Complete Works of Samuel Taylor Coleridge* (New York: Harper, 1854), vol. 5, p. 113, we find this statement: "Any scheme of Christianity which does not arise out of, and shoot its beams downwards into the scheme of nature, but stands aloof as an insulated afterthought, must be false or distorted in all its particulars." In *Aids to Reflection* (1825; London: Pickering, 1839), pp. 313–14, he complains that Descartes, in order to submit the various phenomena of moving bodies to geometrical construction, abstracted from corporeal substance all of its positive properties, and "instead of a world created and filled with productive forces . . . left a lifeless machine whirled about by the dust of its own grinding." In the same work, p. 107, he speaks of "the language of God himself, as uttered by nature," which needs to be attended to as surely as the words of Scripture, and again of nature as "God's amanuensis, a statute-book, as it were, dictated by God." In a lesser known work, *Theory of Life*, ed. Seth B. Watson (London, 1848), pp. 95, 147, he points to the interconnectedness and interdependence of all things in nature, the human realm not excepted, and of life as act and process, adumbrating in some sense the organicism exemplified by Whitehead. Charles Gore in his earlier writings was also an influence. In his Bampton Lectures, published as *The Incarnation of the Son of God* (London: John Murray, 1891), p. 40, we find a statement typical of the volume: "in theology

worthy of the name, the sequence and fundamental unity of nature and grace, of creation and redemption, are always insisted upon." While he did not maintain this position consistently in his later writings, he strongly reasserted it in his Gifford Lectures, *The Philosophy of the Good Life* (London: John Murray, 1930), esp. pp. 239, 296f., and 300, where in opposition to Karl Barth he says: "God as transcendent and acting from without must never be separated in our thought from God as universally and in all men immanent and inwardly operative." The *Lux Mundi* school of theology, of which Gore was a leader, was generally important for me, particularly the writings of J. R. Illingworth. His essay in *Lux Mundi* (London: John Murray, 1889), "The Incarnation and Development," pp. 152–53, places great emphasis on the cosmic dimension of theology and laments the tendency in Christian thought to tear the sacred and secular asunder. The world is here regarded as an "organism," a system in which, "while the parts contribute to the growth of the whole, the whole also reacts upon the development of the parts, and whose primary purpose is its own perfection, something that is contained within and not outside of itself, an internal end." His major works, *Divine Immanence* (London: Macmillan, 1898), *Reason and Revelation* (London: Longmans, Green and Co., 1902), and *Divine Transcendence* (London: Macmillan, 1911), are notable for their depth and illustrative detail. William Temple in *Mens Creatrix* (London: Macmillan, 1911), *Christus Veritas* (London: Macmillan, 1924), and *Nature, Man and God* (London: Macmillan, 1934), one of the great works of modern Anglican theology, extends the *Lux Mundi* perspective, demonstrating, especially in the later work, a marked indebtedness to Whitehead's philosophy of organism, yet subordinates nature to history in a decisive way. Charles Earle Raven, *Natural Religion and Christian Theology* (Cambridge: Cambridge University Press, 1953), although showing the same subordination, made an important contribution to the theology of nature and grace, as did his *Science, Religion and the Future* (New York: Macmillan, 1943) and his *Christianity and Science* (New York: Association Press, 1955). Hughell Edgar Fosbroke (1875–1957), for many years dean of the General Theological Seminary, had a great many sensible things to say about nature in relation to grace that were formative to my own point of view. See Edward French, ed., *God in the Heart of Things* (Greenwich, CT: Seabury, 1962), a collection of Fosbroke's essays and addresses. The last theologian I will mention here—there are others who could be mentioned, e.g., J. V. Langmead Casserley whose *Graceful Reason: the Contribution of Reason to Theology* (Greenwich, CT: Seabury, 1954) is a superb study and example of Anglican divinity—is W. Norman Pittenger, whose process theology has made a significant contribution to understanding the relation of nature and grace. Although I should not want to lay at his door the particular tack I take in this book and certainly not its specific suggestions, he has exercised an influence on my thought for many years, for which I am very grateful. Of his numerous books, the following are of special pertinence: *The Word Incarnate*

(New York: Harper, 1959), *Christian Understanding of Human Nature* (Philadelphia: Westminster, 1964), *God in Process* (London: SCM Press, 1967), *The Lure of the Divine Love: Human Experience and Christian Faith in a Process Perspective* (New York: Pilgrim Press, 1979), and *Catholic Faith in a Process Perspective* (Maryknoll, NY: Orbis Books, 1981). It remains to be said that Anglican theologians generally have taken nature with a seriousness seldom accorded it in post-Reformation theology. I believe that the point of view presented in this book has its roots in a continuing tradition of thought and life, however untraditional some of its suggested directions might appear to be.

Index